# VINOVIA

# VINOVIA

## THE BURIED ROMAN CITY OF BINCHESTER IN NORTHERN ENGLAND

### IAIN FERRIS

AMBERLEY

*To my brother, Mark Ferris*

First published 2011

Amberley Publishing
The Hill, Stroud
Gloucestershire GL5 4EP

www.amberleybooks.com

Copyright © Iain Ferris 2011

The right of Iain Ferris to be identified as the Author of this work has been asserted in accordance with the Copyrights, Designs and Patents Act 1988.

All rights reserved. No part of this book may be reprinted or reproduced or utilised in any form or by any electronic, mechanical or other means, now known or hereafter invented, including photocopying and recording, or in any information storage or retrieval system, without the permission in writing from the Publishers.

British Library Cataloguing in Publication Data.
A catalogue record for this book is available from the British Library.

ISBN 978-1-4456-0128-1

Typesetting and Origination by Amberley Publishing.
Printed in Great Britain.

# Contents

|  | Acknowledgements | 6 |
|---|---|---|
|  | Image Credits | 9 |
|  | List of Images | 10 |
|  | Preface | 15 |
| ONE | Antiquaries and Early Archaeologists at Vinovia | 23 |
| TWO | The First-Century Fort | 39 |
| THREE | The Second Fort and Two Successive Praetoria | 57 |
| FOUR | The Mid- to Late Fourth-Century Praetorium and Bath Suite | 76 |
| FIVE | From Roman Britain to Anglo-Saxon England and Beyond | 115 |
| SIX | Object and Economy, Religion and Ritual | 136 |
| SEVEN | A Military Base, a Centre of Power | 158 |
|  | Notes | 172 |
|  | Bibliography | 179 |
| APPENDIX | Archaeological Excavations, Surveys and Observations at Binchester 1877–2010 | 185 |
|  | Index | 189 |

# *Acknowledgements*

In 1891 the Reverend R. E. Hooppell published his book *Vinovia: A Buried Roman City in the County of Durham*, a study of the Roman fort of Binchester that still stands today as a vital resource for understanding the history of the site. I have consciously echoed Hooppell's book title in the title of my own work in recognition of the lasting significance and ongoing importance of his work.

Earlier this year (2010) my major research monograph on archaeological excavations at Vinovia – Binchester Roman Fort – was published by Durham County Council, presenting to the academic community the detailed results of two major campaigns of excavation at the site, in 1976–1981 and 1986–1991, and setting these results in their broader historical and geographical context. This present book is intended for a less specialised audience and aims to summarise and distil the masses of information presented in that monograph into a more manageable form suited to the needs of an informed lay audience interested in Roman Britain and the history and archaeology of the Roman north. Although not intended as a guidebook to the site, it is hoped that *Vinovia* might inspire readers who have not been to Binchester to visit the site and that it will provide follow-up reading for those who have already been to see there what is undoubtedly the best-preserved Roman military bathhouse in Britain.

I first became involved in studying the archaeology of Binchester Roman Fort in April 1977, when I arrived there to take up a job directing excavations on the site. The project was sponsored by the Manpower Services Commission (MSC), a government job-creation project of the time run by Rick Jones (now Dr), then Antiquities Officer at the Bowes Museum. He had launched preliminary investigations at the site the previous year. I continued working at the site until 1981, when funding from the MSC ran out. The principal supervisory members of the MSC team, with the project more or less for the duration, were Gordon Walker (now Dr Gordon Turner-Walker), Louisa Gidney, Jeremy Evans (now Dr), Tony Sanderson and John Grey.

Between 1986 and 1991 further excavations at the site were co-directed by Dr Rick Jones, then working at the University of Bradford, and Simon Clarke (now Dr). Although not involved in those excavations, I was kept abreast of new developments at Binchester by Rick and Simon. In 1994, funding for post-excavation analysis and reporting of both the 1976–1981 and 1986–1991 campaigns of work came through

*Acknowledgements*

the generous involvement of English Heritage, leading to the publication of the Binchester monograph in 2010, and I would particularly like to thank Dr Pete Wilson, Barney Sloane and Jim Leary, all of English Heritage, for their support of the project at different times and in often trying circumstances.

I would like to heartily thank all the specialist contributors to the now-published monograph report for helping it get there in the end. I have drawn upon these specialist reports again here for information presented in this present book in many instances. Thanks, then, to: Steve Allen (ceramic tiles), Dr Peter Marshall, Dr Alex Bayliss and colleagues (radiocarbon dating), Dr Lynne Bevan (so-called small finds and painted wall plaster), the late Dr Thomas Blagg (architectural stonework), Dr Julie Bond and Julia Cussans (animal bones), Rebecca Nicholson (bird bones), Dr Anthea Boylston and Sharon Norton (human bones), Dr Jeremy Evans and Dr Steven Willis (Roman coarse pottery), Dr Adam Gwilt (querns), Kay Hartley (mortaria), Professor Martin Henig (intaglio/gemstone), Donald Mackreth (brooches), Dr Gerry McDonnell and Adam Russell (ironworking residues), Kirsty Nichol (stone), Dr Sarah Paynter (scientific analysis of Roman glass), Professor Jennifer Price and Sally Worrell (Roman glass), Stephanie Rátkai (post-Roman pottery), Dr Richard Reece (coins), Dr Roger Tomlin (inscriptions and graffiti), Felicity Wild (samian pottery), Dr David Williams (amphorae), and Dr Rob Young (prehistoric worked flint).

Thanks are also extended to: Niall Hammond, Samantha Middleton and Jane Whittaker of the Bowes Museum for organising access to Binchester finds and records over the years; Dr Rick Jones and Dr Simon Clarke for doing the same at the University of Bradford in the 1990s and more recently; and Gordon Walker, Sandy Morris, Ann Biggs and Louisa Gidney of the original Binchester and Bowes Museum team for their preparation of an archive in the early 1980s whose integrity has stood the test of time and on which I have again drawn freely in this present book.

Dr John Rainbird is thanked for commenting on my interpretation of the results of his work at the site in 1971. Most thanks, though, go to Rick Jones, with whom I have shared innumerable fruitful discussions about Binchester over the years, and with whom I have written a number of papers on our work at the site. Indeed, many of the theories about Binchester put forward in this book owe a great deal to Rick's thoughts about the site, shared with me in conversation and in our joint publications. It is still a matter of great regret to me that Rick was unable to contribute towards the publication of the Binchester excavations, as originally envisaged.

Wessex Archaeology and *Time Team* are thanked for allowing me to refer to their work at the site in 2007, and the *Time Team* staff, particularly Billie Pink, are thanked for showing me around their open trenches on site. Many thanks to Dr David Mason of Durham County Council for information on his new campaign of work at the site, started in 2009. His co-director, Dr David Petts, is also thanked for showing me around the excavated areas in both 2009 and 2010.

Dr Chrissie Freeth is thanked for scanning most of the plates that appear in this book from a multitude of discrepant slides and photographic prints. I am indebted to Julian Parker for scanning the Roach Smith drawings to turn them into digital prints. The excellent drawn illustrations in the volume are variously the work of Mark Breedon, Nigel Dodds, John Prudhoe, Miranda Schofield and Gordon Turner-

Walker. I would like to thank Dr Simon Clarke for providing a slide taken during the 1986–1991 excavation campaign and Dr Julie Gardiner of Wessex Archaeology for providing digital images of the mausolea uncovered by *Time Team* at the site, and to both Simon and Julie for permission to reproduce those pictures here.

The staff of the Institute of Classical Studies Library, London, and the British Library, London, were unfailingly helpful in obtaining books and journals for my reference.

Above and beyond the call of duty, my colleague and wife Dr Lynne Bevan read and commented on a draft of the book, much to the benefit of the finished work. At Amberley Publishing I would like to thank Alan Sutton and Peter Kemmis Betty, for commissioning this book in the first place, and Louis Archard for his editorial advice.

Finally, thanks to the people of Bishop Auckland and District who took such an interest in excavation work at Binchester in the 1970s and 1980s and to whom this story of years of discovery is also dedicated.

# *Image Credits*

The majority of the photographic images in this book come from the Binchester photographic record for the 1976–1981 and 1986–1991 excavations, with on-site excavation photos from the 1976 season being taken by Rick Jones, the 1977 season by Iain Ferris or Rick Jones, between 1978 and 1981 by Iain Ferris, and between 1986 and 1991 by Simon Clarke or Rick Jones. Credits for other photographic images are as follows: images 34, 35 and 91, copyright Wessex Archaeology; image 62, Dr Simon Clarke; image 86, John Wilkins; images 31, 87, and 92, Iain Ferris.

All the drawings reproduced here as images were originally prepared for the monograph volume *The Beautiful Rooms Are Empty: Excavations at Binchester Roman Fort, County Durham 1976-1981 and 1986-1991* by Iain Ferris, published by Durham County Council in 2010.

# List of Images

PREFACE

1 View towards Binchester fort, on hilltop covered in trees, across the Wear Valley.
2 Site location plan.
3 Plan showing main excavated areas, excluding the 2009–2010 work.
4 View of the upstanding earthwork ramparts on the east side of the fort.
5 View of the consolidated remains of the mid-fourth-century bathhouse under the wooden sheds, and the commandant's house.

CHAPTER ONE: ANTIQUARIES AND EARLY ARCHAEOLOGISTS AT VINOVIA

6 Woodcut illustration by H. W. Rolfe made in 1854 and showing the mid-fourth-century hypocaust as displayed underground at that time (from C. Roach Smith's 1854 *Collectanea Antiqua*).
7 The ramparts and an associated culvert, as recorded by Mr Proud and Revd Hooppell in the nineteenth century. Drawing by J. W. Taylor (from R. E. Hooppell's 1891 *Vinovia*).
8 The underfloor of the fourth-century bathhouse as recorded by Mr Proud and Revd Hooppell in the nineteenth century. Drawing by J. W. Taylor (from R. E. Hooppell's 1891 *Vinovia*).
9 The extant hypocausted first room of the mid-fourth-century bathhouse, as recorded by Mr Proud and Revd Hooppell in the nineteenth century. Drawing by J. W. Taylor (from R. E. Hooppell's 1891 *Vinovia*).
10 The circular hypocausted room in a building in the vicus, as recorded by Mr Proud and Revd Hooppell in the nineteenth century. Drawing by J. W. Taylor (from R. E. Hooppell's 1891 *Vinovia*).
11 Part of a stone building alongside Dere Street, as recorded by Mr Proud and Revd Hooppell in the nineteenth century. Drawing by W. Heatlie (from R. E. Hooppell's 1891 *Vinovia*).

*List of Images*

12 Part of a stone building alongside Dere Street, recorded by Mr Proud and Revd Hooppell in the nineteenth century. Drawing by W. Heatlie (from R. E. Hooppell's 1891 *Vinovia*).
13 A stone-lined well in the vicus, as recorded by Mr Proud and Revd Hooppell in the nineteenth century. Drawing by W. Heatlie (from R. E. Hooppell's 1891 *Vinovia*).
14 A dedication slab to Aesculapius and Salus found in the nineteenth century (from R. E. Hooppell's 1891 *Vinovia*).
15 Inscribed altar to Jupiter Optimus Maximus and the Matres Ollototae (from Hooppell 1892).

## CHAPTER TWO: THE FIRST-CENTURY FORT

16 Beam trenches of the first-century timber building cut into natural.
17 Beam trenches of the first-century timber building cut into natural, one excavated, the other unexcavated.
18 Beam trench of the first-century timber building cut into natural and truncated by a pit. The baulk into which the trench runs presents a section through the earliest horizons on the site.
19 Plan of the first-century timber praetorium, or commandant's house (called Phase 2 in the stratigraphic schema for the 1976–1981 and 1986–1991 excavations).
20 Block plan reconstruction of the first-century timber building.
21 Plan of second-century industrial features and rubbish dump (called Phases 3–5 in the stratigraphic schema for the 1976–1981 and 1986–1991 excavations).
22 Second-century furnace/oven.
23 Tray or pallet of animal bone in final phase of second-century dump.

## CHAPTER THREE: THE SECOND FORT AND TWO SUCCESSIVE PRAETORIA

24 Plan of first stone praetorium or commandant's house (called Phase 6 in the stratigraphic schema for the 1976–1981 and 1986–1991 excavations).
25 Hypocaust in the first stone praetorium.
26 Hypocaust flue in the first stone praetorium.
27 Wall and ovens in the first stone praetorium.
28 Plan of second stone praetorium, or commandant's house (called Phase 7 in the stratigraphic schema for the 1976–1981 and 1986–1991 excavations).
29 Furnace room, or praefurnium, in the second stone praetorium.
30 Wall and associated mortar floor in the second stone praetorium.
31 Excavations underway in the civilian settlement or vicus in 2010.
32 Geophysical survey plot of part of the fort and civilian settlement or vicus (courtesy of Geoquest Associates).
33 Geophysical survey plots of part of the fort and civilian settlement or vicus (courtesy of Geophysical Surveys of Bradford).

34 Excavation of a mausoleum in the civilian settlement or vicus by *Time Team* in 2007 (copyright Wessex Archaeology).
35 Excavation of a mausoleum in the civilian settlement or vicus by *Time Team* in 2007 (copyright Wessex Archaeology).

## CHAPTER FOUR: THE MID- TO LATE FOURTH-CENTURY PRAETORIUM AND BATH SUITE.

36 Plan of the first phase of the mid-fourth-century stone praetorium, or commandant's house (called Phase 8A in the stratigraphic schema for the 1976–1981 and 1986–1991 excavations).
37 Two ritually deposited pots from the foundations of the mid-fourth-century praetorium, or commandant's house.
38 Sectioned sequence of mortar floors in the first phases of the mid-fourth-century stone praetorium, or commandant's house.
39 A tile flue of the first phase of the mid-fourth-century stone praetorium, or commandant's house, before excavation.
40 Plan of the later phases of the mid-fourth-century stone praetorium, or commandant's house (called Phases 8B–8E in the stratigraphic schema for the 1976–1981 and 1986–1991 excavations).
41 Mid-fourth-century bathhouse foundation trench.
42 Animal carved on the south-western corner of the mid-fourth-century bathhouse.
43 Mid-fourth-century bathhouse interior. In situ opus signinum floor and box flue tiles in first hot room, or tepidarium.
44 Elevation of wall inside the mid-fourth-century bathhouse.
45 Mid-fourth-century bathhouse interior. Louisa Gidney giving radio interview in underfloor area of first hot room, or tepidarium.
46 Mid-fourth-century bathhouse interior. Few remaining pilae stacks of second hot room, or laconicum, and view towards plunge bath.
47 Mid-fourth-century bathhouse interior. Flue arch from western praefurnium, or furnace room.
48 Mid-fourth-century bathhouse interior. Surviving pilae in third hot room, or caldarium, and part of remnant flue to northern praefurnium, or furnace room.
49 Mid-fourth-century bathhouse interior. Remnant of flue of northern praefurnium, or furnace room.
50 Mid-fourth-century bathhouse interior. Remnant of flue of northern praefurnium, or furnace room.
51 Mid-fourth-century bathhouse. Western praefurnium, or furnace room, fully excavated.
52 Mid-fourth-century bathhouse. Northern praefurnium, or furnace room, fully excavated.
53 Painted wall plaster with part of the leg of a bather or an athlete visible.
54 Charcoal store under excavation in kitchen of altered residential ranges of the mid-fourth-century stone praetorium, or commandant's house.

*List of Images*

55 Two new rooms added to the east side of the mid-fourth-century bathhouse.
56 Later fourth-century flagged courtyard.
57 Later fourth-century flagged courtyard, with triple-arched entranceway into the extended bath complex.
58 Later fourth-century flagged courtyard, with close-up of one of the pier stones of the triple-arched entranceway into the extended bath complex.
59 Later fourth-century flagged courtyard, looking onto threshold leading into the courtyard off the fort's main road, or via principalis.
60 Later fourth-century blocking wall in the residential ranges of the mid-fourth-century stone praetorium, or commandant's house.
61 Later fourth-century rebuilt furnace in the northern praefurnium, or furnace room, of the bathhouse.
62 Inscription naming the Ala Vettonum found in situ in the northern praefurnium, or furnace room, of the bathhouse (courtesy of Simon Clarke).
63 Block plans of the mid-fourth-century stone praetorium, or commandant's house, through all phases of its life (called Phases 8A–8E in the stratigraphic schema for the 1976–1981 and 1986–1991 excavations).

## CHAPTER FIVE: FROM ROMAN BRITAIN TO ANGLO-SAXON ENGLAND AND BEYOND

64 Plan of late Roman to sub-Roman activity (called Phase 9 in the stratigraphic schema for the 1976–1981 and 1986–1991 excavations).
65 Late Roman to sub-Roman metalworking furnace fully excavated.
66 Late Roman to sub-Roman slaughterhouse, looking onto stone platform and rough stone wall.
67 Late Roman to sub-Roman slaughterhouse, showing close up of stone platform and animal bones in situ close to platform.
68 Late Roman to sub-Roman stone flagged antler working area to north of Roman bathhouse.
69 Late Roman to sub-Roman activity. Robbed-out archway in the northern praefurnium, or furnace room.
70 Butchery marks on a white-tailed sea eagle bone.
71 Anglo-Saxon female skeleton buried with grave goods.
72 Anglo-Saxon burial with grave goods.
73 Anglo-Saxon grave goods from burial.
74 Human bone. Sheath of new bone on left humerus of an Anglo-Saxon skeleton, probably the result of congenital syphilis.
75 Escomb church.
76 Plan of medieval features (called Phase 11 in the stratigraphic schema for the 1976–1981 and 1986–1991 excavations).
77 Medieval beam trench and posthole.

## CHAPTER SIX: OBJECT AND ECONOMY, RELIGION AND RITUAL

78 Part of a decorated South Gaulish samian bowl of the late first or early second century. Alongside gladiators appear figures tossed by a bull and a sacrificer.
79 Graffito list of names on tile, probably a detail of men working at a military tilery.
80 Ceramic tile stamps; the NCON stamp and the VIV stamp.
81 A bone weaving comb.
82 A silver spoon, probably in use in the fourth-century praetorium, or commandant's house.
83 A selection of glass, stone, ceramic and bone gaming counters and a bone die, probably used for gaming in the fourth-century praetorium, or commandant's house, and its bath suite.
84 A selection of bone pins.
85 Armea graffito on a tile.
86 Carved intaglio or gemstone in an iron ring (photograph by Robert Wilkins).
87 A jet dog, possibly a knife handle, found during excavations in 1971.
88 Facepots from the nineteenth-century excavations of Mr Proud and Revd Hooppell.
89 Graffito on one of a pair of ritually deposited pots.
90 Anthropomorphic stone figure from the foundation trench of the mid-fourth-century bathhouse.
91 Excavation of a mausoleum in the civilian settlement, or vicus, by *Time Team* in 2007 (copyright Wessex Archaeology).

## CHAPTER SEVEN: A MILITARY BASE, A CENTRE OF POWER

92 Excavations underway on a fourth-century stone barrack block in 2010.
93 The fort rampart at the north-east corner, with a culvert, as recorded by Mr Proud and Revd Hooppell in the nineteenth century. Drawing by W. Heatlie (from R. E. Hooppell's 1891 *Vinovia*).
94 Reused fragment of an inscribed altar naming the Ala Vettonum from the northern fourth-century praefurnium, or furnace room.
95 Anglo-Saxon female skeleton and grave goods laid out in a sand tray at the Bowes Museum, Barnard Castle.
96 A circular hypocausted room forming part of a building in the vicus, as recorded by Mr Proud and Revd Hooppell in the nineteenth century. Drawing by W. Heatlie (from R. E. Hooppell's 1891 *Vinovia*).
97 The arches leading to the underfloor of the first room of the mid-fourth-century bathhouse, as recorded by Mr Proud and Revd Hooppell in the nineteenth century. Drawing by W. Heatlie (from R. E. Hooppell's 1891 *Vinovia*).
98 The mid- to late fourth-century praetorium house at its grandest.

# *Preface*

Binchester Roman Fort, Roman Vinovia, sometimes Vinovium, lies on a hilltop spur about two kilometres (around one and a quarter miles) north of the modern town of Bishop Auckland in County Durham, between the River Wear and the River Gaunless. Most visitors to the site today approach it either by car or on foot from Bishop Auckland market place. The route goes past The Sportsman Inn public house, down the very steep and narrow Wear Chare, and along Dial Stob Hill, the road that skirts the banks of the Wear itself. If lucky, you will catch a blue-flash glimpse of kingfishers there on the way. The road now passes over historic Jock's Bridge, built in 1819 and today a Grade II-listed structure, follows the bend in the river, and forks off up the steep, wooded slope, as indicated by the signage. The visitor then passes on his or her left the large, presently disused Binchester Hall, for many years a hotel and, in the latter stages of its life, a nursing home, before reaching the displayed remains of perhaps the best-preserved Roman military bathhouse in Britain here at Binchester.

The Roman fort is a scheduled ancient monument, most of it under grass today, with a relatively small area of the fort around the fourth-century stone commandant's bathhouse consolidated and displayed for public viewing under the guardianship of Durham County Council. The Roman fort controlled the bridge crossing over the River Wear, which carried Dere Street, the main Roman road north, from York to Corbridge and beyond. It also lay at the node of a network of other roads leading both to the east and to the west. Binchester fort lay between the fort at Piercebridge to the south and those at Lanchester and Ebchester to the north.

The first fort at Vinovia, a turf-and-timber fort, was founded in the later first century AD, its defences possibly enclosing an interior area of around 7.14 hectares (17.66 acres). The second fort here, built in stone in the Antonine period, was also a large fort, though smaller than its predecessor, with an enclosed area of about 3.6 hectares (9 acres). The ramparts of the second fort survive in part today as upstanding, grass-covered earthworks and, as mentioned above, stone buildings in the central part of the second fort are displayed to the public. For part of its history at least, it was garrisoned by an auxiliary cavalry unit, the Ala Vettonum. It is also known to have housed at various times a unit of Frisians (the Cuneus Frisiorum), the Numerus Concangiensium, and perhaps detachments of the Sixth Legion and,

1 View towards Binchester fort, on hilltop covered in trees across the Wear Valley.

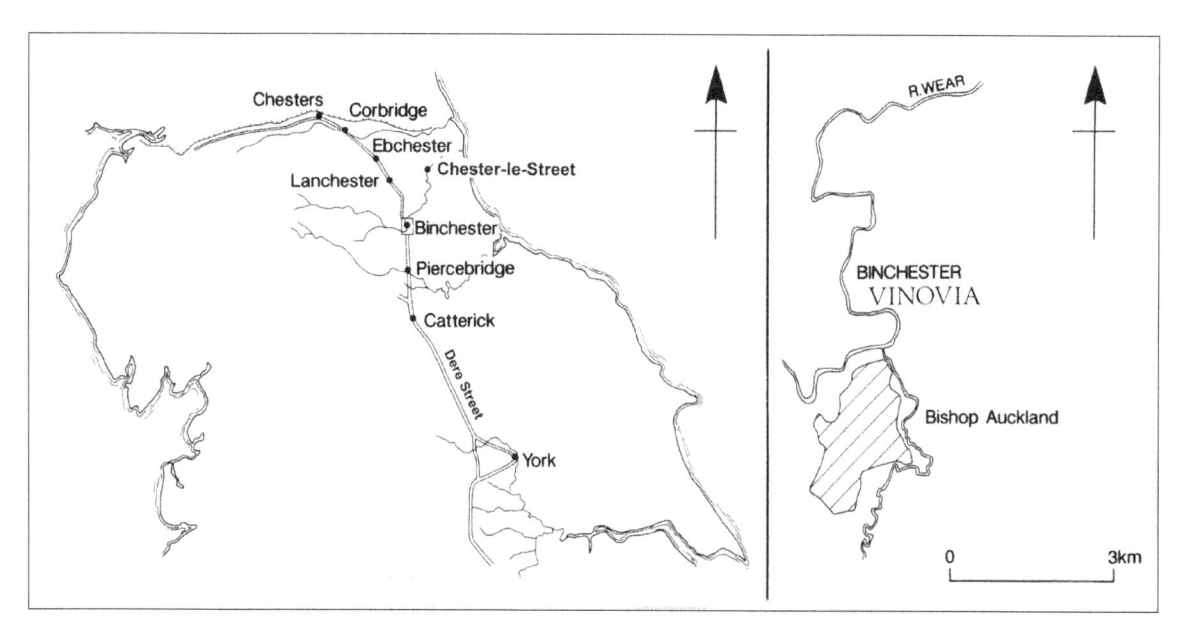

2 Site location plan.

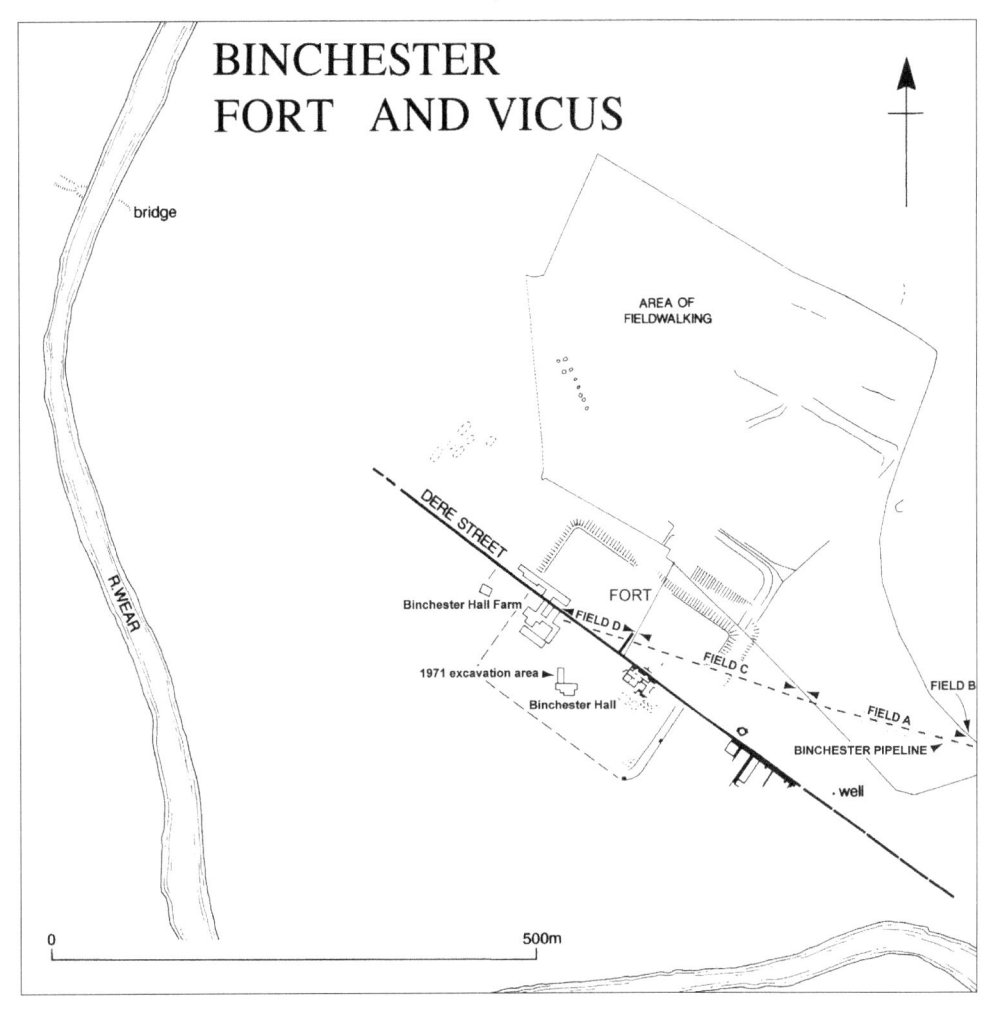

3 Plan showing main excavated areas, excluding the 2009–2010 work.

in its early years, the Ninth Hispana Legion. Around the second fort grew up a very large civilian settlement or vicus, making the total Roman settlement area about 12 to 16 hectares (30 to 40 acres). In fact, it was probably larger, as new survey work is suggesting that the vicus was much more extensive than previously thought.

It has been suggested that the two variant alternative Latin names for the site, Vinovia and sometimes Vinovium, could represent an early and a later form of the name.[1] The site name, perhaps significantly, appears in Ptolemy's *Geography* of *c.* AD 140–150, in the *Antonine Itinerary*, and in the late Roman *Ravenna Cosmography*. It occurs on an inscription from the site, thus irrevocably confirming the identification of site with place name, and also appears on one of the Vindolanda writing tablets. The meaning of the Latin name Vinovia/Vinovium is unknown, and though it was first suggested in the eighteenth century and continues to be promulgated today that the Vin- element of the place name is linked to the Latin word *vinum*, meaning wine, this derivation is highly unlikely. So too is a suggested 'British or Celtic' origin for the name and its translation as 'water's edge'. The later name of Binchester is easier and more

4 View of the upstanding earthwork ramparts on the east side of the fort.

obvious to explain, with Old English *Binn* and *ceaster* or *Binnan* and *ceaster* meaning 'settlement within a fort or camp' and 'manger or stall within a fort or camp'.

A substantial part of the fort on the west has been lost through erosion caused by the River Wear, though the rapid rate of erosion recorded in the 1920s and 1930s seems to have slowed somewhat in the present day. The fort's defences survive as impressive upstanding earthworks on the north-east side and on parts of the north-west and south-east sides. Geophysical survey in 1979 located a corner tower marking the south corner of the fort.

Aerial photographs from the 1950s[2] revealed the cropmark presence of another apparently military enclosure beyond the north-east side of the visible fort, and while this was at one time thought to represent an annexe it is now considered to represent part of the defences of the earlier fort here.

The site has been recognised since the sixteenth century, when it was mentioned by John Leland, but was first substantially investigated in the late nineteenth century by John Proud and the Revd R. E. Hooppell. These excavations recovered traces of substantial internal buildings, principally the fourth-century stone praetorium and its associated bathhouse, and a large civil settlement or vicus, where were recognised traces of both some very large individual structures and at least three consecutive major phases of stone building. For many years Binchester was the only example of a civilian settlement at a northern fort where any excavated details of the buildings were

5 View of the consolidated remains of the mid-fourth-century bathhouse under the wooden sheds, and the commandant's house.

available. However, aerial photographs from the 1950s and 1960s[3] indicated that the vicus was even larger than supposed by Hooppell, extending not only over the area to the south-east of the fort but also to its north-east and on the north-west on the scarp slope down towards the River Wear.

Excavations by Kenneth Steer in 1937 examined part of the fort defences and recovered evidence for the presence of buildings over the line of the infilled ditch, a relationship subsequently confirmed elsewhere in the fort through geophysical survey. In the 1960s John Rainbird, on behalf of the then Ministry of Works, carried out rescue excavation in the fort interior and found evidence for, among other things, a period of considerable industrial or semi-industrial military activity. He also uncovered part of what is now known to be an extensive Anglo-Saxon cemetery within the former fort defences.

Most excavation, though, has been confined to the area inside the fort around a very well-preserved late Roman bathhouse, to the south-west of the fort's via principalis, first examined in detail by Proud and Hooppell, and which had been partially exposed by a local amateur archaeological research group and placed in the guardianship of Durham County Council in the 1960s.[4] This bathhouse was partially displayed inside a wooden building and was open to the public. Excavation by Durham University under Brian Dobson and Michael Jarrett was conducted to the east of this building in 1955. The most extensive research campaign since the nineteenth century began in 1976, continued to 1981 and resumed in 1986, being finally completed in 1991. The excavations led to the extension of the protective building and a fuller interpretation of the site for visitors. Subsequent work at the site was on a relatively small scale, usually undertaken in response to proposals for building work here, until the visit of television's *Time Team* to the site in 2007. In 2009, with public interest in the site reawakened, a new, large-scale, five-year international field project began, run jointly by Durham County Council, Durham University and Stanford University.

The 1976–1981 and 1986–1991 excavations at Binchester aimed to provide contextual information for the planned consolidation and display of the bathhouse to the public. By examining the full sequence of deposits at the site, it soon became clear that the stratigraphy at Binchester held the key to the elucidation of many of the then-current research questions in northern Roman military studies. It also raised new and fundamental questions about both the early and the late to sub-Roman periods, both on this specific site and more widely.

The complex picture of Binchester's history revealed by archaeological excavation has been simplified here to enable a clear picture to emerge, as was intended when the project's research aims and objectives were first defined.[5] In studying Roman military archaeology, it is all too easy to become intellectually isolated in a seemingly hermetically-sealed academic field concerned solely with the minutiae of the military world, endlessly analysing fort sizes and layouts, tracking changing military dispositions on a chronological and geographical basis, and cataloguing the smallest changes or variations in the use of items of military equipment. That is not to say that these are not important aspects of the ancient world to study, but it is often too easy to lose track of the central aim of all academic ventures in the arts and humanities, that is to connect with the lives of individuals and with their contemporary societies.

The late 1970s and 1980s excavations at Binchester had six main academic aims and objectives, and these have informed both the structure of the academic monograph publication of 2010 and of this present book. Firstly, Binchester has been analysed as a settlement site rather than simply as a military establishment, and this has been achieved through the definition of the social and economic character of the settlement, both at specific periods of time and over the extended period of time represented by the exceptionally high quality archaeological record.

Secondly, change over time at Binchester has been studied in detail in terms of site character and function, as was possible through analysis of the unusually detailed excavated sequence and finds assemblages, and this change has been viewed on a wider, regional basis, as well as in terms of changing frontier activities within the structure of the western Roman Empire.

Thirdly, the mechanisms of Roman army supply between the first and fourth centuries AD have been considered, in particular in relation to the exploitation of local raw materials and resources and the on-site production of artefacts and materials, especially with regard to the industrial-scale metal production attested at Binchester in the second century.

Fourthly, the structure, workings and context of an important late Roman house as represented by the fourth-century commandant's house and bath suite at Binchester have been dissected. A complex series of alterations and changes to the original house have been analysed in terms of social changes, as well as changes in military structure.

Fifthly, the specific issues of continuity and transition from the late Roman period into the sub-Roman and earlier medieval periods have been addressed. Again, this is a field of study that has had to take cognisance of regional, national and international study of this crucial transitional period. The extended and complex late Roman and sub-Roman to Anglo-Saxon sequences at Binchester contained substantial finds assemblages of pottery, animal bone, and small finds in particular and proved to provide sufficient secure samples to allow a scientific dating programme to be brought to bear on this material.

Lastly, site formation processes have been studied in order to try to characterise the various finds assemblages from the deeply-stratified and well-preserved sequence, both on a phase-by-phase basis and in terms of longer-term trends of acquisition, use and discard within the overall finds assemblage.

This book consists of seven chapters. Chapter One acts as an introduction to the history of the antiquarian and early archaeological exploration of the Roman site at Binchester. Chapter Two presents an examination of the evidence for the earliest timber fort on the site and discusses the historical context for the foundation of a fort here as part of the broader Roman strategy for the north of Britain. In Chapter Three the later stone fort is described and discussed, with particular, extended attention being paid to the first two phases of stone building within this fort. In Chapter Four attention is turned to the fort in the mid-fourth century and the building here of a massive commandant's house, or praetorium, the remains of whose bathhouse is on display to the public today.

Chapter Five concentrates on describing and discussing what happened at the site after the Roman army had abandoned the fort and how the fourth-century praetorium was reused for purposes other than its original military and administrative role. The use of the site for the location of an Anglo-Saxon cemetery will also be discussed, as well as the later activity on the site in the medieval and post-medieval periods. In Chapter Six attention will be turned away from the historical and archaeological sequence and towards a discussion of certain aspects of everyday life at the fort between the first and fifth centuries, as reflected in the material culture of the site, that is in the objects recovered by excavation both in the 1976–1981 and 1986–1991 excavations and during earlier and later campaigns of work. Finally, in Chapter Seven, there will be presented an overview of the significance of Vinovia/Binchester in terms of what excavation there tells us about the Roman military north and, most particularly, about the late Roman transition in this region. Academic footnotes and a short bibliography then follow. Finally, in an appendix, a chronological gazetteer of archaeological fieldwork at the site is presented.

It is hoped that the book will act as introduction to the site of Vinovia for the informed lay reader interested in Roman Britain in general, as well as for undergraduate students of archaeology. The provision of basic academic notes and a short bibliography should allow those wishing to pursue in more depth the more complex aspects of the study beyond the book's main narrative to do so with relative ease.

Remarkably, there has been no accessible book-length study of Vinovia/Binchester published since the nineteenth century, in contrast to the availability today of numerous books on other northern Roman fort sites. There have, however, been numerous articles on the site published in academic journals and a recent academic monograph by the author, though the site is often not mentioned beyond passing in more general books on the Roman northern frontiers. This present book will hopefully fill an evident gap in the market.

Iain Ferris<br>
Birmingham<br>
April–December 2010

CHAPTER ONE

# *Antiquaries and Early Archaeologists at Vinovia*

Binchester Roman fort – Vinovia or Vinovium – has attracted the attention of antiquarians and archaeologists since the sixteenth century and it is intended here to provide a summary review of discoveries at the site from that time up to the end of the nineteenth century. Some of this work is highly significant, some of it less so, but the summation here of the results of all such work at Binchester should allow the contextualisation of the results of the later, larger and more scientific excavation campaigns to be undertaken. It also provides a sad reminder of how little of the early archaeological work undertaken at the site has been fully published and how many of the finds made before the mid-nineteenth century have been destroyed, lost or otherwise dispersed, often with the crassest of motives.

The principal antiquarians whose work will be discussed here are John Leland, William Camden, John Horsley, William Hutchinson, John Cade, Charles Roach Smith, John Proud and the Revd R. E. Hooppell.

## A POORE VILLAG

In 1540 John Leland visited County Durham and Northern England as part of his wider journey around the country. In his published *Itinerary* he described Binchester as 'now a poore villag stondith on the South side of the Were,' where 'as I roode on the South side, [I saw] a little Fosse, and indicia of old Buildinges. In the ploughid feeldes hard by thys village hath and be founde Romaine coynes, and other many tokens of Antiquity. Betwixt Auckland and Binchester is an exceeding fair bridge of one arch upon Were.'[1] It is interesting that Leland not only saw a contemporary village or small settlement here, probably with its origins in the medieval period, but also Roman buildings, presumably inside the fort but probably also in the area of the vicus. That these structures had not by then been completely robbed out or levelled is extraordinary, though the destructive effect of ploughing at this time on archaeological deposits in those parts of the site now turned over to agriculture is apparent from his description of regular finds of Roman coins and other artefacts.

Some forty years or so later, on a visit in 1586, William Camden provided a somewhat fuller account of the site that he published in his *Britannia*, along with a description of a number of inscribed stones discovered there:

> ... the remaines of an ancient city not now a-dying, but dead many yeeres ago, standing on the brow of a hill ... wee call it at this day Binchester, and it hath in it a very few houses. Yet it is very well knowne to them that dwell thereabout, both by reason of the heapes of rubbish, and the reliques of walles yet to be seene, as also for peeces of Romane coine often digged up there, which they call Binchester Pennies, yea and for the Inscriptions of the Romans.[2]

Again, it is noteworthy that Camden too saw structural remains on the site.

Both John Horsley in his *Britannia Romana* of 1732[3] and William Hutchinson in *The History and Antiquities of the County Palatine of Durham* of 1794[4] described visits to the site and reported on finds made there, their interests mainly being focused on the inscribed stones and altars and other artefacts found at Binchester, though Horsley, interestingly, made note of the traces of buildings in the area of the vicus. Hutchinson also made note of the discovery of a Roman cremation urn found during the building of a bridge 'over the river Gaunless, in the park at Bishop Auckland, in the year 1757', 'about a quarter of a mile from Binchester'.[5] A more contemporary allusion to this latter discovery was made by Bishop Richard Pococke who, writing in May 1760, noted that 'they lately found in the park several urns like common potts; some with burnt bones in them, and lately two or three full of earth.'[6] Hutchinson is also responsible for passing down to us an excellent story about a superstition concerning a fragment of Roman sculpture found at the site. He recounts how a stone relief sculpture of Priapus was used for some time as a weight for a cheese press at the farmhouse here, there possibly having been a link made in the finder's eye between ancient fecundity and present agricultural bounty. But when the cheese curdled and wasted, the farmer's wife's ire was turned on the malignant influence of the deity whose previous munificence she had taken for granted.

Hutchinson also took time to describe old Binchester Hall, which stood on the site, within the area defined by the ramparts of the stone fort. This building was demolished in 1835 and a new hall built, probably because the old structure was now perilously close to the edges of the rapidly eroding hillside by the River Wear. He described the old hall as

> a fine old building of the stile used in Queen Elizabeth's time, composed of a centre and two wings, the south wing having a noble semi-circular window projected from a bracket, the north wing is modernized; the hall is furnished with old armour, and the [Roman] antiquities before noted. Behind the house, on the brink of the hill, is a short but delightful terrace, commanding the picturesque prospects of the vale of Wear, with a side view of Bishop Auckland.

The old hall was drawn by Nathaniel Buck[7] around seventy years before Hutchinson's visitation and appears in the background of an illustration of Auckland Castle and its surrounding landscape published as a print in 1728. The print quite clearly shows the large mansion house within a walled garden set in landscaped grounds and with a separate smaller structure outside the main compound. In around 1778 a distant view towards the hill on which Binchester fort and hall stood was drawn by the touring Swiss illustrator Samuel Hieronymous Grimm of Burgdorf[8], but this picture includes little useful detail to add to the discussion here. At the time of the demolition of the old hall in 1835 it was reported by local historian Peter Fair,[9] who lived nearby, that 'this ancient seat has been pulled down and rebuilt on a very beautiful plan by the late owner, the Honble. Thomas Lyon, except one part used in building the present farmhouse near the site of the old mansion.'

It is principally to Camden, Horsley and Hutchinson that we owe our knowledge of the many carved and inscribed stones found at Binchester up to the 1850s that are now lost, as will be described below. Others were subsequently recorded by Samuel Lysons in his *Reliquaiae Britannico-Romanae* of the earlier nineteenth century, and by J. C. Bruce in his *Lapidarium Septentrionale* of the 1870s.

Camden recorded an altar bearing the inscription '[M]atrib(us) o[lloto(tis)] | CartoXval | Marti Vetto(num) | Genio Loci | Lit Ixt' ('To the Mother Goddess Ollototae ... Cavalry Regiment of Vettonians ...').[10] This was the first intimation that the auxiliary cavalry unit of Vettonians was in garrison at Binchester at one point in the fort's history. The significance of the cult of the Mother Goddesses at Binchester is of great interest and will be discussed more fully in Chapter Six. This find was the first of a number of altars dedicated to the Matres to be recovered from the site. Horsley reported on two more such altars: the first inscribed 'Deab(us) | Matrib(us) O[l]lot(otis) | T[i]b(erius) Cl(audius) Quin | tianus b(ene)f(iciarius) co(n)s(ularis) | v(otum) s(olvit) l(ibens) m(erito)' ('To the mother Goddess Ollototae Tiberius Claudius Quintianus, beneficiarius of the governor, willingly and deservedly fulfilled his vow');[11] and the second 'Mat(ribus) | sac(rum) | Geme | llus | v(otum) s(olvit) l(ibens) m(erito)' ('Sacred to the Mother Goddess; Gemellus willingly and deservedly fulfilled his vow').[12] A third altar reported on by Horsley was more fragmentary and while it too might have been a dedication to the Matres, only a partial inscription reading 'v(otum) s(olvit) l(ibens) m(erito)' ('... willingly and deservedly fulfilled his vow'),[13] survived.

A second altar dedicated by the cavalry regiment of Vettonians was reported on in J. C. Bruce's *Lapidarium Septentrionale* of 1870–5 but had been found much earlier, around 1760. The inscription on this altar read 'Sul[e]ui[s] (?) | [ala] Vett[on(um)] | CANN | v(otum) s(olvit) l(ibens) m(erito)' ('To the Suleviae the Cavalry Regiment of Vettonians ... willingly and deservedly fulfilled its vow').[14]

Evidence for the presence of a later military unit stationed at Binchester – the Cuneus Frisiorum – was provided by another inscribed altar reported in Samuel Lysons' *Reliquaiae Britannico-Romanae* of 1801–17. The inscription read 'mandus | ex c(uneo) Fris(iorum) Vinovie(nsium) | v(otum) s(olvit) l(ibens) m(erito)' ('... from the formation of Frisians of Vinovia, willingly and deservedly fulfilled his vow').[15]

Another highly significant inscribed stone, in this case a large tombstone, was also published by Lysons. The tombstone was not actually found at Binchester itself; rather it was seen in or some time before 1813, built into a causeway leading to a footbridge over the Bell Burn, about a quarter of a mile north of the fort. The tombstone inscription read 'D(is) M(anibus) s(acrum) | Nem(onius) Montanus dec(urio) | vixit ann(os) XL Nem(onius) | Sanctus fr(ater) et coher(edes) | ex testamento fecer(un)t' ('Sacred to the spirits of the departed: Nemonius Montanus, decurion, lived 40 years. Nemonius Sanctus, his brother, and his joint heirs set this up in accordance with his will').[16]

All seven of these inscribed stones are now lost to us. Shortly after their destruction, in 1858 there was found another altar at the site bearing a partial inscription: 'F]ortunae | Sanctae | M(arcus) Val(erius) | Fuluianu[s] | preaf(ectus) eq(uitum) | v(otum) s(olvit) l(aetus) l(ibens) m(erito)' ('To holy Fortune Marcus Valerius Fulvianus, prefect of cavalry, gladly, willingly, and deservedly fulfilled his vow').[17] This stone can now be seen in the collection of the Chapter Library, Durham Cathedral.

One of the more curious antiquarian contributions to the study of Binchester was made by John Cade in 1783 and published two years later in *Archaeologia*, in a short note entitled 'Conjectures on the Name of the Roman Station Vinovium or Binchester'. This need not concern us long, however. In this paper, Cade advanced the theory that Binchester 'was sacred I apprehend to Bacchus, and derived its name Vinovium, from the festivals instituted there in honour of that Deity.' Cade's supporting evidence for a significant or lasting Bacchic cult cell here is hardly convincing, consisting of

> a priapus, at present in the possession of Farrer Wren, Esq the proprietor of the Station ... a small bronze image of that Deity, which had probably been a symbol worn by the Bacchae or female priestesses, as there is a perforation in its lower part ... [some] curious fragments of bowls and vases encircled with vine branches ... [and] a large bass relief of a fawn with an altar.[18]

Cade's theory then that the Vin of Vinovia/Vinovium, and indeed of other Roman sites beginning with Vin-, derived from *vinum*, the Latin word for wine, and hence from some spurious connection to the god Bacchus, can thus be seen to be somewhat tentative, if not actually absurd.

Previously little commented on by academics studying the history of Binchester fort is a number of letters written to Robert Surtees of Mainsforth in 1805 and 1808 by Dr Thomas Sherwood of Bishop Auckland,[19] detailing both the discovery of further Roman remains at Binchester and the cynical destruction of some of these remains and of finds from the site by the local landowner, Mrs Lyon. While Mrs Lyon is not directly blamed for the first act of vandalism in 1805, she is certainly deemed culpable for the second one in 1808, the robbing of building materials from a Roman structure.

> She suffered the work people to pull down and destroy the greatest part of the building and even sold the bricks to people in Auckland ... Mr Bailey of Chillingham has just called here and has cursed Madame L. black and blue for selling the Roman bricks – you must compose a new paragraph in Latin on this occasion.

Mary Lyon, née Wren, had married Thomas Lyon and had inherited the Binchester estate from her father in 1794, after the Wren family had held the estate for around 200 years.

It is likely that the adverse publicity surrounding the Lyon family's cavalier attitude to the Roman remains on their estate brought a halt to further damage being done at the site, at least for a short while. Indeed, around 1815, purely by chance, the hypocausted commandant's bath suite on display at the site today was discovered, being at the time completely buried under pasture. A horse and cart traversing the field in which the bathhouse was sited fell into a large hole caused by the collapse of part of the underlying hypocaust, thus revealing the existence of this building to the then-landowner, Charles Lyon, who had the structure partially cleared to make it safe and had a brick vault built over part of the remains, accessed down a set of steps from the surface, terminated by a trapdoor in the field. This benevolent attitude towards the ancient structure was quite a turnaround from the attitude of other members of the Lyon family only a short time before. Astonishingly, this arrangement for protecting and giving access for viewing of the building lasted up until the 1960s.

However, this new interest in the site's Roman past unfortunately was not long held by the estate's owner, with disastrous consequences, as is shown by three accounts of what happened at Binchester around 1832, all written some years after the event.

Canon James Raine, writing in 1852, sadly noted that

> the extensive and important collection of Roman altars, and other sculptured stones, which had been within the camp or in its precincts from time to time, and which had long been preserved with care in an outbuilding of the Mansion House were, with one exception, destroyed by the owner of the estate, in the construction of the underground works of a coal pit, before it was sold to the Bishop. That exception was an altar which had not been broken up.[20]

This presumably relates to Charles Lyon's disastrous attempt to sink a mine shaft on nearby Binchester Flatts Farm, at Newton Cap Flatts, an undertaking abandoned in 1832. Two years later, in 1854, Charles Roach Smith reported that 'one of my many correspondents tells me that a considerable number [of inscribed stones] were left for years in a courtyard and farmhouse [at Binchester], and were ultimately used for building materials'.[21] More information on this terrible piece of cultural vandalism is provided by Revd R. E. Hooppell, writing almost forty years later. Hooppell tells us that:

> In the early part of the present century there was, it is believed, a large and deeply interesting collection of Roman antiquities at what was then, and had been for many generations, Binchester Hall. The latest inheritor of the Hall, however, determined on coal-winning. He sank a pit, and much money in it. He broke up also, and sent down the pit, along, doubtless, with considerable quantities of other stones, the Roman altars and other sculptured remains which his ancestors had found and treasured, as material to be used by the masons employed beneath ... The late Canon Raine ... arrived on the spot one day, just in time to save the last altar of the collection from the fate which had overtaken its compeers.[22]

Hooppell reported in his *Vinovia* volume that the pit was by then (1891) flooded out and that there was no chance of the lost Binchester stones ever being recovered;

6 Woodcut illustration by H. W. Rolfe made in 1854 and showing the mid-fourth-century hypocaust as displayed underground at that time (from C. Roach Smith's 1854 *Collectanea Antiqua*).

however, later in the same volume he corrected his previous assertion that the pit was flooded, but without giving any source for this new information.

The first academic reporting of the 1815 discovery of what is now known to be the bath suite of the fourth-century commandant's house was made by Charles Roach Smith almost forty years later, in his *Collectanea Antiqua*,[23] following his visit to the site in autumn 1854. Roach Smith reported that:

> the walls of the station, on the north-east, are yet to be traced, notwithstanding they have evidently been resorted to as quarries for building stone by generations of landed proprietors; but with one half, at least the lords of the soil have more successfully done what they liked with their own, and not one stone is left standing upon another. The buildings within the station have also long since been pulled down, and over their ruins the earth has accumulated to the depth of five or six feet.

He then went on to briefly discuss the bathhouse's hypocaust, which he went through the trapdoor and down the steps to examine, his report being accompanied by two drawn views in the form of etchings made by H. W. Rolfe. The first etching shows a side-on view of the three open arches giving access to the underfloor of the hypocaust, along with the protective brick tunnel vault and the access steps. The second is a face-on view of the three tiled arch openings, with a number of the stacks of pilae tiles supporting the hypocaust floor being visible through the central arch. Roach Smith's description of the remarkably preserved building apparently helped draw regular streams of visitors to the site, all eager to experience the unusual thrill of going underground with candles and lanterns to examine the Roman remains. This growing local interest was going to lead, in a very short time, to the launching in 1879 of a well-funded, well-planned and well-executed campaign of archaeological excavations at the site.

## A BURIED ROMAN CITY

The excavations that began in 1879 were directed by John Proud, a well-known and respected solicitor from Bishop Auckland, 'a gentleman who has ever been foremost in promoting every good work connected with science, or religion, or social progress in his locality', and the Revd Robert Eli Hooppell, then-rector of nearby Byers Green, near Spennymoor, and by then a respected northern antiquarian. Their excavations were extensive and in many ways acted to set the agenda for the interpretation of Binchester for many years to come, almost up to the launching of the major campaign of excavations here in 1976. Proud and Hooppell's work, of course, included the uncovering of much of the fourth-century commandant's house and bathhouse on which the 1976–1981 and 1986–1991 campaigns were subsequently focused and analysis of which forms the core of this present book. They also examined parts of the fort's defensive circuit of ramparts and a number of stretches of the Roman road passing through the fort and vicus and, highly significantly, a number of stone buildings in the vicus itself.

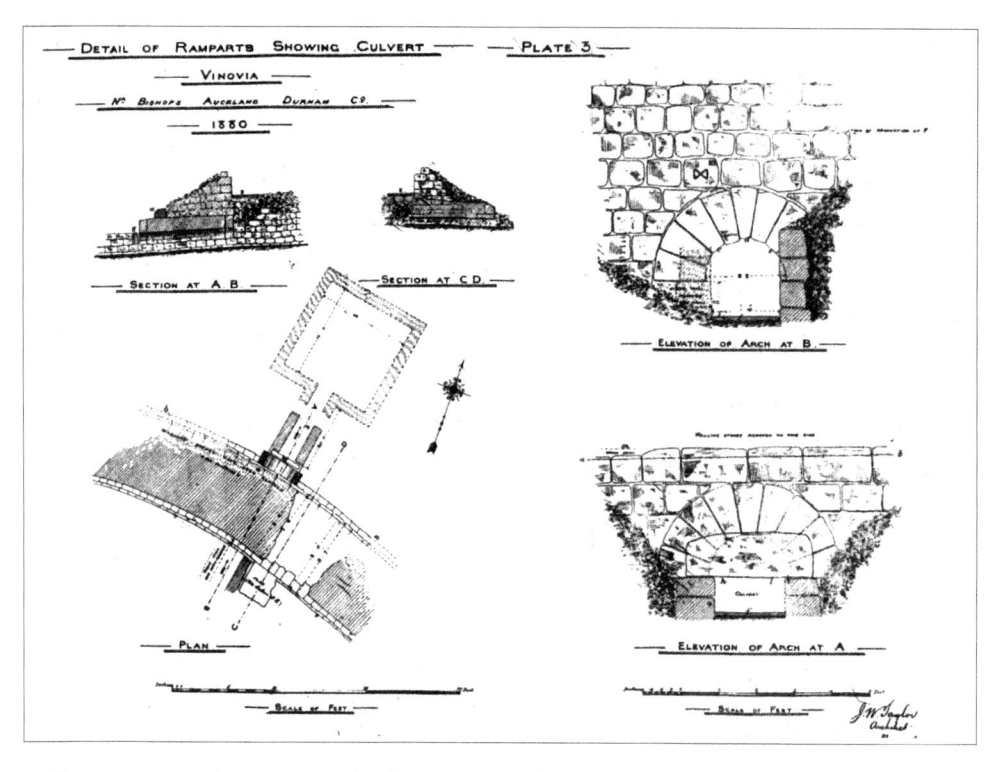

7 The ramparts and an associated culvert, as recorded by Mr Proud and Revd Hooppell in the nineteenth century. Drawing by J. W. Taylor (from R. E. Hooppell's 1891 *Vinovia*).

The excavations were reported on in a number of illustrated talks by Hooppell to meetings of the British Archaeological Association which were later published in the association's journal[24] and in a public lecture at Bishop Auckland Town Hall, which also went into print due to popular demand.[25] Hooppell later brought all this information together, along with much new material, in his 1891 book *Vinovia: A Buried Roman City in the County of Durham*,[26] after which this present book is named. Hooppell's publication of the work at Binchester is greatly enhanced by its inclusion of superb and highly accurate plans and elevations of the fourth-century bathhouse, prepared by and credited to J. W. Taylor, an architect of Newcastle upon Tyne, and, to a lesser extent, by line drawn sketches of excavated features by W. Heatlie. A number of Taylor's original hand-coloured plans can be found in the archaeological archives of Newcastle University.

Proud and Hooppell's excavation campaign was launched by the examination of parts of the fort defences, including the cutting of at least five trenches at various points along the eastern rampart, which was found to survive to some height, to be up to 8 feet 6 inches in thickness, and to be faced with large stone blocks, as might have been expected, and set on a bed of large river cobbles, in places recorded as being 30 feet wide. A culvert pierced the rampart in one place and fed into a 10-foot-square structure outside the fort. Signs of burning on its floor led to Hooppell interpreting this below-ground feature as being a possible 'Mithraic cave', later, he thought, turned over to use as a kiln.

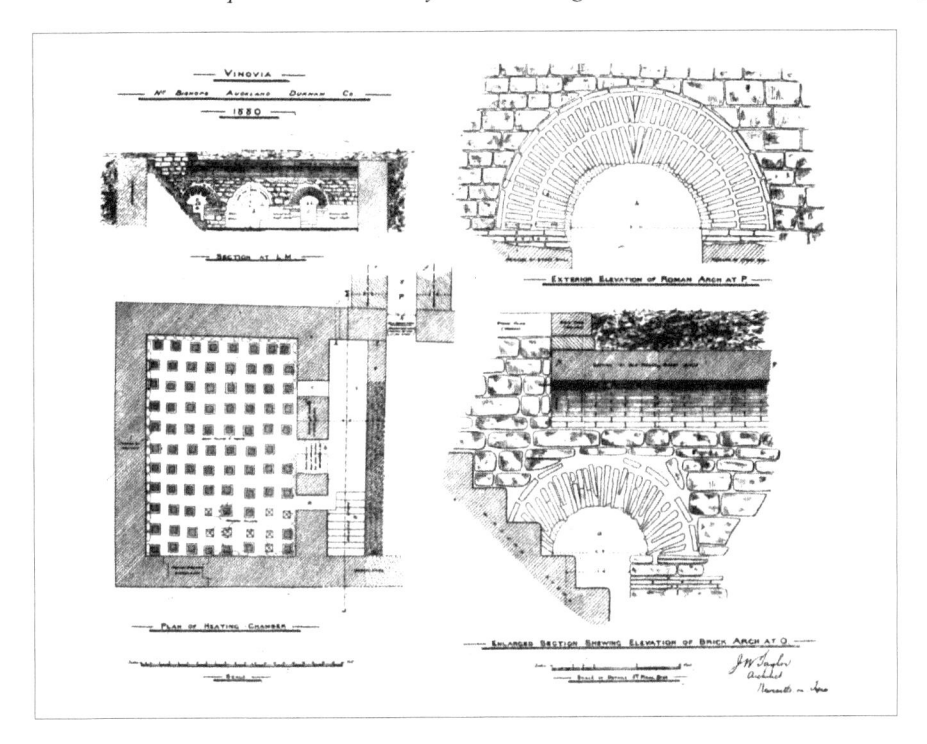

8 The underfloor of the fourth-century bathhouse as recorded by Mr Proud and Revd Hooppell in the nineteenth century. Drawing by J. W. Taylor (from R. E. Hooppell's 1891 *Vinovia*).

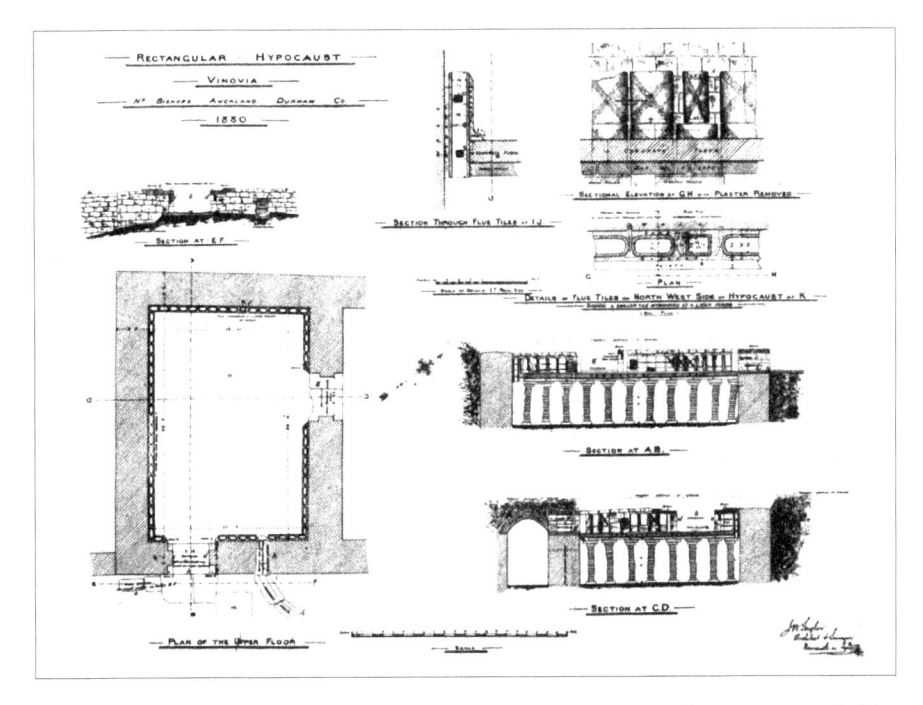

9 The extant hypocausted first room of the mid-fourth-century bathhouse, as recorded by Mr Proud and Revd Hooppell in the nineteenth century. Drawing by J. W. Taylor (from R. E. Hooppell's 1891 *Vinovia*).

Inside the fort, Proud and Hooppell understandably concentrated their efforts on elucidating the history of the large, hypocausted bathhouse which had been the focus of public interest in the site almost since its accidental discovery in 1815 and certainly since its existence had been brought to wider public attention by Roach Smith's publication of drawings and a description of the building in 1854. This bathhouse will be discussed in detail in Chapter Four and so only the briefest summary of the Victorian work on the building will be given here.

The main aim of the work on this building was entirely admirable, in that it was 'to make the most exact survey of it, and to put on record every detail connected with it'. This was most certainly achieved by the making of the excellent survey drawings by the architect J. W. Taylor, whose plans and elevations of the building form a remarkably accurate record invaluable to archaeologists even today. Proud's workmen started excavation by removing the deposits overlying the largely intact floor of the first room of the bathhouse, the warm room or tepidarium, in the process probably inadvertently removing all evidence for the very late Roman or early post-Roman disuse or reuse of this part of the building. The plan of the second room, a dry hot room or laconicum, was then recovered, though here the floor and most of its underlying hypocaust had already been destroyed and robbed out. Part of the third room, a wet hot room or caldarium, was also opened up, again with the floor already destroyed here, along with its related small plunge bath. Neither of the bathhouse's furnace rooms was located or examined.

Outside the bath building, to the east, a large expanse of a stone-paved courtyard was exposed, including a system of stone gutter channels servicing the bathhouse, and much of the plan of a range of residential rooms lying to the south-west was revealed, principally by following wall lines with slit trenches. Solid concrete floors were exposed inside some of the rooms and part of a ruinous hypocaust, represented only by a few surviving pilae, or floor-supporting tiles, was uncovered. Two short lengths of stone walls of another stone building lying across the other side of the Roman road from the bathhouse were also located, trenched and planned. Although recorded on his published plans, these rooms and buildings away from the bath suite unfortunately received little or no discussion in the text of Hooppell's book and his interventions here in fact were to create significant subsequent problems of interpretation for those of us excavating in the same areas in the 1970s and 1980s.

For many years, Proud and Hooppell's excavations in the vicus remained the most extensive exploration of a vicus attached to a northern fort. Outside the fort ramparts to the east, parts of a number of buildings were excavated, including a circular bathhouse room connected to other rooms in a much larger building, though Hooppell did not recover the overall plan of this structure. The circular room had a stone bench around its walls and Hooppell surmised that the roof might have been supported by a central column, though this is perhaps unlikely. Inside the circular room were found seven or eight terracotta bobbins, as Hooppell termed them, each about 6 inches in height and pierced through lengthways. Even Hooppell was at a loss when it came to suggesting an identification and purpose for these objects. At a later date these items were interpreted as being spacers from a pottery kiln, used to separate rows of stacked pots inside the kiln during firing, but they have most recently

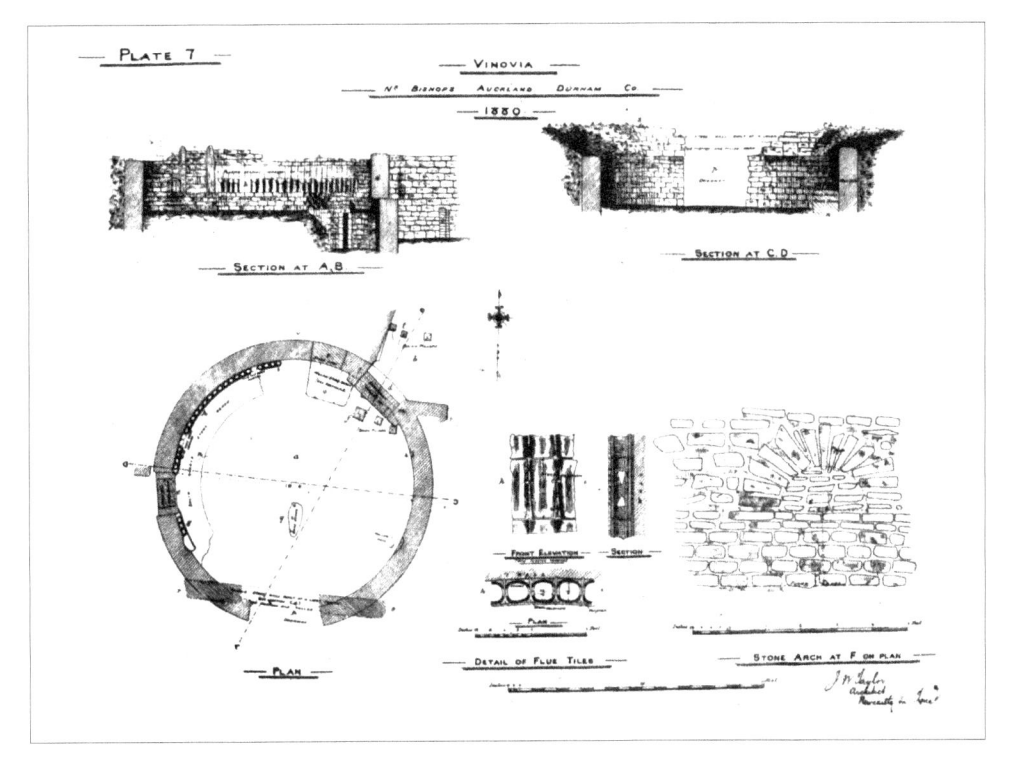

*10 The circular hypocausted room in a building in the vicus, as recorded by Mr Proud and Revd Hooppell in the nineteenth century. Drawing by J. W. Taylor (from R. E. Hooppell's 1891 Vinovia).*

been re-identified as spacer bobbins used in building work. A copper alloy strigil, an implement used by bathers to scrape clean their oiled skin, was also found inside the circular room.

On the western side of Dere Street – Hooppell calls it Watling Street in his published reports – were excavated a series of strip buildings facing directly onto the road. While close together, these buildings did not share party walls. Hooppell suggested that these were of a number of distinct phases. The longest of these buildings[27] was '91 feet long and 25 feet 8 inches wide' and its walls survived in places up to ten stone courses in height, with a door at its eastern end opening onto the Roman road. Though the interior of this building was not cleared out by the workmen, Hooppell was able to note the absence of an interior hypocaust and that there was a dividing wall inside the building, creating two rooms or cells, one 64 feet long, the other 21 feet in length. Hooppell wondered whether this building could have been a Christian church but despite its size it is likely that all the buildings examined in the vicus had a shared function, combining domestic space with commercial or workshop space.

Stretches of the Roman road itself were also examined, including the abrupt termination point of the road on the western plateau edge. A well, now on the western plateau edge in Binchester Plantation Woods, was partially excavated and a collection of pottery was recovered from its backfill, including part of a head pot or face pot.

One of the most significant individual finds of the Proud and Hooppell campaign of work was a large fragment of a decorated dedication slab or votive tablet with an

*11 Above left:* Part of a stone building alongside Dere Street, as recorded by Mr Proud and Revd Hooppell in the nineteenth century. Drawing by W. Heatlie (from R. E. Hooppell's 1891 *Vinovia*).

*12 Above right:* Part of a stone building alongside Dere Street, recorded by Mr Proud and Revd Hooppell in the nineteenth century. Drawing by W. Heatlie (from R. E. Hooppell's 1891 *Vinovia*).

*13 Left:* A stone-lined well in the vicus, as recorded by Mr Proud and Revd Hooppell in the nineteenth century. Drawing by W. Heatlie (from R. E. Hooppell's 1891 *Vinovia*).

14 A dedication slab to Aesculapius and Salus found in the nineteenth century (from R. E. Hooppell's 1891 *Vinovia*).

inscription, about three quarters of the stone surviving intact. The main inscription reads '[Aesc]ulapio [et] saluti [pro salu]te alae Vet[tonum c(iuium) (Romanorum) M(arcus) Aure[lius...]ocomas me [dicus u(otum) s(oluit)] l(ibens) m(erito)' (translated as, 'To Aesculapius and Salus for the welfare of the Cavalry Regiment of Vettonians, Roman citizens, Marcus Aurelius [...]ocomas, doctor, willingly and deservedly fulfilled his vow').[28] The bearded, balding, toga-clad figure of the healing god Aesculapius, his toga draped over his left shoulder, leaving much of his upper torso exposed and naked, looks out directly at the viewer and stands next to and holds the hand of the heavily damaged image of his daughter Salus, whose head and face, left shoulder and general outline only survive intact. In his left hand the god clutches a wooden spar or staff, around which is entwined a serpent, a traditional symbolic attribute of the god. Although his full name does not survive on the dedication slab, there is no doubt that the dedicator of the stone, despite having the Roman forenames Marcus Aurelius, was an ethnic Greek, especially given that most of the doctors serving in the Roman army would likewise almost certainly be of Greek origin. Luckily, this stone was found some time after most of the other inscribed and sculptured stones from Binchester had been disposed of as ballast down a local coal mine, as detailed above, and it now is now part of the collections at the Old Fulling Mill Museum, Durham University.

Two further inscribed stones were recovered, though the second of these may in fact simply have borne tooling marks rather than a formal inscription. The first was an altar fragment inscribed, 'Mat[ribus... | trib(unus) [... | inst(ante) [... | IRI[...' ('To the

Mother Goddess ... tribune ... under the direction of ...').[29] The discovery of this altar added further conclusive evidence for the one-time existence of a Matres cult here at Binchester. The altar is now in the Old Fulling Mill Museum, Durham University. The second stone remains in situ at the site, being built into a culvert outlet on the inner face of the rampart at the north corner of the fort.[30]

Two pieces of fragmentary statuary were also recovered. The first fragment comprised part of what was probably a decorated tombstone bearing the legs and lower torso of a soldier. Unfortunately, this fragment did not include any inscription or dedication. The second broken fragment is perhaps of more interest and is part of a relief sculpture of a female deity, identified by Hooppell as Flora, Roman goddess of flowers, fertility and spring, depicted in a diaphanous dress, with braided hair and holding a cornucopia or horn of plenty. Ever ready to read archaeological discoveries as religious metaphors, a failing that is perfectly understandable given his profession, Hooppell noted that the circumstances of the discovery of this statue fragment – broken, turned face down and reused as a part of the foundation deposit for fourth-century flagstone courtyard blocks as they over-rode a drain channel – immediately brought to his mind a Biblical parallel: 'It furnished to the writer's mind, an irrefragable evidence of the wide-spread extension of the Christian religion in Britain during the latter part of the Roman occupation of the land. When the writer saw it, he could not but be reminded forcibly of some words of the prophet Jeremiah respecting a once powerful but afterwards degraded and insulted king, "Is this man Coniah a despised, broken idol?"'[31]

While there is no doubt about the importance of the work carried out at Binchester by Proud and Hooppell, a note of caution must, however, be sounded about their excavation methodology. The standard of their work was very much of its time and would not be in any way acceptable today. Both were antiquarians with little or no experience of archaeological fieldwork, directing teams of labourers who were opening up and clearing areas principally with picks and shovels rather than carefully excavating in the manner of professional field archaeologists of the twentieth and twenty-first centuries.

The excavation strategy in the areas selected for examination generally conformed to locating solid stone walls and then following the lines of those walls in narrow slit trenches. Plans of individual rooms within larger structures could thus be recorded without the interiors of the rooms necessarily being excavated. When room interiors were excavated, the workmen simply shovelled off archaeological deposits until they hit a solid floor or until it was decided that excavation would cease at a particular level. Any evidence in the form of postholes or beam slots for any ephemeral timber structures overlying these floors would simply not have been recognised.

There was no detailed written record made of individual layers or features, as would be made today, nor was there any coherent strategy for the recovery of finds. Many finds were simply missed by the inexperienced workmen and were backfilled into the trenches at the end of the excavation. The careful hand re-excavation of a number of Proud and Hooppell's original trenches during the mid- to late 1970s campaign of work at Binchester led to the recovery of a large quantity of such missed finds, including pottery, coins and other so-called small finds. When finds were recovered

15 Inscribed altar to Jupiter Optimus Maximus and the Matres Ollototae (from Hooppell 1892).

by the workmen their exact findspots were often not recorded, nor were most of the retained finds marked with any identifying codes to help future researchers reconstruct their findspots. Recording the contexts in which finds are recovered is one of the most crucial tasks of archaeologists today and in not doing this, a great deal of important information about the site was simply lost by Proud and Hooppell.

The final pre-twentieth-century discovery at Binchester to be reported on here was the find of an inscribed altar made in 1891, by chance, by workmen digging pipe trenches just outside the fort, to the south-east. The inscription on the altar read: 'I(oui) O(ptimo) M(aximo) | et Matrib | us Olloto | tis siue Tra | nsmarinis | Pomponius | Donatus | b(ene)f(icarius) co(n)s(ularis) pro | salute sua | et suorum | v(otum) s(olvit) l(ibens) a(nimo)' ('To Jupiter, Best and Greatest, and to the Mother Goddess Ollototae, or Overseas, Pomponius Donatus, beneficiarius of the governor, for the welfare of himself and his household willingly fulfilled his vow').[32] This altar is now in the new Great North Museum: Hancock, Newcastle University.

Thus it can be seen that antiquarian interest in the Roman remains at Binchester between the sixteenth and twentieth centuries was both a blessing and a curse. On the one hand, we owe our knowledge of the inscriptions on a number of now destroyed altars and other sculptured stones to the assiduous transcriptions of the texts made by antiquaries such as Camden, Horsley, Hutchinson, Bruce and Lysons, for example; without these records we would be unaware of the identification of a number of the military units in garrison at Binchester at various periods, and of the great significance of the cult of the Mother Goddesses – the Matres – at the site. On the other hand, antiquarian interest generated an impetus towards the amassing of a private collection at the site of altars, inscriptions, pottery and coins and other finds, leading ultimately to the dreadful act of cultural vandalism that was the stones' disposal down a nearby colliery shaft. Very few of the finds from Binchester recorded by antiquarians can be located today.

The excavations at the site begun in 1879 by Proud and Hooppell constituted a break with the antiquarian past. Firstly their work involved systematic excavation, albeit unscientific in its methodology compared to archaeological techniques employed today, rather than just the collection of stray finds. Their interest was equally focused on both the elucidation of the chronology of the site and of the layout of both the fort and its vicus, a quite revolutionary objective at the time in academic research terms. They were as equally interested in structures and buildings as they were in coins and pottery and other Roman finds. Finally, both Proud and Hooppell, although still to us apparently gentlemen antiquarians in nature and temperament, saw their work as serving some higher cause, in Hooppell's case a social purpose inextricably linked to religious mores, and most importantly their work was intended to generate local interest and pride. Their motives were not too dissimilar to those behind many community archaeology projects today.

Hooppell's moral imperative behind the excavations is well summed up by his closing remarks in a lecture on Binchester he delivered in 1879 in Bishop Auckland town hall:[33]

> the exploration of Binchester has conferred a great boon on Science, has given the inhabitants of Bishop Auckland an insight into their past history, of which I feel sure they cannot, will not, be other than proud, and has helped to demonstrate, what all true study of antiquities plainly shows, that God has made of one blood all nations of men, and that the duration of the human race upon this earth has not been excessive, and is not likely to be indefinitely prolonged.

CHAPTER TWO

# The First-Century Fort

## DATING THE EARLY FORT

There is some artefactual evidence for pre-Roman activity on the Binchester hilltop, some of it dating to a considerable time before the founding of a fort here. A small collection of prehistoric worked flints was recovered from the site in the 1920s by James McIntyre, though largely without a detailed stratigraphic provenance, and almost one hundred flints were recovered during excavations in the 1976–1981 campaign of work in the centre of the fort, along with a fine leaf-shaped arrowhead found during fieldwalking in 1978 to the north-east of the fort.

Most of this excavated flint was recovered from secondary contexts, that is redeposited in later Roman horizons, though some of the material from the buried soil that lay directly over the natural gravels at a depth of 2–3 metres below the present field surface may represent a contemporaneous group. The majority of the flints were flakes, chips and chunks, none of which was closely datable. However, the leaf-shaped arrowhead could represent Neolithic activity in the area and four scrapers and two cores may be of Mesolithic or Neolithic date. Most of the raw material used seemed to be from local pebble sources and was similar to the raw material used for prehistoric flint tool production elsewhere along the Wear Valley.

Though the second-century AD geographer Ptolemy listed Binchester as a 'city of the Brigantes', there is as yet no archaeological evidence of a later prehistoric presence on the site and it must therefore be assumed that though Binchester certainly lay deep within the territory of the late pre-Roman Iron Age tribe of the Brigantes there was no Brigantian settlement site here on the hilltop. The founding of the first Roman fort must therefore have been on virgin land. The main question must then be when the first fort was established here.

When studying Roman Britain, caution needs to be exercised in trying to marry the historical records of the period with the evidence provided by the archaeological record. While these two very different types of evidence sometimes happily match, on other occasions slight mismatches or even contradictions can emerge. However, for the early history of northern Britain following the Roman invasion of AD 43 there is a sufficiently opaque set of accounts of the Roman political and military actions and interventions here against which the archaeological evidence from a site such as Binchester can be assessed.[1] A brief summary of the broad historical accounts will now be given, followed by an analysis of the independent dating evidence for the first fort at Binchester provided by archaeological excavation of deposits and features of that fort.

After the initial invasion and Claudius's triumphal celebration of victory at Camulodunum (Colchester), and later in a triumph on his return to Rome, the Roman forces moved out from the south-eastern area of England where their initial campaign had been focused and, in the next few years, moved westwards and northwards. Claudius's victory, though partial in terms of actual territory conquered in Britain, had not simply been a military one and diplomatic ties and accords had been made with a number of indigenous British tribes whose the loyalty and cooperation were secured under threat of military intervention or retribution should they in any way renege on their agreement with Rome. It is generally accepted that the Brigantes of northern Britain were among these client tribes, their territory probably including most of England north of York and part of southern Scotland.

We are told by the Roman historian Tacitus that eventually splits emerged among the tribal leadership of the Brigantes and that loyalty became divided along pro-Roman and anti-Roman lines, positions respectively taken by Queen Cartimandua and her consort or husband Venutius. These very real tensions led to political and social instability in the tribal area, probably along with economic problems, and almost inevitably the Roman army was eventually forced to move in to bolster the pro-Roman faction and to restore order.

The collapse of the Brigantian kingdom was, however, an extended process. In AD 47 a minor armed insurgency seems to have taken place there and, though it was quashed by Roman forces, no permanent occupation of the territory took place at this time. In AD 51 the defeated tribal leader Caratacus fled from mid-Wales to the north, where he hoped to find a safe haven with the Brigantes. However, Cartimandua handed him over to the Romans, probably in order to enhance her pro-Roman credentials, and in so doing sent him to his eventual death in Rome. During the governorship of Aulus Didius Gallus, AD 52–57, another, more serious, armed rebellion occurred in Brigantian territory, attributed to the plotting of Venutius, but once again this was put down by Roman arms. Cartimandua and Venutius were now separated both by irreconcilable political differences and by a romantic schism, with Cartimandua now recorded as ditching her former consort and provocatively taking up with his one-time shield carrier Vellocatus. In AD 69 the Brigantian kingdom finally fell apart, with the exiled Venutius staging one final attempt to seize power for the anti-Roman faction and succeeding temporarily. Cartimandua was rescued by Roman forces and evacuated south. The situation in Brigantia was now totally out of control and unacceptable to Rome on any level. A formal invasion of the territory and its occupation was now inevitable.

Quintus Petillius Cerialis was appointed governor by the Emperor Vespasian and between AD 71 and 74 he is recorded as conquering the Brigantes and setting in place an infrastructure of roads and forts to control the newly-conquered territory. A later governor, Gnaeus Julius Agricola, AD 77–83, again concentrated Roman efforts on the pacification of northern Britain and according to his son-in-law, the Roman historian Tacitus, achieved total conquest, a triumph subsequently allowed to slip by changes in imperial policy. Agricola's campaigns, taking his forces into Scotland, would probably have involved the further reorganisation of northern military deployments to allow such an extended campaign to be properly backed up by reserves of both men and equipment and, equally importantly, of supplies. The founding of a fort at Binchester must therefore have occurred either under Cerialis or under Agricola and indeed there still continues to be debate about this choice today, though present evidence favours an Agricolan foundation date of *c.* AD 80, as will be discussed shortly below. Agricola is generally credited with the construction of the line of forts along Dere Street – Piercebridge on the River Tees, Binchester on the River Wear, Ebchester on the River Derwent and Corbridge on the Tyne – which formed a coherent military system at this time.

The dating evidence for the earliest activity on the Binchester site comes principally from finds made in the lowest archaeological levels excavated in the central part of the fort during the 1976–1981 campaign of work. Four coins of the Emperor Vespasian, AD 69–79, and a Republican denarius, *c.* 97 BC, were recovered, along with a small but significant pottery assemblage of around ninety sherds which included Terra Nigra pottery, a Lyons ware indented beaker, and vessel fragments from a number of samian vessels including part of a Neronian/early Flavian Dragendorf 29 vessel, which, along with the ceramic and coin evidence from the succeeding phase, would seem to suggest a date of *c.* AD 80 for this phase and thus for the founding of the first fort here.

More recently, in 2007, *Time Team* excavated a trial trench across the defences of the early fort, as will be described shortly. Initially, on the *Time Team* broadcast and on its back-up website,[2] much was made of the recovery here of 'one small piece of [samian] pottery ... [which] ... provided dating evidence that this early fort was in use in the 70s A.D. ... [that Binchester] was one of the fort's from [Cerialis's] campaign.' However, the follow-up published report on the work did not repeat this bold assertion, based as it was on the recovery of a single small sherd of pottery, and until further work takes place on the earliest levels at the site an Agricolan date for the first fort, as established by the examination of the 1976–1981 finds, must stand.

The later stages of the first fort's existence cannot again be formally linked to the historical record. That there was some kind of unspecified trouble in the north in AD 118 is attested by the issuing in AD 119 of the so-called Britannia capta coins by the Emperor Hadrian, with their provocative depiction of a subdued personification of the province. The establishment of the frontier of Hadrian's Wall in the AD 120s, following the earlier use of the Stanegate frontier, tied Binchester firmly into this system of military strength-in-depth in the north. The first fort at Binchester would appear to have come to the end of its life around AD 120–130.

## THE FORT'S DEFENCES AND INTERNAL BUILDINGS

No part of the early fort is visible to visitors to the site today and indeed there has been little archaeological examination of the buried remains of this fort. The fort buildings would have been of timber and the rampart defences of turf and timber, as was the case for all Roman forts of this period, whether legionary or auxiliary, though a stone-built bathhouse might have been expected, perhaps outside the defences. The fort's defensive circuit on its north-eastern and eastern sides was recorded by aerial photography in the 1950s and has more recently been plotted and mapped by geophysical prospection. An abortive attempt to examine these early defences on the north-east side was made in the 1970s. During the three-day excavation at Binchester by the *Time Team* archaeologists in 2007, a small trench was excavated through the eastern defences. Results were somewhat inconclusive but otherwise unsurprising. The excavators concluded that several separate episodes of excavation and backfilling of a number of large defensive ditches, including in one phase a double-ditch defence, were represented in the northern part of their trench, while in the central zone it was surmised that the line of the rampart crossed this area, though no rampart deposits were present, and at the southern end of the trench a metalled road surface was identified, along with part of a possible beam slot of a timber building and a patch of clay floor.

The overall size of the first fort at Binchester can be estimated at around seven hectares (about 17.5 acres), survey indicating that the north–south axis of this early fort was about 290 metres (approximately 951 feet), potentially making it much larger than the second, later fort which succeeded it and on present evidence the largest auxiliary fort in northern Britain at that time.

The interior of the early fort has only been examined archaeologically in two relatively small areas: most extensively in 1976–1981, beneath the stone fourth-century commandant's house now consolidated and on display at the site today, and in a smaller area in 1971 during the building of an extension to what was then Binchester Hall Hotel. The account here will concentrate on the sequence and remains found in the 1976–1981 area. During excavation here work was subject to a number of health and safety restrictions, so that all pre-fourth-century archaeological deposits had to be excavated in small box areas rather than in open areas, the areas diminishing in size with depth, making interpretation of deposits and features of these early phases difficult, though not impossible. Correlating deposits from one area with those from another was done during post-excavation analysis.

The natural gravel subsoil was encountered at a depth of 2–3 metres (about 6.5–10 feet) below the field surface here. A buried soil survived over most of the excavated area, the dark upper surface of which was interpreted as representing the base of a former turfline, the turf itself having been stripped off most of the area before building work began for the fort, perhaps for use in the building of the ramparts. There was also evidence at this horizon for the clearing of vegetation, including shrubs and bushes and larger trees whose positions were marked by a number of infilled tree boles. The fills of these features were generally sterile of finds and consisted of old soil and natural subsoil mixed together. Some of these features did, though, contain Roman finds, as did a large rectangular pit. Its fill, of very mixed grey-orange clay silt with clay, pebbles and charcoal, contained two coins, a small assemblage of pottery, some animal bone, iron nails and stone, but not enough to suggest that it was a rubbish pit as such. It had possibly once been lined with timber to act as a water tank and then was subsequently used for rubbish disposal at the end of this phase of site clearance and preparation. Another square pit contained a cess-like deposit and may have been dug as a latrine pit for the convenience of the work party of soldiers preparing the site.

Evidence for site clearance or preparation ahead of the commencement of building work has been widely attested by excavation at numerous Roman fort sites throughout Britain. At Rocester, Staffordshire, for instance, a large number of irregular, infilled holes were interpreted as representing the positions of bushes or shrubs cleared away in the early to mid-second century ahead of the construction of a barrack block there.[3]

The rubbish left behind by the work party repaid close analysis, particularly the ninety or so pottery sherds and the smaller assemblage of vessel glass. Among the pottery there was a noticeable proportion of finewares present, something that might indicate high-status activity in the area of excavation or nearby. As already mentioned, notable imported wares included Terra Nigra vessels and some Lyons ware, though York was identified as the source of almost a fifth of the pottery from the phase. Among the glass vessel fragments were pieces from a mould-blown vessel and a conical/convex jug. The mould-blown cup is an extraordinary and rare find, bearing a Greek inscription of a type otherwise unknown in Roman Britain. The inscription in translation reads either, 'Wherefore art thou come? Rejoice,' or, 'Enjoy yourself as long as you are here.' Again, its presence suggests high-status activity on the site at this period.

Among the 300 or so animal bones discarded, presumably mostly food waste, were represented cattle, sheep and pig, in order of magnitude, with a dog, horse and red deer also being present in the assemblage.

Following the preparatory clearing of the site and the disposal of rubbish, the ground was now levelled, ready for the construction of a large timber building here. The lines of the main walls of the building were represented by beam trenches into which the main horizontal timbers would have been laid, with the main vertical timbers forming the main frame of the building being jointed into the horizontal timbers at or just below floor level. Many of these timbers had been left to rot in situ in their original beam trenches; other beam trench lines were represented only by robber trenches dug to extract the timbers at the time of the eventual demolition of the building. Internal divisions, made by doors or screens and so on, were marked by post holes, stake holes or slots and gullies of various kinds which remained as so-called negative features to be recorded by the modern excavators. Floors would have either been of pegged timbers or of puddled clay, depending on the function of individual rooms. Evidence suggests that glass windows would have been provided, decorated plastered walls in most rooms, and an oak shingle or stone tiled roof. Hearths made of laid ceramic tiles or packed stones might have existed in some rooms. In another was excavated a large pit, possibly originally in use as a latrine pit and containing a small but interesting ritual deposit of finds in its final sequence of backfills, as will be discussed more fully shortly.

The partially recovered plan of the building is at first sight difficult to interpret. The nature of the excavation strategy as detailed above meant that only a fragmentary

16 *Above:* Beam trenches of the first-century timber building cut into natural.

17 *Left:* Beam trenches of the first-century timber building cut into natural, one excavated, the other unexcavated.

18 Beam trench of the first-century timber building cut into natural and truncated by a pit. The baulk into which the trench runs presents a section through the earliest horizons on the site.

plan could be recovered in the major, central area of the excavation where fifteen separate, unconnected box-areas were excavated at different times, while in the two more isolated, outlying, excavated box-areas to the north-west and the south-east the timber building remains excavated could conceivably belong to other structures. It is not possible to identify confidently any of the beam trenches as being the outer walls of the building, which fact again creates problems of interpretation.

If all of these features do belong to a single building, then it has dimensions of at least 30 metres (about 98 feet 6 inches) east–west by 21.5 metres (about 70 feet 6 inches) north–south. The potentially large size of the building and its suggested high-status function, as indicated by the examination of the associated finds assemblage, probably mean that it can be identified as the early fort's commandant's house (in Latin the praetorium), or, less likely, as the headquarters building, or principium, dating, it is thought, to AD 80–90.

The most noticeable element of the extrapolated groundplan in the central, southern zone is a very large rectangular area or room, referred to on the plan reproduced here as Room 2/1, internally subdivided into six separate and more-or-less equally sized units which on the plan are labelled Room 2/1a–2/1f for ease of description. To its east lies what may be a corridor, beyond which are parts of further rooms, and to its west two further rooms.

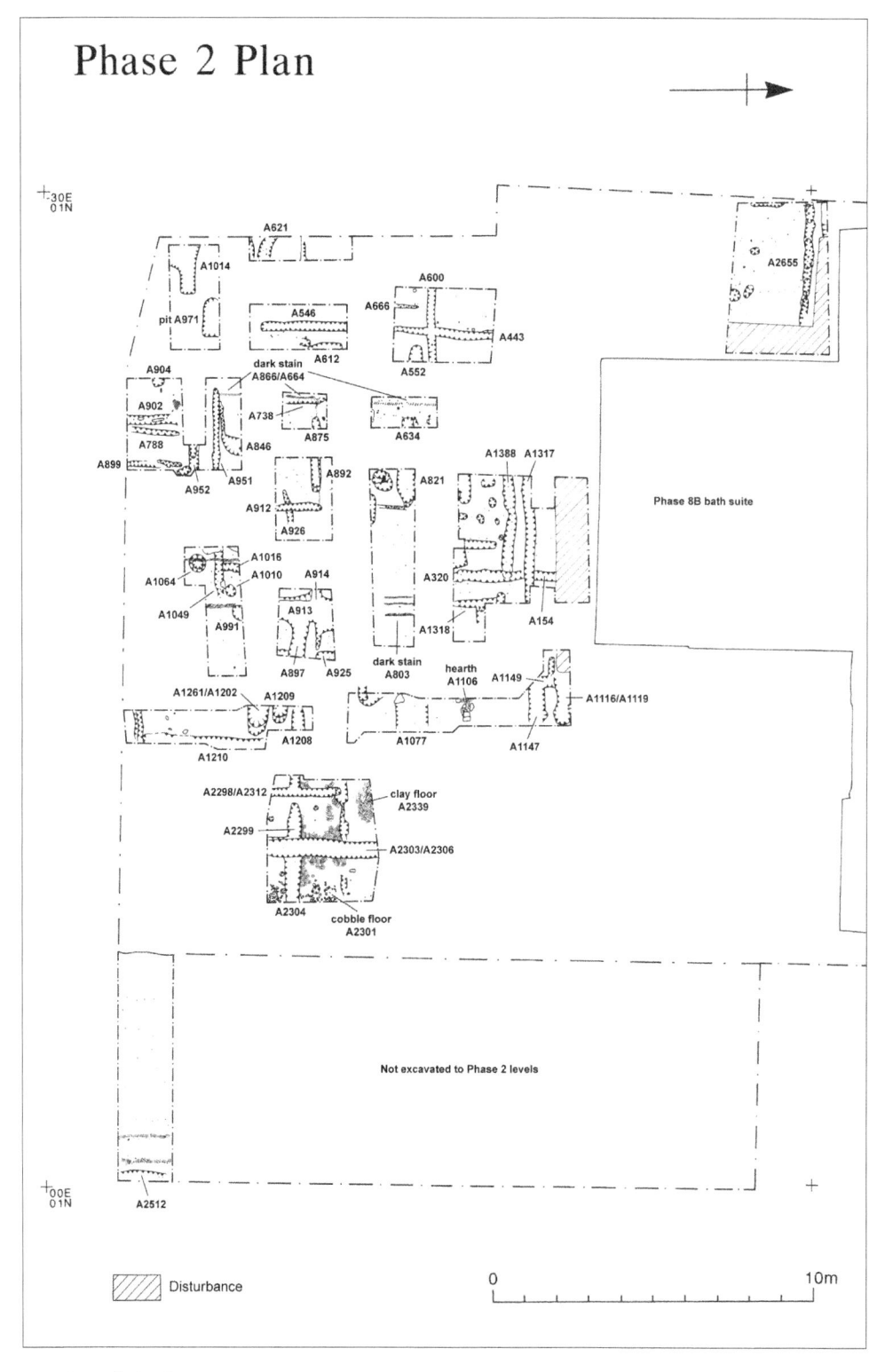

19 Plan of the first-century timber praetorium, or commandant's house (called Phase 2 in the stratigraphic schema for the 1976–1981 and 1986–1991 excavations).

*The First-Century Fort*

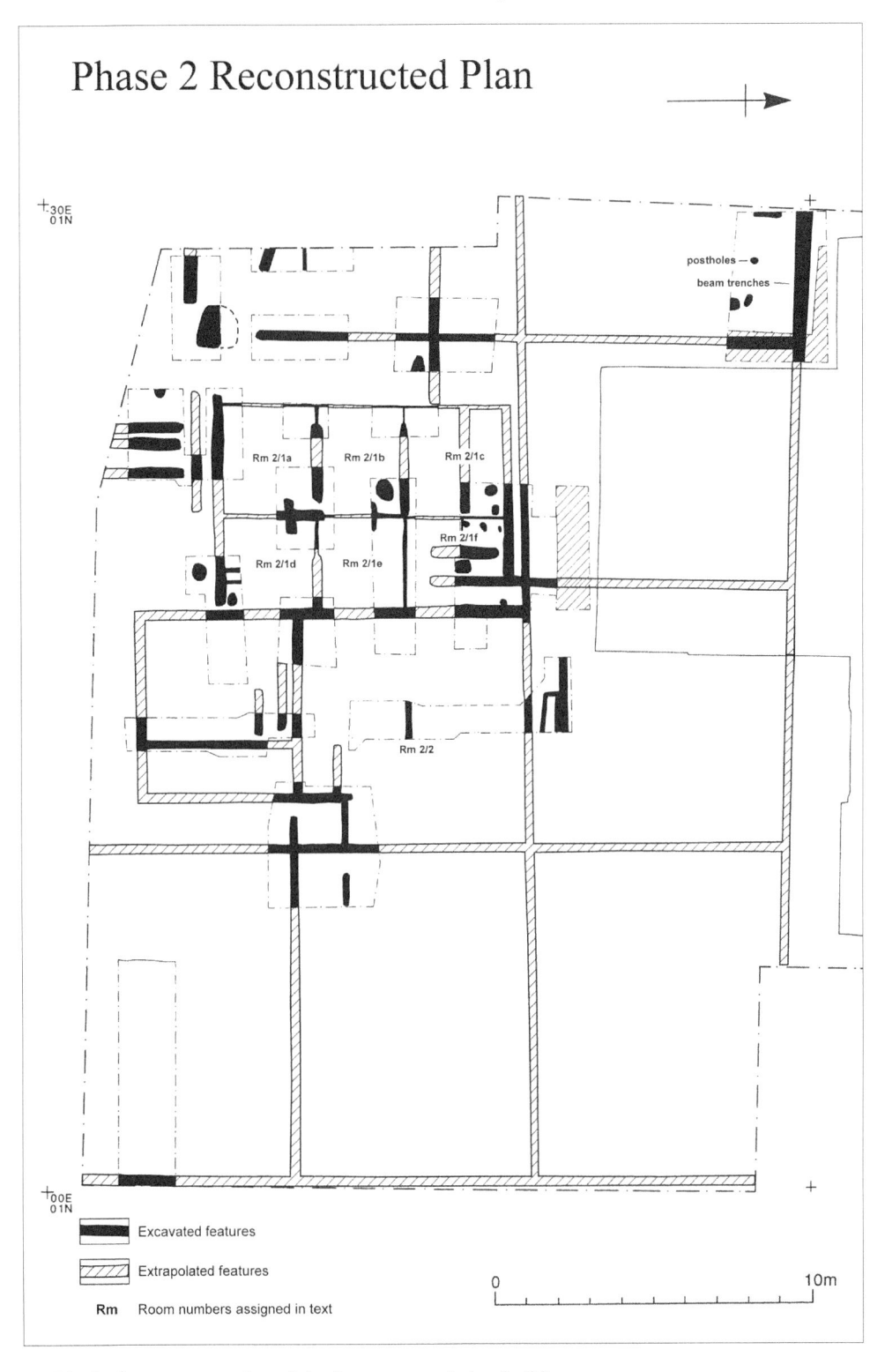

20 Block plan reconstruction of the first-century timber building.

Parallels for the form of praetoria and principia can be sought at other sites. A perusal of published comparanda of fort plans[4] throws up a number of possible parallels, though, of course, no definitive answer can be provided here given the uncertainty over whether there is one building represented at Binchester in this phase or parts of two or more separate structures. If it was a single building, the Binchester structure, at 30 metres by 22.5 metres, is roughly the same size of the Fendoch timber praetorium, at 30 metres by 20 metres;[5] however, few of the plan elements of the Binchester and Fendoch buildings appear to correspond. One of the most striking elements of the Binchester plan, as noted above, is the group of six more-or-less equal-sized rooms in the south-west of the building; similar, but not identical, rows of rooms can be seen in the Valkenburg 1 principium.[6] There is again the potentially complicating factor that the Binchester building, if a praetorium, could have taken the form of a praetorium with adjoining compound, as at Inchtuthil.[7]

Inside the Binchester building almost no clues were provided as to the function of individual rooms, either by the excavated structural evidence or by analysis of the finds made there. However, of particular interest was a pit in one of the rooms in the south-western part of the excavated structure. This feature stood out for several reasons: firstly because of its shape and form, there being no other pits represented elsewhere on the site at this period; secondly because of its apparent original function; and thirdly because of the unusual assemblage of finds recovered from its backfill.

This large, deep pit was straight-sided, with a flattish base. The number and nature of the finds within the backfill did not indicate its use as an ordinary rubbish pit, while the greenish tint of some of the soil in the backfill suggested the one-time presence here of organic rubbish. The finds were most unusual, in that there must have been a number of whole pots dumped into or carefully placed in the pit, one pot being a buff flagon and the others of rustic ware, as well as oddities like a fragment of a lamp chimney – an object more often associated with Roman religious sites – and a bronze seal box, a personal item associated with the writing and conveying of messages, an assemblage of items which together suggests that the backfilling of the feature was somehow linked to ritual or religious practice of some kind. The pit's regularity could be explained by the one-time presence here of a timber lining which was removed during the demolition of the building, though no such lining was detectable in the archaeological record.

This large timber building in the centre of the first fort at Binchester was systematically demolished, or rather dismantled, at the end of its life. The majority of the horizontal timbers were evidently dug out, the squared butt ends of the beam trenches being enlarged and rounded by digging to allow the levering out of the timber. In the case of some timbers, digging took place along the whole length of the beam trench and the timber was removed from this robber trench. The horizontal timbers that remained in situ were presumably in a state of decay or of no use, or they were simply too difficult to remove. The upright timbers also seem to have been systematically removed, even from some of the in situ horizontals where void stakeholes suggested that the frame had been simply pulled out. Where evidence suggests that timbers had been morticed into horizontals, it seems that they had been sawn off level with the top of the beam in most cases. A certain amount of rubbish was backfilled into the emptied beam trenches, just as some rubbish had found its way into some of them when originally dug, but otherwise the trenches were remarkably clean of finds. The timber board or plank floors which must have existed in parts of the building were lifted. Therefore, it is not surprising that so few deposits associated with life in the building survived when this is borne in mind.

With such a systematic dismantling, one might have expected to find large quantities of iron nails or fittings at this horizon, but this is not the case, and it may be that the structure relied more on jointing or pegging than on nails to give it strength.

The date of the life of the timber building is suggested by finds analysis, particularly of the samian pottery assemblage, to be *c*. AD 80–90. Indeed, samian characteristic of the Flavian–Trajanic period after *c*. AD 90 was tellingly absent from the phase. The mass of finds from the dumped contexts of the succeeding phase that sealed the backfilled features of the by-then-dismantled structure tended to be late first to early second century in date, which may suggest that the timber buildings lasted for only a short time, though the physical evidence for the renewal of a floor surface in one area and the suggestion of a replanning in another may contradict this.

The overall finds assemblage associated with the timber building was of some interest. Just over 900 sherds of pottery were recovered. Once more, the pottery evidence pointed to this being a high-status building or buildings, as did the glass assemblage. Among the pottery there were high levels of finewares, a bias towards tablewares such as dishes and bowls, and vessels such as beakers, mortaria and lids. The number of storage jar sherds was low and a high proportion of South Gaulish decorated samian was present.

Many sources of supply for pottery were evident at this phase, each generally providing small quantities of vessels. Some pottery derived from local production, including Iron Age-tradition gritted ware, and pottery from York, was well represented. Material from south-east England or the Midlands was also present. Notable imported wares included quite a large range of Terra Nigra vessels, Noyon Gallic mortaria and North Gaulish greywares.

One noteworthy samian vessel from this phase, a Ritterling 9 form, would have certainly been an heirloom piece at the time of its breaking and deposition as such vessels are rarely found after AD 60. As already mentioned above, ritual or religious activity was suggested by the deposition of an almost-complete two-handled flagon and other large pottery fragments in the backfill of the pit in the south-west of the building, along with a quantity of samian pottery and a number of other items such as part of a ceramic lamp chimney and a copper alloy seal box.

In the small assemblage of over sixty glass fragments from the building, two pillar moulded bowls, a facet-cut beaker, three wheel-cut cups and one convex jar/jug were present, vessels which indicate a high-status occupant of the building.

Although there was not a large number of small finds from this phase, functionally there was a marked bias towards personal ornaments and equipment and tools or craft items, along with a piece of worked antler and a piece of jet waste, attesting to some craft activity having taken place at this time.

A surprising amount of painted wall plaster was recovered, most of it bearing a patchy red paint, though two fragments with gold bands on white were also recovered.

About 2.5 kilograms of stone roof tiles were also found, indicating a relatively early exploitation of local stone sources at nearby Binchester Crags. While these could have been used to roof the timber structures of this period, alternatively they may be derived from a contemporary stone or half-timbered building elsewhere in the fort. A small quantity of ceramic tile, mostly comprising fragments of tegulae, may have been used as hearth stones rather than for roofing.

It must be assumed, in the absence of excavation of contemporary early levels elsewhere inside the fort, that the whole fort was cleared of timber buildings at the same time as the demolition of this major building in or around AD 90. Following its demolition and the clearance of the site, the area examined in 1976–1981 was used for an altogether different purpose, suggesting that the function of the fort at Binchester changed significantly at this time, albeit relatively temporarily.

## INDUSTRIAL PRODUCTION IN THE SECOND CENTURY

The central area of the fort where the large timber building described above had once stood was now used for other purposes, starting with rubbish dumping, followed by an intensive period of ironworking and the dumping of associated waste, and ending with another phase of dumping of waste and spoil.

Many of the layers in these three successive dumps contained large quantities of pottery, glass, small finds, ironworking slag, animal bones and so on, and the green colouring of other deposits suggested their derivation from organic waste. There were also, though, many sterile deposits of heavy clay, of sand, and of cobbles, which may have been dumped periodically in this area to cover rotting organic waste matter here.

The first spoil-heap laid down here covered an area of at least 13 metres (around 42 feet 6 inches) north–south by roughly 18 metres (around 59 feet) east–west. The depth of the dump deposit varied. It is likely that the western limit of the area designated for dumping was originally defined by a fence, represented by a north–south line of void stakeholes excavated here. The western fenceline was subsequently dismantled and its former line covered over by dumped spoil. A similar sequence was found in the northern central part of the excavated area, where a small hearth of burnt stones set into a heavy, reddened clay overlay the line of a former beam trench and was, in turn, overlain by dumped deposits. It is possible that a spread of sands and clays in an area to the north-west of the main zone of dumping represented some kind of working surface contemporary with the activity to the south-east.

The next phase of activity consisted of the building and operation of a number of metalworking hearths and ovens in this area and the dumping of waste material, much of it highly charcoal-rich and probably derived from the industrial production processes being carried out here, in a central spoil-heap over the top of the pre-existing dump. This second dump consisted principally of charcoal and over 40 kilograms of iron-smithing slag and other metalworking residues, along with a number of crucible (or possible crucible) fragments, coal, and numerous fragments of daub and baked clay, mixed in with general domestic rubbish in a dirty, grey, silty loam matrix.

## The First-Century Fort

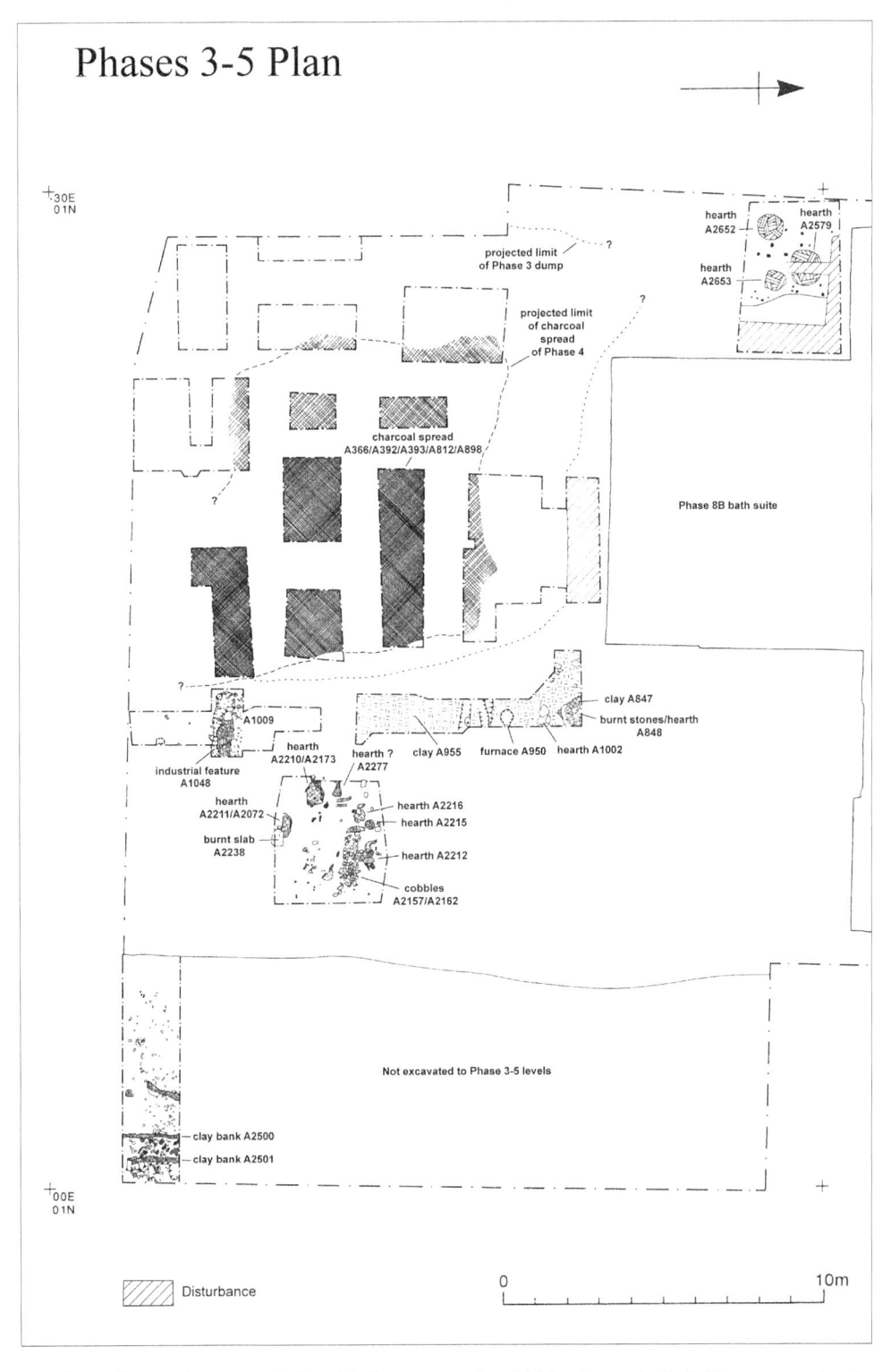

21 Plan of second-century industrial features and rubbish dump (called Phases 3–5 in the stratigraphic schema for the 1976–1981 and 1986–1991 excavations).

22 Second-century furnace/oven.

Three simple hearths or hearth bases lay to the north-west of the charcoal dump, two just to the north-east, along with a keyhole-shaped feature, possibly a furnace, and at least seven hearths and a cobbled working surface or floor lay to the east. Here were also found extensive spreads of charcoal and ash. There was evidence for a number of these so-called hearths having originally had domed roofs made of baked clay.

The phase was probably very short-lived, as one cannot imagine such work being carried out in the open air during a northern winter. At the end of this phase the furnace domes appear to have been staved-in after the backfilling of the pits, and the hearths were all levelled. The dumped material of the second phase remained as an upstanding, low spoilheap in the centre of the area of excavation and the third phase of dumping took place around the outside of this mound.

The deposits of this third dump were again rich in finds, including a group of semi-articulated bones of various animals, cattle, pig and bird, packed closely together in such a way as to suggest, in conjunction with the presence and position of a number of iron nails or fittings, that they were originally joints of meat contained in a shallow wooden box or palette. The uppermost deposits of the dump were formed by a thick and extensive layer of crumbly green-brown clay silt, the colour and aerated nature of which suggested that it either originally comprised pure cess or that it contained significant quantities of organic material which had subsequently rotted down.

Contemporary with the third and last phase of dumping was the laying down to the east of the spoil-heap of a rough cobble road or track, around 3 metres (almost

*23 Tray or pallet of animal bone in final phase of second-century dump.*

10 feet) in width and aligned north–south on the line that would later become the via principalis (or main road) of the subsequent second fort at Binchester. A second layer of cobbles in sand in the west probably represented a patch or repair to the original road surface.

The first phase of dumping is dated as beginning *c.* AD 90–95/100, almost immediately after the demolition of the timber building, the second phase as *c.* AD 95/100 and the third as *c.* AD 110/120 – AD 120/130. In other words, this area of the fort was utilised for non-domestic purposes for around forty years.

In total, the deposits of this phase contained almost 4,800 sherds of pottery and around 6,000 animal bones, along with numerous other finds. The functional analysis of the pottery, alongside the structural evidence, confirmed a change in function of this area of the fort, with fewer finewares being present in these phases than in the timber building phase and a marked bias towards storage vessels such as jars, as opposed to tablewares, though this changed towards the top of the dumped sequence.

In the pottery assemblage locally produced oxidised wares were particularly significant in all three dump phases, and local reduced ware continued to be important. Pottery from York was less important in proportional terms than it had been in the timber-building phase. Imported Noyon Gallic mortaria and North Gaulish greywares were also represented. A small proportion of Black Burnished ware (BB1) pottery from south-west Britain appeared in the assemblage in the last phase of dumping. The samian was still mainly South Gaulish in origin, with a small amount of Central Gaulish material appearing towards the end of the phase. It is also worthy of note that three fragments from a briquetage salt container came from the second phase of dumping.

Ritual or religious activity in the first phase of dumping is perhaps suggested by the presence of half of a samian Dragendorf 37 vessel and half of a samian Dragendorf 18/31 vessel in the same context. Again, a large, virtually complete jar recovered from a context in the second phase may also be of significance. Although the finding of complete or near-complete pottery vessels often indicates ritual or religious activity, rather than this being the case here, as has been suggested by pottery specialists, there is probably a more mundane explanation for the presence of the vessel: it might have contained water used by the workers in the industrial activity of this phase. At the end of the third phase there are a number of indications that the uppermost dumping levels could represent a so-called closing deposit. Further indications of possibly ritual or religious activity towards the end of this phase come from the recovery of a more-or-less complete mortarium from the uppermost layer and three very large parts of highly-decorated samian bowls, all Dragendorf 37s, from another part of the same deposit.

The amount of vessel glass in these dumped phases varied, with little in the first two episodes of dumping and over 200 pieces retrieved from the third phase. In the first phase only two vessels were represented, a pillar moulded bowl and a conical/convex jug, and in the second only four vessels: a cast vessel, a mould-blown beaker, a facet-cut beaker and a conical/convex jug. However, the cast vessel, a rectangular tray or plate, is facet-cut and unparalleled in Britain. In the Roman period such a vessel would have been an expensive rarity. The mould-blown beaker, decorated with horizontal spiral scroll mouldings, is again of a rare type in Britain. The twelve vessels represented in the third dump phase were three facet-cut beakers, a wheel-cut cup, two convex jars/jugs and six conical/convex jugs. One piece of glass manufacturing waste came from each of the second and third phases of dumping.

Twenty-seven small finds of copper alloy, iron, lead, glass, bone, jet or shale and stone came from the first two phases of dumping, including a copper alloy pendant, a copper alloy toilet implement, a junction loop from a horse harness, part of an iron window grille, seven glass beads, parts of two lead pigs, a ceramic gaming counter, a bone weaving comb, a bone die, a bone handle, part of a quern, a hone, and a few pieces of sawn shale and un-worked shale. Twelve iron hobnails from shoes or boots also came from deposits of these two phases, along with a whole shoe sole formed of dozens of fused hobnails.

From the third phase came forty-five small finds, two-thirds functionally biased towards personal ornaments and equipment and a third towards fixtures and fittings. The finds included three copper alloy brooches, a copper alloy pin, two copper alloy finger rings, a seal box, parts of a patera and another copper alloy vessel, three items of horse harness, an iron finger ring with intaglio, fifteen glass beads, an antler ring, a bone die, part of a quern, a hone, a stone pot lid, and eight pieces of unworked shale. A whole shoe sole formed of dozens of fused hobnails was also found. Over 80 kilograms of stone roof tiles came from this phase, this large dump of material suggesting demolition of a nearby building. There was almost 20 kilograms of ceramic tile from this phase, again mainly roof tiles where identifiable.

The animal bone assemblage of around 6,000 bones was the most substantial assemblage from any period on the site, with the exception of the much larger assemblage from the very late Roman or sub-Roman phases. As might be expected, cattle, sheep and pigs were the best represented species, in that order, with, perhaps surprisingly, many other species being present to a much lesser extent, including horse, red deer, roe deer, dog, domestic fowl, duck, goose, swan, oystercatcher, raven and fish. Other environmental material included around 150 shell fragments, mostly of the common blue mussel and of the common European oyster, with the common winkle, the common European cockle, the common limpet, the soft-shell clam and the giant-razor shell each being represented by a few shells only.

The large quantity of ironworking slag from the second phase of hearths and dumping, a very significant amount indeed, suggests that smithing on a semi-industrial scale was taking place in this period. Among this material was a significant quantity of hearth lining, which confirms the structural evidence for hearths operating within the excavated area. The smaller but still-significant amount of ironworking slag from the third dump phase either suggests that metalworking on a semi-industrial scale was continuing to take place in this period, following its commencement in the second phase, or that much of this material was residual and was in fact derived from the earlier activity. The metallurgical analysis of the residues was also of great interest. The analysed slags from the second phase were consistent in both mineral composition and texture, indicating a closely controlled production process or the production of a narrow range of artefacts. This equally applied to analysed slags from the first and third phases.

In the excavations carried out in 1971 adjacent to the Binchester Hall Hotel as it then was,[8] a similar horizon of hearths and hearth bases was encountered, although here associated with timber structures and a gravel surface, along with a great deal of charcoal and metalworking residues. At least sixteen possible hearths and a keyhole furnace were recorded here. This activity was dated to the first half of the second century and is therefore probably broadly contemporary with the dumping and industrial activity recorded to the south and discussed in detail above. If similar contemporary metalworking is interpolated as also having taken place over the whole of the as-yet-unexcavated area between the two archaeological sites then it would therefore appear that at least 0.5 hectares (over an acre), and probably considerably more, of the interior of the fort at Binchester was turned over to industrial production at this period.

The second-century industrial phase at Binchester provides another new perspective on Roman frontier bases. It is now apparent that much of the interior of the fort at Binchester at that time was used for industrial production, rather than for the barracks and conventional buildings of contemporary forts. This raises many questions about the organisation of Roman military supply systems at this time. This is a pattern to be found at other sites in northern Britain and in Wales at about the same period. The Roman army seems to have been managing the supply of its own specialised requirements, an intermediate stage between importing its own supplies into newly occupied territory and the full economic integration of the frontier region. Some forts, at least, were therefore not just fighting bases with their occupation determined by the need to contain hostile natives.

At the site of Ribchester a considerable number of similar metalworking hearths has been excavated and, again, much slag recovered, this activity starting at a slightly later date than at Binchester. Many of the Ribchester hearths were related to a building of mid-Hadrianic date.[9] However, it was in the succeeding period, around AD 120–125, that larger-scale metalworking took place, producing quantities of material above and beyond the needs and requirements of the immediate settlement and its occupants. Parallels for the industrial activity were sought by the excavators at Caerhun in north Wales, where a small industrial annexe was attached to the fort, and at the Scottish site of Newstead, where timber buildings with furnaces were found within the southern annexe.

In a northern military context, evidence for metalworking has been found on some of the turrets on Hadrian's Wall, at Sewingshields milecastle, and at the forts of Housesteads, Vindolanda, Stanwix, Carrawburgh, South Shields, Newcastle and Piercebridge,[10] although in these cases the evidence of structures and finds is not strictly comparable to activity at Binchester.

The civilian settlement or vicus outside the fort at Manchester contained a large area set aside from the early second century to the third century for metalworking,[11] both for iron smithing and, to a lesser extent, for iron smelting. Whether metalworking took place in a military-controlled annexe or was a spontaneous civilian response to military needs and requirements is uncertain. The same uncertainty over the control of production away from forts or fort annexes, whether it was military, civilian, domestic, industrial, tributary or tax-linked, applies to other northern sites where metalworking has been identified.

Evidence both from an examination of the uppermost deposits belonging to this industrial phase at Binchester fort and analysis of the finds from these deposits suggests that after the cessation of the large-scale industrial activity and the associated dumping here, this part of the fort subsequently remained open and unbuilt-on for some time. That a large part of the fort, and possibly even the whole establishment, had been turned over to use as a works depot of some kind in the earlier second century looks likely from the present evidence. Certainly the extensive area of metalworking hearths at this period suggested by their contemporary presence both in the area excavated in 1976–1981 and that excavated in 1971 points towards this interpretation. There must, though, have been some buildings within the fort at this time, for even if Binchester did operate as a production and distribution centre, it would be necessary to accommodate the worker soldiers, their officers and overseeers, and to have sufficient secure storage buildings for goods and raw materials, and for the stabling of horses and protective sheltering of waggons for transporting goods.

When building work did take place again in the central area of Binchester, it was to construct the first of three successive stone commandant's houses, or praetoria, dating from the mid-second to the mid-fourth century. These buildings will be described in the next two chapters.

CHAPTER THREE

# *The Second Fort and Two Successive Praetoria*

Pottery evidence indicates that there was a considerable gap between the end of the earlier second-century industrial activity and related dumping in the central area of the fort at Binchester and the start of the next phase of activity here in the Antonine period. This new phase of activity marks a major change at the site, with the entire fort now being replanned and resurveyed to become a smaller military establishment than its predecessor. Substantial stone ramparts were now constructed and buildings inside the new defensive circuit were now also constructed in stone, in whole or in part, as will be seen below. It is probably around this time that the vicus or civilian settlement was established, though there could have been a small cluster of timber buildings outside the first fort that so far has not been detected by the rather limited excavation that has taken place here. This will be discussed further below.

The broader context of the abandonment of the first fort at Binchester in AD 120–130 and the building of a new, smaller fort here in the mid-second century needs to be considered briefly.[1] The theatre of Roman military operations had moved further north from Hadrian's Wall in the subsequent decades after its construction and inauguration as a permanent frontier, leading to the establishment of the new Antonine Wall frontier in Scotland and its eventual abandonment in the 160s, with an accompanying return south to Hadrian's Wall.

Following this, the appointment of a number of governors with solid reputations in a crisis, men such as Sextus Calpurnius Agricola, suggests frontier problems, even if the historical accounts do not specify the nature of the problems at these times. In the third century the northern frontier would appear to have been relatively peaceful, apart from the campaigning carried out during the reign of Septimius Severus in Scotland. In the fourth century a series of apparent crises occurred, according to the historical sources: in AD 305/306, Constantius Chlorus is recorded as campaigning in northern Britain and dying at York; in AD 315 Constantine, we are told, celebrated a victory in Britain, presumably one achieved in the north. Little is known of activity on the northern frontier and beyond in the next two decades and there is therefore no historical context in which to interpret the apparent upgrading in importance of Binchester fort, as seems to have occurred in the mid-fourth century, and will be described in Chapter Four.

## THE SECOND FORT: THE DEFENCES AND VIA PRINCIPALIS

The ramparts of the second fort have been sectioned in a number of places, in three different campaigns of work: firstly, in the nineteenth century under Proud and Hooppell, as was detailed above in Chapter One; secondly, in 1937 as part of the exploratory excavation carried out by Kenneth Steer; thirdly, and most recently, in 1977, when the present author and a team conducted a watching brief on a water pipeline trench that cut through the rampart at one point.[2]

The 1937 campaign of work saw the excavation of eight trial trenches across the line, or suspected line, of the defences. Although perhaps the dating of the pottery recovered from some of the trenches might now be questioned, nevertheless important information about the construction of the ramparts emerged from this work. A stone curtain wall of large-faced ashlar blocks, about 2.5 metres (just over 8 feet) wide at the base, had been set on a 3.3 metres (almost 11 feet) wide cobble foundation that itself rested or was embedded into a clay bank that the excavator took to be the remains of part of the circuit of the clay rampart of the earlier fort. At the east angle of the fort, part of a small structure, possibly an angle tower or corner tower, was recorded. Steer's work also confirmed that the defensive fort ditch on the south-east side was around 12 metres (just over 39 feet) wide and 3.5 metres (around 11 feet 6 inches) deep and that, some time after its backfilling, stone buildings had been built over part of its line. Finally, one trench encountered part of a drain whose outlet was into a stone-built cistern or water tank, similar to a tank discovered by Proud and Hooppell in the nineteenth century.

None of the fort gates has been examined archaeologically, although it is provisionally planned that excavation of the north-west gate will take place some time in the near future as part of the new five-year campaign of research excavation that began on the site in 2009. Work has, though, been carried out on what was at first thought to be an interval tower on the inside face of the south-east rampart of the fort. This feature, approximately 2.4 metres (8 feet) by 5.5 metres (18 feet), with deep foundations and infilled with stone rubble, which showed up clearly on aerial photographs, was the focus of a small excavation in 1957 and was subsequently reinterpreted as being a platform for housing a ballista or piece of military field artillery which had been added to the rampart as a secondary feature.[3]

The replanning of the fort also led to the establishment of a new roadline through the fort as its via principalis. The roadline of this period has only been examined in one small trench in the centre of the fort and here it was found that the line of the approximately 3 metres (almost 10 feet) wide rough cobble track that had existed here towards the end of the life of the first timber fort was now followed by a more substantial road surface of rammed cobble gravel, at least 4–5 metres (just over 13 feet to around 16 feet 6 inches) in width, increasing to 6 metres (over 19 feet 6 inches) in width in the subsequent phases, and being serviced by stone gutter channels to cope with surface run-off water.

## THE SECOND STONE FORT: INTERNAL BUILDINGS

Our knowledge of the internal layout of the interior of the second stone fort comes almost entirely from geophysical survey plots. Limited excavation took place in 1995 in the former Binchester Hall Hotel walled garden, and stone walls of an unidentified Roman building, probably the principium or headquarters building, were uncovered; in 1996 a very small part of a stone building, possibly a barrack building, was partially excavated in the north-east quadrant of the fort; and in 2005 stone walls of what the excavators assumed to be another barrack building were encountered close to the former Binchester Hall Hotel building.[4] Excavation of another, complete barrack building began in 2009 and is due to continue for several more seasons. These, though, are all possibly fourth-century stone buildings.

So once more, it is in the central area of the fort, where the two major campaigns of excavation took place in 1976–1981 and 1986–1991, that we know most about the nature of the stone buildings of the second fort, both in terms of the date and sequence of building here, in terms of understanding the dynamics of change here on the northern frontier between the second and fifth centuries, and in terms of connecting with the lives of military personnel within the fort through the study of finds of artefacts made in association with the structures, and about the social and economic basis of life here.

That there was a time-lapse between the laying down of the upper part of the three-phase dump and the construction of the first stone building was suggested not only by the pottery record but also by the degree of disturbance noted in the uppermost horizons of the extensive spread of green silt clay which formed the top of the dump in most areas examined by excavation, which suggests that it had been exposed to the elements for some time and trampled. In addition, at some time before the construction of the stone building, a number of features, including two groups of stakeholes, six in a linear alignment and perhaps forming a temporary fenceline, two isolated clay pads and a number of pits had been cut into, or through, the upper dump surface. The pits lay in the north-west of the excavated area and may have been open and continued in use during part of the life of the first stone building.

Some of the logistical problems of excavation at Binchester in 1976–1981 have already been outlined above, but particularly relevant to the excavation of features and layers associated with the three successive stone buildings was the perpetuation and reuse of wall lines and building plans from one phase to another. This meant that not only were wall lines followed by one phase after another but also that the actual fabric of early walls in some cases was incorporated into that of later buildings. Such constructional practices often made the interpretation of the excavated stone building remains difficult, particularly for the earliest of them. During excavations in 1976–1981, the problem was partially alleviated by the fact that for much of this period a stonemason worked on the site to consolidate those walls which were necessary to the display of the latest, fourth-century building remains. Thus, during the recording and stripping down of some walls, the opportunity was presented for a detailed study of their build and of their foundations, which often threw light on parts of the plan of the two earlier stone structures. At this horizon the excavation of box-areas was no longer a necessary strategy to employ, so most of the stone buildings were examined in plan.

60 *Vinovia*

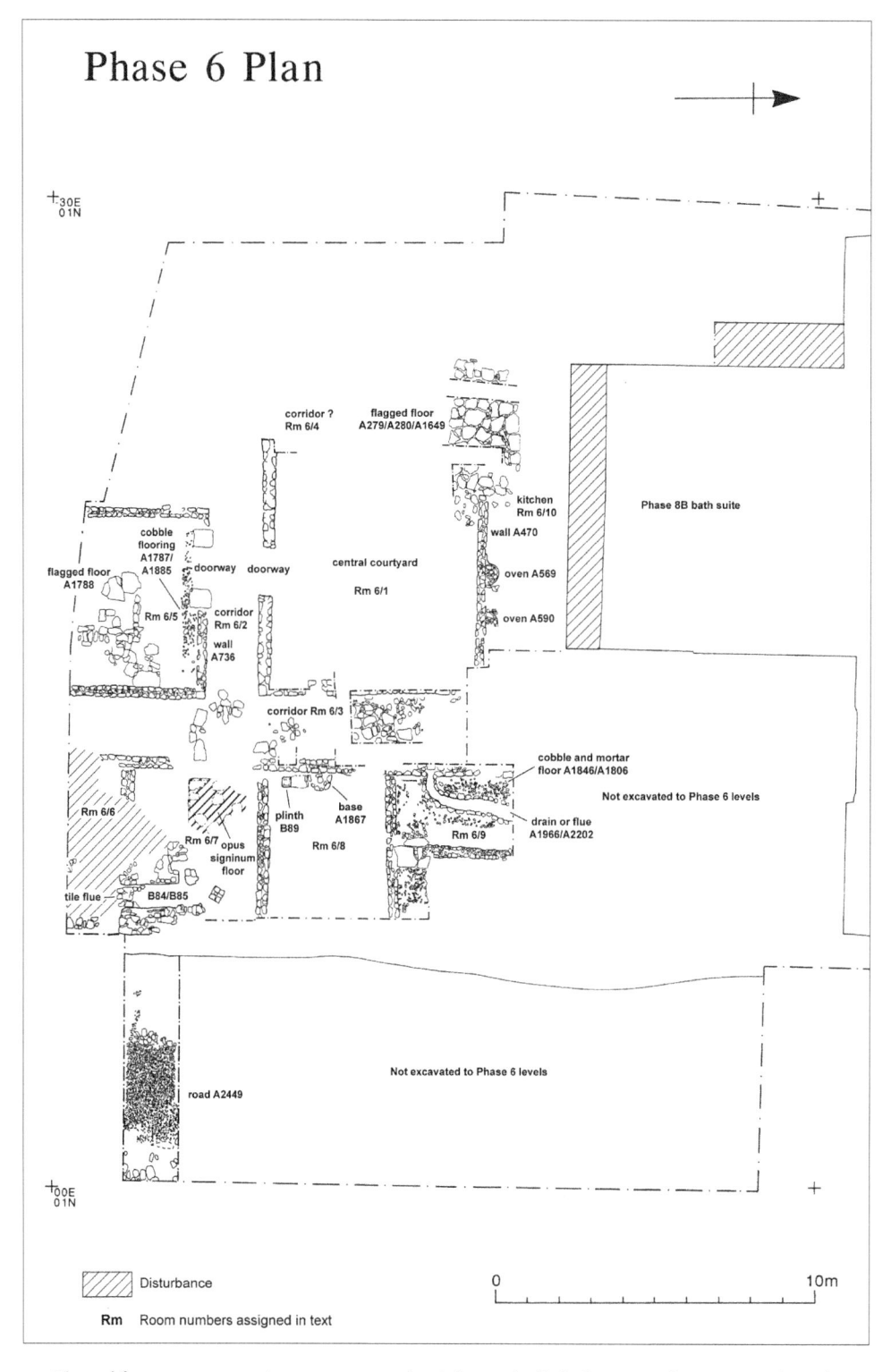

24 Plan of first stone praetorium or commandant's house (called Phase 6 in the stratigraphic schema for the 1976–1981 and 1986–1991 excavations).

## THE FIRST STONE PRAETORIUM

The first stone building excavated in 1976–1981 was a large courtyard building, a commandant's house, or praetorium, with narrow walls, suggesting that it was a half-timbered construction. It had at least one hypocausted range. Only part of the building lay within the area of excavation, though it had dimensions of at least 20 metres (around 65 feet 6 inches) east–west by 16 metres (around 52 feet 6 inches) north–south. The walls of this phase, surviving between one and six courses along different stretches, were built of faced sandstone blocks and were quite narrow.

Where foundation trenches were dug, they tended to be very shallow indeed and were backfilled with loose earth and small, angular stone rubble. The upper surfaces of these trench fills appeared to have been rammed. Other walls merely sat on shallow footings of angular stone rubble in a matrix of orange, sandy mortar, or were built on carefully prepared surfaces of large cobbles or cobble flagstones.

Finds suggest that the building was roofed with pegged stone roof tiles and had painted plaster walls, substantial concrete floors, architectural adornments and a hypocaust system. It took the form of a number of rooms arranged around an unroofed central courtyard, the rooms being separated from one another in some cases by narrow passages or corridors which themselves bounded the open area on at least two sides.

The central courtyard area, of which three boundary walls were recognisable and the line of the fourth reasonably certain, was uniformly surfaced with cobbles, with there being some evidence for occasional repairs to the surface having been carried out during the life of the building. The courtyard surface may have been correspondingly added to as floor levels within the building were raised.

To the south and to the east of the courtyard were two narrow corridors providing access both into and out of the courtyard and to ranges of rooms to the south and to a hypocausted suite to the east. It is uncertain whether there was a similar corridor to the west of the courtyard, while to the north there would appear to have been a kitchen range. The south and east corridors were surfaced with rough cobble flagging and rammed small cobbles. The flagstones were heavily worn and, in one or two places, repaired with a secondary surfacing.

The eastern hypocaust range, aligned north–south, was of considerable interest and will be considered here first. It consisted of four rooms which will now be described, starting in the south. A massive medieval robber pit had destroyed the presumed stokehole of the hypocaust in the southernmost excavated room of the range and had destroyed any internal features here. However, substantial spreads of a burnt purple silt loam found here could well represent material cleaned out of the hypocaust flue and the stokehole.

The hypocausted room itself was to be much altered in the succeeding phase and, again, had been greatly disturbed by medieval intrusions and stone robbing and by the nineteenth-century excavators. However, much of the flue from the stokehole beyond survived, the angled setting of the tiles that formed the sides of the flue suggesting that they originally formed an arched tunnel. The flue channel was floored by a single layer of flagstones, which were heavily burnt and crumbly, laid over the top of a make-up

25 Hypocaust in the first stone praetorium.

level of thick, pure clay, also burned to a red-pink colour. The tile pilae stacks of the hypocaust, which had once supported its floor, were held together by a pink opus signinum cement, and in plan formed an apsidal end to the structure. A squarish tile feature at the end of the flue may well have represented a base upon which stood a metal tank for the purpose of heating water.

The base of the hypocaust was formed by a red-pink concrete, opus signinum floor, into which the pilae tiles were set. The upper floor did not survive in situ but, taking into account the height of the surviving pilae stacks, the underfloor was probably only about 0.3–0.4 metres (1 foot) in height. Directly to the west of this hypocaust was found a large deposit of broken-up or cut-up chunks of red-pink opus signinum flooring that may represent debris from the demolition of part of the structure, perhaps again in the medieval period.

In the late 1870s the workmen of Mr Proud and the Revd Hooppell uncovered part of this hypocaust, removing any deposits that had built up in the area and immediately backfilling their trenches once a rudimentary plan had been made showing the positions of a number of the pilae stacks. This appears on Plate 4 in Hooppell's *Vinovia: A Buried Roman City*, but no mention is made of this hypocaust in the text, perhaps because of a lack of understanding as to how this hypocaust fitted in with the other remains at the site.

Further north, the third excavated room in this range was a room with little in the way of surviving internal features. However, on the western side were two surviving features that perhaps attest to the one-time importance of this room. The northernmost of these features was a single well-cut and squared stone block, almost a low plinth

26 Hypocaust flue in the first stone praetorium.

in form, with a raised, flat, smooth upper surface. This stone plinth may have formed a base for a column or a statue. The second feature consisted of six cut stones, set in a white mortary matrix and forming a semi-circular pediment up against the western wall of the room. Again, this may have been a base for a statue.

Also inside the third room, against the southern face of the wall, along the western part of its line, was cut a sub-circular hole into which had been placed a decorated samian pottery bowl before it was backfilled with mixed grey-brown clay, opus signinum lumps and mortar. This must be a ritual deposit, presumably for dedicatory purposes connected with the completion of the building. There is, though, the slight possibility that this could represent a secondary deposition, since no floors or key deposits sealed the backfill of the hole.

In the fourth, most northerly excavated room of this range, an extended sequence was revealed. The primary solid mortar and cobble floor had been cut through by a stone-lined channel with a mortar base, aligned roughly south-west to north-east, with a kink in its line to the south. Its floor sloped gently northwards, and it was backfilled with a dark mixed silt and patches of charcoal. Part of its flagstone capping survived to the south. None of the stones forming the lining of the feature were burned, but thin spreads of heavily burned material to the west of the channel and overlying the contemporary floor may have been cleared out of the channel since they were so similar in consistency to the channel fill. Given all the evidence it is difficult to say whether this was a flue or a drain, though the latter seems more likely. It was probably later in this phase that the doorway between the two northernmost rooms in this range was blocked, rather than this occurring in the succeeding phase.

27 Wall and ovens in the first stone praetorium.

To the north of the courtyard lay a room which has been interpreted as a kitchen, because of the presence of ovens there. In the north of the room the massive foundation trench dug for the fourth-century bath suite had destroyed all earlier deposits and features in this area. The southern wall of the room survived to only one or two courses in height and was plastered on both faces, the base colour being white, but, since the plaster survived as little more than a stain on the ground, nothing can be said about decorative schemes. Into the northern side of the wall were set two ovens, one semicircular in shape and consisting of a patch of stone rubble, some of it heavily burnt, set in a very loose pink, powdery mortar mixed with cobbles. The second oven only retained a vaguely quarter-circle shape outside the line of the wall, but partly set back into the wall itself survived two burnt clay linings, indicating that the oven would have been completely circular at its base but with only half projecting northwards beyond the wall face. Presumably the first oven would have been of a similar build. Burnt material, presumably cleared out from the two ovens, was found spread over the partially surviving floor of the room. After the ovens went out of use there is evidence for a number of successive re-floorings in this room, highlighting again the longevity of this building.

This building was subsequently refurbished, with there being evidence for the re-laying of floors, the application of a second layer of wall plaster in one room, the blocking of a number of doorways, and the addition of a new range of rooms, though only a small part of this new range could be excavated. The lifespan of the building appeared to be long, as is also suggested by analysis of the finds from this phase.

The latest coins found in association with this building were an issue of Antoninus Pius, AD 138-161, and one of Septimius Severus, AD 193-211. It was uncertain whether two later coins, of Julia Maesa, AD 217–222, and Philip, AD 244–249, belonged to deposits of this phase or the succeeding one. The pottery found included no material later than the end of the second century and there was much residual material. There was a foundation deposit of a complete Dragendorf 37 samian vessel in a context dated AD 135–60 which appeared to be contemporary with a primary wall. Nene Valley colour-coated ware was present, as was Rhenish ware.

Overall, the pottery looked like a small Antonine group contaminated by much residual material. One of the coins, coming as it did from the make-up of a tertiary floor level, demonstrated that the building was still in use in the early third century. The overall site evidence would therefore suggest that the phase started in the Antonine period and that the first stone building continued to be occupied until it was partially demolished and partially reused in the succeeding phase in the later third century, although there is no ceramic evidence for the latter part of its occupation.

The finds assemblage from the building was not large, but it was of some interest in determining the nature of life in the fort at this time. There were just under 500 sherds of pottery from this phase. The high status of the building was shown by a marked functional bias towards tablewares, particularly bowls, though jars still remained a relatively large component of the overall assemblage. Levels of finewares were also significant.

Black Burnished ware pottery (BB1 and BB2) from manufactories in the south-west was now a significant component of the pottery assemblage. Fineware supplies included significant quantities of samian and Nene Valley and Rhenish ware colour-coated wares. Mancetter mortaria from the Midlands now dominated the market in these vessels. Amphorae, including Gallic wine amphorae, appearing for the first time, were noticeably quite significant. Ritual or religious activity was almost certainly attested by the careful deposition of a samian Dragendorf 37 bowl in a small hole, though the vessel was subsequently disturbed by later activity and some of its sherds were broken and scattered in other layers.

Though there was a substantial decrease in the amount of vessel glass in this phase in comparison to the last phase of dumping, the vessels represented were of great interest. A colourless flask decorated with wheel-cut lines was of a type of vessel relatively rare in Britain, while part of a possible so-called Mercury flask, often bearing the god's image, was also present. One piece of glass manufacturing waste also came from this phase. Small finds from this phase were few, though the presence of six pieces of unworked shale might suggest shale working at this time.

A significant amount of painted wall plaster came from the building, most of it bearing a patchy red paint, though a number of small fragments featuring red and gold banding on white or cream grounds was also recovered. Just over 6 kilograms of stone roof tiles were recovered, this quantity, while not great, suggesting that some form of stone-tiled roof was associated with the building of this period. The distribution of the tile suggests roofing around a courtyard aisle. Twenty-eight kilograms of ceramic tile was collected from this phase, mainly flue-lining tiles and pilae tiles from the hypocaust that was to continue in use into the next building phase.

Little food waste in the form of animal bone came from this phase, though the presence of around forty shell fragments, mostly again of the common blue mussel and the common European oyster, with a few shells of the common winkle and the common European cockle, shows that seafood formed part of the diet here in the praetorium.

At the end of its long life the first stone building was only partially demolished, to be followed in the late third century by the construction of a second, all-stone, praetorium, which lasted in use until the mid-fourth century. In places the second structure duplicated the plan of the first stone building and reused some of the earlier wall foundations, though where this occurred there was always a widening of the stretch of earlier wall being reused. Otherwise, in other areas the lines of second building walls were often only traceable by the survival of their diagnostic cobble-and-clay foundations.

While in this second stone building the residential rooms of the building differed in layout from those in the earlier stone house, the earlier hypocausted range or bath suite remained very much the same in its basic ground plan in the later phase. Few layers or floor surfaces associated with the second stone building survived. Like its predecessor, the second stone courtyard house fronted onto the fort's via principalis.

The establishment of the line of the new via principalis had obviously been part of a broader, major replanning of the layout and defences of the fort at Binchester in the Antonine period. The new fort was on a much reduced scale, it would appear, than the earlier fort, though nevertheless remaining at a size greater than many of its contemporaries in the north. The scale of building and investment in large residences in a fort in the period is therefore not particularly surprising, nor is the replacement of a half-timbered building with a fully stone-built house. The second stone praetorium house at Binchester was a grander structure than its predecessor and very much part of a later Roman phenomenon in the north of forts being provided with large, well-appointed residences such as this, as can be seen, for instance, at Piercebridge, Chester-le-Street and South Shields, reflecting the existence of a common elite culture in the later empire to which Roman military commanders belonged.

## THE SECOND STONE PRAETORIUM

As in the earlier stone building, the second stone building comprised a series of ranges around an elongated central courtyard. It had at least two hypocausted rooms, one in a separate bath suite. However, despite the considerable size and scale of the building and its walls, it does not seem to have been particularly grandly furnished. Evidence for painted wall plaster and concrete floors was scanty, while the rather shoddy wall foundations raise questions about the motives behind the rebuilding of the unquestionably elegant earlier structure.

Enough of this building was examined to allow some generalisations to be made about the method of its construction. Firstly, construction trenches were dug, these being usually straight-sided with rounded bases. These trenches were then packed with rounded river cobbles set in a matrix of solid, pure, blue-grey clay. Into the top of the clay matrix were set roughly rectangular, thin slabs of a mellow-coloured flaky sandstone set in a matrix of coarse yellow sand. In places, two courses of this rough stone were recorded. However, so

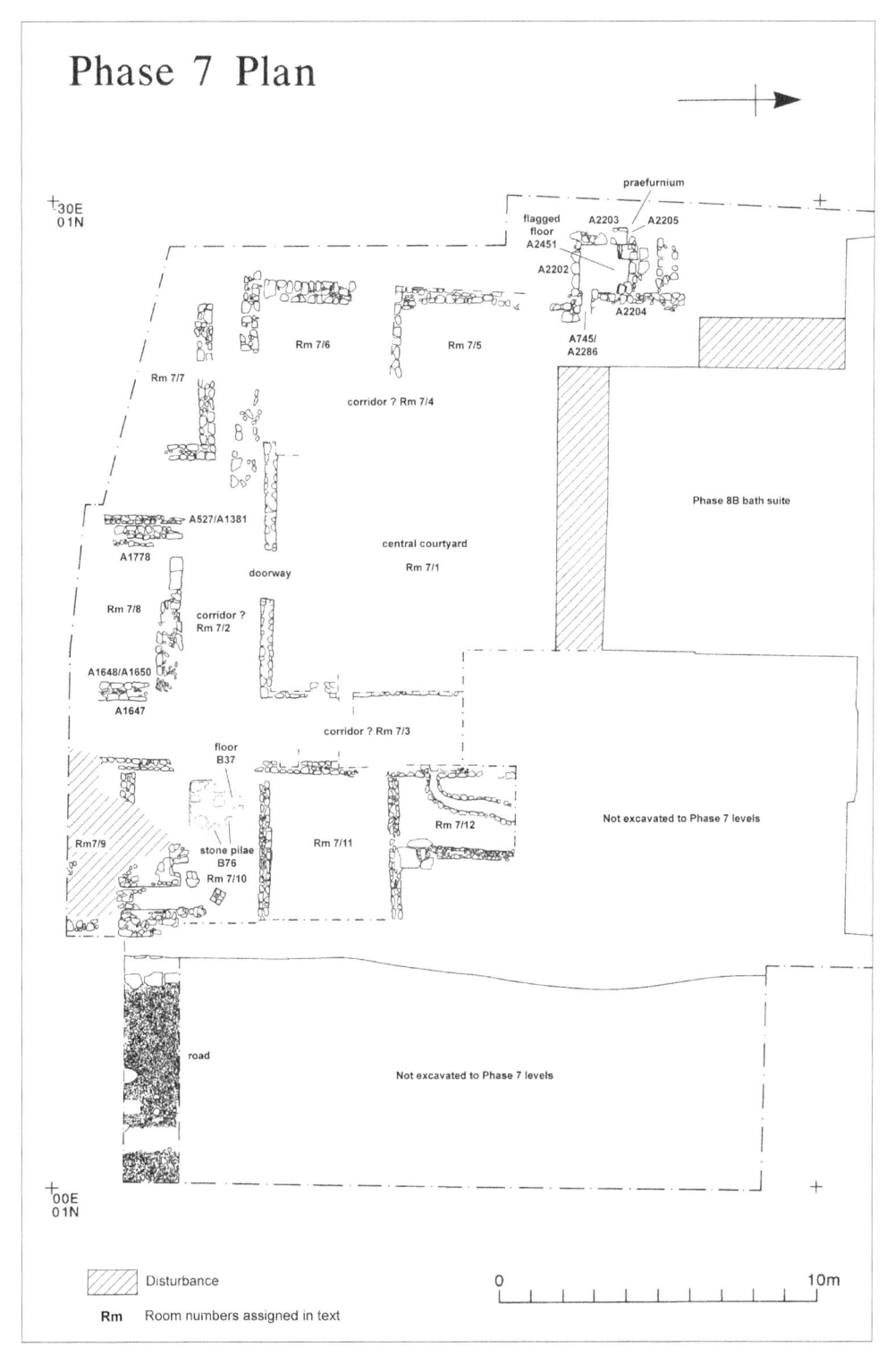

28 Plan of second stone praetorium or commandant's house (called Phase 7 in the stratigraphic schema for the 1976–1981 and 1986–1991 excavations).

complete was the destruction of this building at the end of its life, before the construction of a third stone building, that we have little idea of the appearance of the walls above this rough lower foundation coursing, though we do know that the same yellow flaky stone was also used for wall courses, as this was found surviving in a few places.

Those parts of the earlier structure that were incorporated into the new building scheme were altered accordingly, walls being widened by the addition of a cobble and clay foundation base, not set in a trench but actually above ground, running alongside the inside face of the wall and upon which the normal building pattern was then followed.

Examination of the plan of this phase reveals that our knowledge of its layout is even more sketchy than that for the previous building, but it does show that the arrangement of rooms in the later phase was much more complex.

The apparently open, central courtyard was retained in some form, perhaps indeed enlarged by its extension northwards. In the courtyard the spreading and levelling of deposits is attested, the depth and regularity of this raising of the ground surface presumably being dictated by floor-level changes elsewhere inside the building. The corridors to the south and east of the courtyard, as originally laid out in the earlier phase, were now altered and no longer existed in their original form. The possible corridor to the west may have continued in use.

To the west of the central courtyard, a series of truncated walls and foundation trenches of this phase was excavated, which in plan make little sense. However, the presence of a small stone-built praefurnium, or furnace room, in the north-west suggests that the western walls may all have belonged to a new western range that included at least one hypocausted room. The stone-built praefurnium was very small and probably below ground, approached by two stone steps down. The interior was floored by a single, large, worn, burnt flagstone and a mortar skim. Burning was also noticeable on both faces of the presumed flue, the stones, pink-red in colour, crumbling and flaking. The flue was floored by a mortar skim. Outside the room were found very substantial spreads of burnt material; similar deposits, with occasional large charcoal inclusions, built up inside the room over the flagged floor.

Moving eastwards, only part of the plan of a room survived because of the destruction caused by the digging of the massive foundations of the fourth-century bathhouse. It seems, though, that this was a hypocausted room heated from the small praefurnium, but the evidence for the form of this hypocaust is somewhat lacking. A single pila, a large, squared, burnt stone block, was found here, but there is some doubt about its being in situ since it did not appear to be set into any solid material. In the south-west corner of the room a single large stone slab, covered by a fragment of opus signinum flooring, may be part of the floor surface itself.

The non-hypocausted rooms of the western range were only examined in relatively small areas. Little survived in the interiors of what must have been a number of rooms apart from two small patches of yellow-white mortar flooring and flat stone slabs in the south, a remnant of a pink mortar floor with large stones set into its surface in the central range, and evidence for a further floor, of white mortar, alongside one wall in one place to the north. Above these floors, evidence for occupation deposits was slight.

## The Second Fort and Two Successive Praetoria

29 *Right:* Furnace room, or praefurnium, in the second stone praetorium.

30 *Below:* Wall and associated mortar floor in the second stone praetorium.

To the south of the central courtyard, a number of earlier walls were reused. The suite of rooms with a hypocaust to the east of the central courtyard remained very much the same in its basic ground plan as in the previous phase, when it was first built. One wall was widened by the addition of a cobble and clay foundation on which a layer of masonry survived. One doorway was now blocked.

However, substantial changes were now made to the hypocaust system itself. The apsidal-ended plan was now abandoned and the hypocaust system was enlarged by the addition of further pilae of stone, varying in shape from squared and faced blocks to vaguely rounded stones and to some little-more-than-ordinary building stones placed on end. Many of these stone pilae remained in situ and were burned to a pinky-red colour. In the west of the room, seven or eight shallow holes cut into the basal floor denoted places where stone pilae had been set and subsequently removed. Whether this enlargement of the basic hypocaust plan meant that there was a reciprocal enlargement of the firing arrangements cannot be said, since extensive medieval disturbances had destroyed the area of the stokehole, but certainly no alteration was made to the flue. These alterations would have necessitated the laying of a new floor.

Within the most northerly room of this range, probably late in the phase, a rough drain was built, running roughly east–west in the eastern central part of the room and with an outlet through the eastern wall of the room.

There were just over 1,000 sherds of pottery from this phase, with, as in the preceding phase, a marked functional bias towards tablewares, now both bowls and dishes, and a rising level of jars which constituted a large component of the overall assemblage. Numbers of beakers rose, perhaps significantly, to almost double the level of beakers in the previous phase. Levels of finewares dropped slightly, but nevertheless fineware levels remained significantly high.

Black Burnished ware (BB1) was now the dominant component of the pottery assemblage, accounting for half of the pottery present in this phase and suggesting that this was now brought north in quantity as part of a military supply contract. Fineware supplies included significant quantities of, in particular, Nene Valley colour-coated wares. Mancetter mortaria were now less significant than in the previous phase and Catterick and Oxfordshire mortaria were also present. Amphorae were noticeably less significant than in the first stone phase. The samian from this phase was mainly from central Gaul.

Although the small finds assemblage from this phase was small, functionally there were marked numbers of personal ornaments and equipment, while the presence of eight pieces of sawn and unworked shale might suggest shale working during this phase. The most noteworthy small find was an iron shield boss. Two bone dice and a stone gaming counter attest to some leisure activities taking place inside the building.

A significant amount of painted wall plaster was associated with the building, most of it bearing a patchy red paint, though fragments with red stripes on a white ground, red and gold intersecting bands on a white ground and gold bands on white were also recovered. Just over 14 kilograms of stone roof tiles were also recovered, this quantity, while not great, suggesting that some form of stone tiled roof was associated with the buildings of this period, as in the previous phase. The distribution of the tile once more suggests roofing around a courtyard. Forty-five kilograms of ceramic tile were collected from this phase, mainly roofing tiles, with a smaller amount of flue-lining tiles and pilae tiles.

The crucial coin for dating the construction of this second praetorium was a Barbarous Radiate, AD 270–290, from one of the wall foundation deposits. The non-residual pottery from this phase seemed to be third-century in date but it need not necessarily be later than perhaps c. AD 280–5. The one good group from the phase came late in the sequence and contained burnt mortar, plaster and many nails and therefore could be interpreted as a demolition deposit. This would seem to be of a later third-century date, after c. AD 270. The building was completely demolished and the site coin list suggests a phase of abandonment of the site or of this part of the site in c. AD 260–330. While the site was clearly occupied after this, a gap in the occupation from c. AD 280–5 to c. AD 335 would be possible, although little evidence can be found amongst the ceramics to support or reject this.

## THE VICUS

As noted in Chapter One, Proud and Hooppell's excavations in the Binchester vicus, or civilian settlement, were highly significant, and in some ways revolutionary, in providing evidence for the layout of the settlement and for their recording of the plans of a number of individual buildings here. However, apart from being able to conclude that a number of phases of activity were represented here, no close dating for the start of the vicus nor a date for its demise were offered. Just as the possibility of there being archaeological remains related to early timber structures at a lower level than that of the buildings inside the fort was not considered by Hooppell, no possibility of there having been earlier timber vicus structures was entertained either. Unfortunately, the opportunity to re-examine and date pottery recovered from the vicus trenches of Proud and Hooppell was not available to subsequent generations of archaeologists as much of this material was lost or disposed of and the remainder retained was not clearly labelled with a provenance.

It was not, therefore, until a watching brief was carried out in 1977 on the digging of a water pipeline across part of the vicus that the opportunity could be taken to recover finds from the vicus that might help in dating its origins. Though only a relatively small assemblage of pottery was recovered during this exercise, study of this material suggested to the pottery specialists that the Binchester vicus did not perhaps originate in a fully developed form until the Antonine period, although some settlement must have existed here from shortly after the middle of the second century. There was no evidence to suggest that the Binchester vicus did not conform to the general pattern established for the ending of vici in general in Durham and on Hadrian's Wall, that is ending by the start of the fourth century or a short time thereafter,[5] though other evidence for the presence of at least one late stone building here was provided by Steer's excavation and is perhaps also suggested by the provisional dating of pottery recovered during the 2010 excavation in the vicus.

It is, however, geophysical survey that has transformed our knowledge of the Binchester vicus in the past six years, indicating that its full extent is greater than

72  *Vinovia*

31 Excavations underway in the civilian settlement or vicus in 2010.

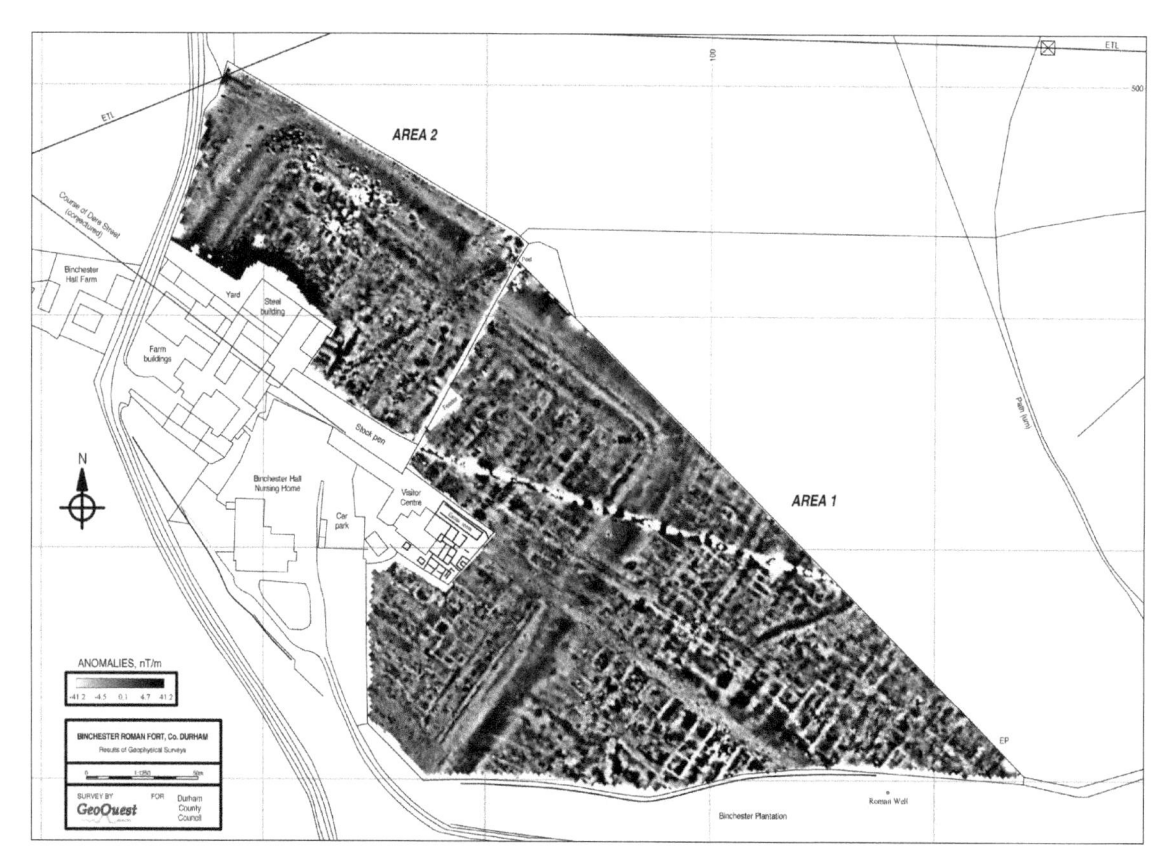

32 Geophysical survey plot of part of the fort and civilian settlement or vicus (courtesy of Geoquest Associates).

33 Geophysical survey plots of part of the fort and civilian settlement or vicus (courtesy of Geophysical Surveys of Bradford).

34 Excavation of a mausoleum in the civilian settlement or vicus by *Time Team* in 2007 (copyright Wessex Archaeology).

hitherto expected and that its layout is more zoned than previously thought.[6] There are indeed plans to further extend the bounds of geophysical survey, to potentially add new information to that presented here. At the moment the survey plots indicate that as well as civilian buildings lining both sides of Dere Street as it emerges from the north-west gate of the fort, buildings, roads and tracks also lie beyond the north-eastern defences of the stone fort, and the whole of the pasture field outside the fort to the south-east contains buildings of one sort or another. A curving road flanked by ditches may be identified on the plots outside the east corner of the stone fort, with a series of ditched enclosures to the east of this suggested road. Some of these ditched enclosures contained stone buildings, subsequently identified as mausolea.

Perhaps the most exciting archaeological discovery made in the vicus since the time of Proud and Hooppell has been the locating and partial excavation of a number of these stone mausolea in 2007 when television's *Time Team* visited Binchester.[7] These features, as already mentioned, had first showed up on geophysical survey plots and were then chosen for further investigation by trial trenching. Once topsoil had been stripped away, it was soon apparent that here was a row of three stone-built mausolea, two of them enclosed within a precinct wall. The largest mausoleum measured

35 Excavation of a mausoleum in the civilian settlement or vicus by *Time Team* in 2007 (copyright Wessex Archaeology).

approximately 8 metres (just over 26 feet) square, the smaller two inside the enclosure 3.3 metres (around 11 feet) by 2.7 metres (around 9 feet), and 1.9 metres (just over 6 feet) by 1.8 metres (just over 6 feet) respectively. The area enclosed by the precinct wall was shown by geophysical survey to be approximately 14 metres (almost 46 feet) by 11 metres (36 feet). A fourth mausoleum possibly lay to the south-east, as indicated by geophysical survey.

An inhumation burial in a grave was found in the large mausoleum, but not fully excavated, and disarticulated human skeletal remains were found inside another. Examination of the bones in the burial indicated that they represented an adult male of approximately 22–30 years of age, while the disarticulated remains could also be identified as being from a robust male. The finding of iron nails suggested that he had been originally buried in a wooden coffin. Two complete pottery vessels were also found in the grave and may have sat on top of the coffin. These comprised a greyware jar with lattice decoration and a Black Burnished ware bowl. It is thought that the two complete pottery vessels from the one mausoleum date to the second century, after AD 150.

CHAPTER FOUR

# The Mid- to Late Fourth-Century Praetorium and Bath Suite

In the area excavated in 1976–1981 and 1986–1991, the construction of the major fourth-century stone building which has been identified as another commandant's house or praetorium marks a key event that perhaps suggests another major functional or administrative change for the fort at Binchester taking place at this time. Though the two previous stone buildings on this part of the site were also in all probability praetoria, they were somewhat smaller in size and certainly less grand in their decoration or appointment. The demolition and clearance of the second of these buildings acted as a prelude to the replanning of this area and the creation of the new, grander structure. A coin of the House of Constantine dated AD 335–345 was sealed beneath a primary opus signinum floor, placing the new praetorium very firmly towards the end, datewise, of a category of late Roman house that seems to be a genuine phenomenon in the northern military zone. Geophysical survey suggests that the overall dimensions of the third and last Binchester stone praetorium, presumably in its final incarnation, were approximately 45 by 65 metres (about 147 feet 6 inches by about 213 feet). It is part of the residential range of this building and its associated bathhouse that lies within the guardianship area today and which is on display to the public.

This building was to see an extended series of alterations and additions, the latest of which take the context of the activity represented there beyond the framework for close dating provided by coins or pottery. Coin supply to the Roman north had then more or less stopped, while the pottery industries had either ceased to make and market their goods or their repertoire had become typologically fossilised and therefore largely undiagnostic.

An account will now be given of the archaeological sequence that starts with the construction of the mid-fourth-century praetorium house and which pre-dates the sub-Roman activity and the Saxon burial of the mid-sixth century. A carbon-14 scientific dating programme utilising charcoal and bone samples from this sequence has allowed a much more nuanced dating of individual parts of the sequence to emerge, though the carbon dates and their use in a mathematical dating programme are not without points of uncertainty.

Though there are, of course, gaps in our knowledge of this phase of building activity, it remains, nevertheless, the most complete and complex of the buildings so far examined at Binchester. Being the latest, as well as the most substantial, building in the centre of the fort has meant that it had withstood well the ravages of time but, conversely, it has also meant that it was highly prone to the unsolicited attentions of stone robbers in the medieval period. Perhaps a threat even greater than that posed by the stone robbers came from the somewhat haphazard excavations of Mr Proud and Revd Hooppell in the late nineteenth century, delvings that greatly complicated the task of the more recent excavators and possibly clouded our picture of the later and most crucial years of this building's life.

During post-excavation analysis of the site records and finds from the 1976–1981 and 1986–1991 excavations, this phase of activity was designated Phase 8 and was divided up into five sub-phases, Phases 8A–8E. This phasing scheme was also followed in the published monograph report on the excavations in 2010 and, for ease and clarity of description, it will be used in this present account as well. It should be noted, though, that these sub-phases are not necessarily separated one from another in time in every case, as will now be explained. The reason for this is the presence of the large bath suite, whose extensions and renovations cannot satisfactorily be linked to changes within the residential part of the building. Phase 8A is the building as initially envisaged and laid out. Phase 8B represents the addition of a new large bath suite to the basic Phase 8A plan. Activity of Phase 8C is limited to the residential quarters and covers the first major change of plan of the 8A rooms. Phase 8B and Phase 8C may, then, possibly be more or less contemporary. The enlargement of the Phase 8B suite into a complicated and more sumptuous bathing complex takes place in Phase 8D. Phase 8E represents the final changes to the plan and the fabric of the Phase 8A/8C house and the subsequent running-down of the building as a residential establishment.

The historical events which coincide with the lifespan of this praetorium are impossible to detect in the archaeological record.[1] In AD 342/343 the Emperor Constans visited Britain to sort out possible frontier problems, once more probably in the north. In AD 360 it is recorded that Roman forces were sent to Britain to deal with the Picts and the Scots, with raids by the Picts, Scots and Saxons following in AD 364. The various crises in the north are reported as reaching some form of boiling point in AD 367–368, the time of the so-called 'great barbarian conspiracy', all the frontiers of the province being attacked, with order eventually being restored by the intervention of Count Theodosius. In AD 396–399 Stilicho is reported as campaigning against barbarians in Britain, presumably including those beyond the northern frontier, and in AD 401–2 he withdrew some troops from Britain, ostensibly to defend Italy against barbarian incursions and raids, probably including some of the troops stationed in northern England. In AD 410 it has traditionally been thought that the Emperor Honorius washed his hands of the troublesome province of Britannia and told its citizens to look to their own defence against the barbarians.[2]

## PHASE 8A: THE THIRD STONE PRAETORIUM

The preceding stone praetorium building was now systematically stripped down to its very foundations and work began on construction of the Phase 8A building. The walls

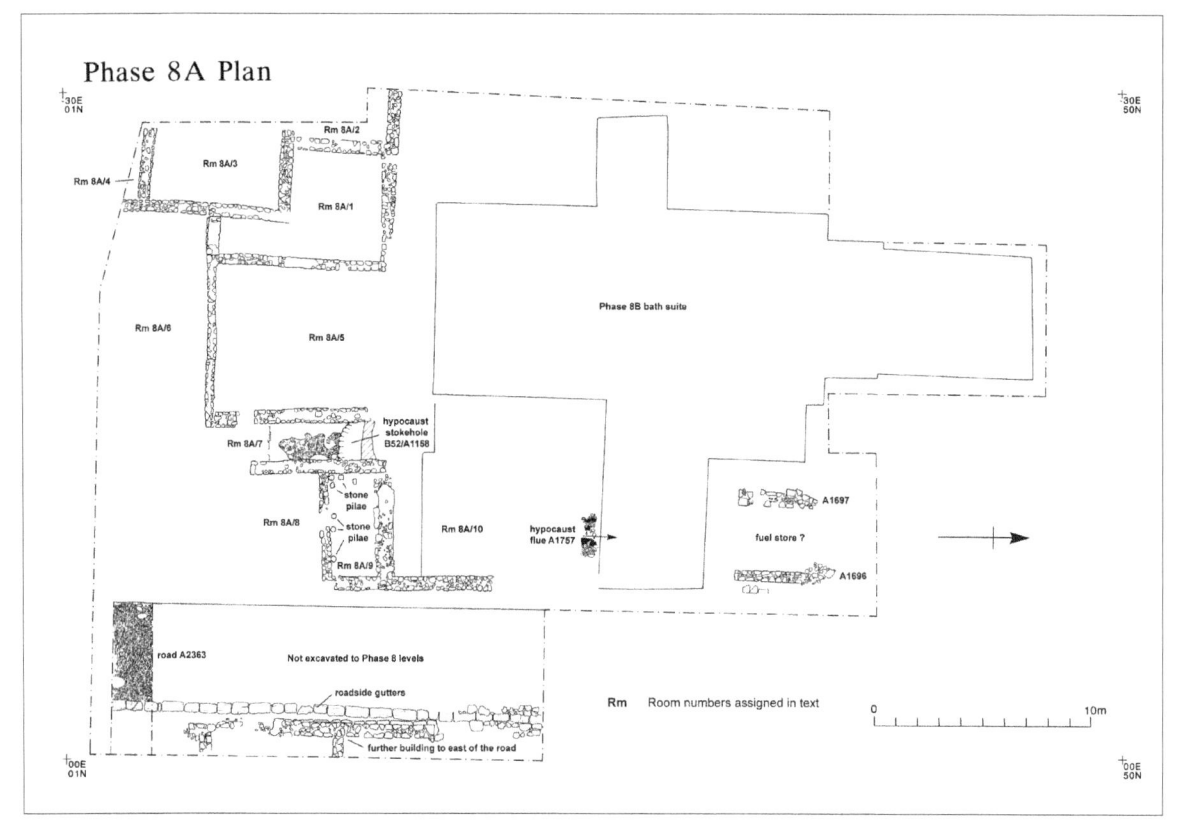

36 Plan of the first phase of the mid-fourth-century stone praetorium or commandant's house (called Phase 8A in the stratigraphic schema for the 1976–1981 and 1986–1991 excavations).

of the new building were extremely well built, of cut and faced sandstone blocks, with seven or eight courses of stone remaining in situ in places. A ritual dedicatory deposit was represented by two clay-lined, circular holes dug into the top of the backfill of one of the construction trenches. Into the first hole had been placed, upside down, a Black Burnished ware pottery vessel, and into the second had likewise been placed, again upside down, another pot, of grey ware, with a circular stone stopper in position over its mouth. It is impossible to say if they contained anything when buried, though the presence of the stopper would suggest that they did. On the shoulder of the grey ware vessel was scratched a graffito.

Another extremely important find for the purposes of interpreting and dating the start of this phase was a coin of the House of Constantine, AD 335–345, from the foundation deposit of mortar and upturned stones for the primary opus signinum floor in one of the residential rooms of the Phase 8A building. The coin provides a secure terminus post quem for the laying of the opus signinum floor and consequently for the whole of the Phase 8A building.

Only part of the Phase 8A building lay within the area of excavation, the only limiting walls of the structure here being the northern and eastern walls. Excavation recovered the partial groundplan of the central part of the building, including a western range that included an L-shaped room (Room 1) and parts of three further

*The Mid- to Late Fourth-Century Praetorium and Bath Suite*

37 Two ritually deposited pots from the foundations of the mid-fourth-century praetorium, or commandant's house.

rooms (Rooms 2–4) west of Room 1, a large central room that more or less duplicated the plan of the preceding phase's courtyard (Room 5), a wide, long corridor or room (Room 6) to the south of Room 5, and an eastern hypocausted range of rooms (Rooms 7–10) to the east of Room 5, with an ancillary building, possibly a fuel store, lying to the north of the building. The individual excavated ranges and rooms of the Phase 8A building will now be considered in detail.

In the western range lay Rooms 1–4. Room 1, to the west of the central courtyard, was the only residential room whose complete plan was recovered by excavation. It was a large, roughly L-shaped room, later sub-divided into smaller units by the building of two further walls. The room was initially floored with a dirty white concrete floor set on a thick foundation of large river cobbles and masonry rubble set on edge. A quarter moulding, a sill or rounded concrete edging for the floor, ran north–south along the eastern wall of the room. In places, plastering covered the moulding.

In the main part of the room, above the primary floor surface and below the north–south running wall inserted across this room in Phase 8C, a very interesting sequence of building activity was recorded. Firstly a new floor of white pebble and concrete was laid, again with a quarter moulding which survived along the northern part of the eastern wall. A third floor, red in colour because of the crushed tile mixed in with the main pebble and mortar matrix, followed. This third floor evidently

38 Sectioned sequence of mortar floors in the first phases of the mid-fourth-century stone praetorium or commandant's house.

suffered from subsidence, dipping dramatically northwards in the northern central part of the room. The subsidence was not a recent phenomenon but, rather, occurred during the Roman period, there being evidence for an attempt to rectify the problem. In the north-east corner of the room a deposit of clean, yellow fine sand, wedge-shaped with its thickest end towards the north, was spread here, doubtless to level the now drastically cracking and dipping floor. A pink-white mortar floor could be seen to overlay the sandy levelling deposit, though it only survived in patches. Away from the problem area a patchy brown clay overlay the floor, this being the only occupation deposit attested in this particular room. The general absence of occupation debris is not really surprising, since not only was the cleaning of a solid concrete floor an easy matter but it was hardly likely that rubbish deposits would have been allowed to accumulate inside the building.

Access to Room 1 was provided by no fewer than four doorways, one from Room 2 in the west, one from Room 3 in the south, a third from Room 6, and the fourth from Room 5. The first of these had a threshold with a solid opus signinum surfacing and it may be that all the doorways were so rendered.

Room 2, to the west of Room 1, was only just within the area of excavation and consequently little of the room was available for examination. About half of Room 3, to the south of Rooms 1 and 2, lay within the area of excavation. The primary floor of yellow mortar inside the room was set on a foundation base of soft, pale-brown sandy mortar. In places, the floor was overlain by a mixed brown clay with charcoal, possibly an occupation deposit, while elsewhere there was evidence for repairs to the floor surface itself. Room 4 lay to the south of Room 3, but only part of its northern party-wall with Room 3 and its east wall lay within the area of excavation.

In the central range were two rooms, Rooms 5 and 6. Room 5 roughly corresponded to the area that had been a central courtyard in the preceding building. Access to this room was through a doorway from Room 1 to the west and through one in the eastern wall from Room 6. To the south of Room 5 lay Room 6, a large part of which lay within the excavated area. Room 6 may have been a corridor, or it is possible that it is part of a central, open courtyard. Over a thick make-up deposit of brown-yellow clay were spread here small cobbles, opus signinum and rough paving. Over these was laid a thick deposit of rough cobbles in a silty matrix.

In the eastern, hypocausted range were four further rooms, Rooms 7–10. Very little of this range was available for excavation as much of it lay beneath later features – opus signinum floors and the flagstoned courtyard of Phase 8D – and therefore had to be left in situ. A praefurnium or furnace room (Room 7) containing a stokehole lay to the west of the main range which comprised at least three separate rooms (Rooms 8–10, numbered from south to north). To the south it is very possible that the earlier hypocaust that had operated in both the first and second stone praetorium phases may have been refurbished and reused in this Phase 8A range.

The stokehole for the furnace that serviced this hypocausted suite was in Room 7, to the west of the range. A narrow stone-built arch in the east wall of the room linked the stokehole with the underfloor of the hypocausted room, Room 9, to the east. This arch was later blocked by its infilling with soil and stones set on edge, the hole then being covered by a flagstone set on edge. The flue itself was well constructed, with a stone-lined base, and was infilled with charcoal deposits.

Room 8, the southernmost room of the range, was a relatively plain room. A light orange-brown sandy mortar with pebbles appeared to be the remains of a floor that covered much of the room, a small patch of white mortar flooring in the southern central area possibly being a repair to the primary floor. A doorway in the eastern wall of the room was later blocked, but a number of mortar-covered flagstones on a bedding of tile chips in silt may represent the in situ threshold for this entrance. It is also possible that this may represent the site of a small mortar-lined foot-bath or plunge at the entrance to the room.

Room 9, directly connected to Room 7 by a flue arch, as noted above, was examined in detail. Here, in a small area, the Phase 8D flagstones were lifted in order to examine earlier features, this particular area being chosen because of the presence here of a flattened Phase 8A wall whose course was visible to the east where flagstones had been robbed out. The wall had been flattened in Phase 8D to allow flagstones to be laid over its line. It was thought likely that some of the flagstones here had already been disturbed by the nineteenth-century excavations; the Revd Hooppell, probably referring to this area, noted that 'beneath the pavement in one place were found a great number of broken stone hypocaust pillars, which had belonged to an earlier structure, and which were laid carefully against the wall, in order, side by side. That must have been done by the builders, or, at any rate, by the pavers of the hall.'[3]

*39 A tile flue of the first phase of the mid-fourth-century stone praetorium or commandant's house before excavation.*

The significance of this will now, hopefully, become clear. Beneath deposits representing the demolition, backfill and levelling of the Phase 8A were found spreads of pure charcoal overlying the remains of a mortar floor forming the base of the hypocaust underfloor. A number of red, burned stone pilae, including two with circular sections, were found inside the room. Further burnt stones, which may be pilae from this hypocaust, were found in the Hooppell backfill deposits over the flagged courtyard.

Room 10, to the north of Room 9, was not examined. Further north still, in an area where Phase 8D flagstones had been robbed out, was recorded part of what has been interpreted as a hypocaust flue, consisting of two opposed rows of north–south aligned tiles forming a channel backfilled with a mixed, burned red-brown clay. The tiles were squared, like the classic ceramic pila tile, and set on a thick blue grey clay. Most interesting of all, though, was the fact that one of the tiles was stamped with the retrograde NCON stamp, previously thought to be exclusively associated with tiles in the later Phase 8B bathhouse.

Outside the Phase 8A building to the north of the eastern hypocausted range lay a related ancillary structure formed of two low, parallel stone walls, both aligned north–south and about 3 metres (almost 10 feet) apart. The wall to the east survived in the south to only one or two courses in height, and in the north to two or three.

It was butt-ended in the south, the northern end of the wall having been destroyed. The wall to the west survived to only one course, the stones at the southern end of the wall being heavily burned. Again, this wall was butt ended and of a similar length to the other wall. At the southern end of the area between the two walls was a spread of a thick black charcoally loam. This structure would appear to represent the stone foundations of an open-ended shed, probably a fuel store, an external structure outside of, but linked to, the hypocausted eastern range to the south.

Finally, to the east of the easternmost wall of the Phase 8A praetorium building, ran the line of the main fort road, the via principalis. The contemporary road surface was composed of small, rammed pebbles in a matrix of orange sand and lay flush with a sequence of stone gutter channels to the east. No guttering existed to the west but, rather, there was evidence here for a channel flanked by two low banks of clay and backfilled with earth and cobble rubble, presumably kicked off the road. The upper surface of the road survived exceptionally well, with only one possible infilled rut being recorded in its upper surface.

On the eastern side of the road, and most probably contemporary with the Phase 8A building on the western side, was part of another building, the majority of which lay outside the excavated area. Nevertheless, it can be seen to have been a substantially fronted structure, with internal divisions and a doorway or threshold recorded. No part of its interior was excavated.

There were around 750 sherds of pottery recovered from deposits of Phase 8A, with a marked functional bias in this assemblage towards tablewares, particularly dishes, and a rising level of jars, jars being a large component of the overall assemblage. Beaker levels dropped quite dramatically from the preceding phase. Levels of finewares remained quite high. Among the pottery there were two developed Huntcliff vessel types, suggesting the assemblage extends in date up to at least around AD 350–5, when the type first appears, and painted Crambeck parchment ware was also present, again making the group extend beyond *c.* AD 350–5.

The pottery supply in this phase was dominated by Black Burnished ware (BB1) products. One of the ritually-deposited jars was a BB1 pot contemporary with the phase of its deposition, the other, its mouth sealed by a circular stone stopper or pot lid and with a graffito on its neck reading 'ANDRUS ARCE', was an earlier pot contemporary with activity of the first stone building. This early vessel could have been dug up during Phase 8A construction works, recognised as an earlier ritual dedicatory pot, and then reburied.

There is a substantial increase in the amount of vessel glass in Phase 8 in general, but only two vessels were represented in Phase 8A: a beaker with horizontal cordons and a tubular unguent bottle. One piece of glass manufacturing waste came from this phase.

Although the Phase 8A small finds assemblage was relatively small, it can be seen that functionally there was a marked concentration of personal ornaments and equipment in particular. A noticeable increase in the number of jet artefacts, three times more than in the previous seven phases together, and the presence of an unfinished jet pin head and nine finds of jet/shale waste, one comprising sixty individual pieces of jet found in association with the unfinished pin head, sawn shale and unworked shale, indicate without doubt the working of these materials here on site during this period.

A large assemblage of painted wall plaster was associated with the building, most of it bearing a patchy red paint as a base colour, though fragments with red stripes on a white ground and green stripes on gold were also recovered. However, the most interesting individual fragments came from the western range in the house, from where three fragments bearing floral or foliate motifs in green and brown on a cream ground and blue-grey ground were recovered. From the same room there also came a fragment painted with brown and red slashes of paint on a cream ground and another with red and yellow bands on a cream ground.

This phase sees the first appearance of ceramic tiles stamped NCON, with all other recorded examples occurring in later Phase 8B, both in archaeological contexts and in situ in the standing remains of the bath suite, and residually in later phases. The ceramic tile from this phase included both roofing tiles and a smaller quantity of pilae tiles. Just over 30 kilograms of stone roof tiles came from this phase.

The small amount of animal bone included was dominated by cattle, sheep and pig, in order of magnitude, with a cat, three dogs and four birds, including domestic fowl, also being present in the assemblage.

## PHASE 8B: THE BATHHOUSE

This sub-phase is connected specifically to the addition of a large bath building to the plan of the Phase 8A building and with the bathhouse's praefurnia or furnace rooms and related landscaping. Certainly, the Binchester Phase 8B bathhouse is the most well-known of the remains at the site and the building was known about for many years before the 1970s campaign of excavation began, as has been detailed in Chapter One.

Following the examination of large parts of the bath building in the nineteenth century by Proud and Hooppell, the structure was not examined again until 1969.[4] The hypocausted first room, and a less well-preserved second room, were then covered by a wooden protective shed and the backfill over the floors was removed; this shed was later extended to take in half of a third room and all of a small plunge bath. The excavation of the area covered by this new extension was directed in 1972 by W. C. Fawcett and J. Rainbird.[5] Thus, by the time the major series of excavations began on the surrounding parts of the building in 1976, the interior of the bath suite was largely cleared out. Yet despite the amount of previous work done in and around the bath, no clear idea really existed of the relationship between the bath and the rest of the house, of which the bath formed only a small part, and even the date of the bathhouse was uncertain.

To make way for the digging and laying of foundations for the building of the new bath structure, a certain amount of demolition of parts of the Phase 8A building evidently had to have taken place at this time. Of course, it is impossible to say how much demolition actually did occur, the problem being compounded by the fact that so large was the Phase 8B building that whole rooms of the Phase 8A building could have been demolished and their former area taken in by the bath suite without a single indicator of their ever having existed surviving.

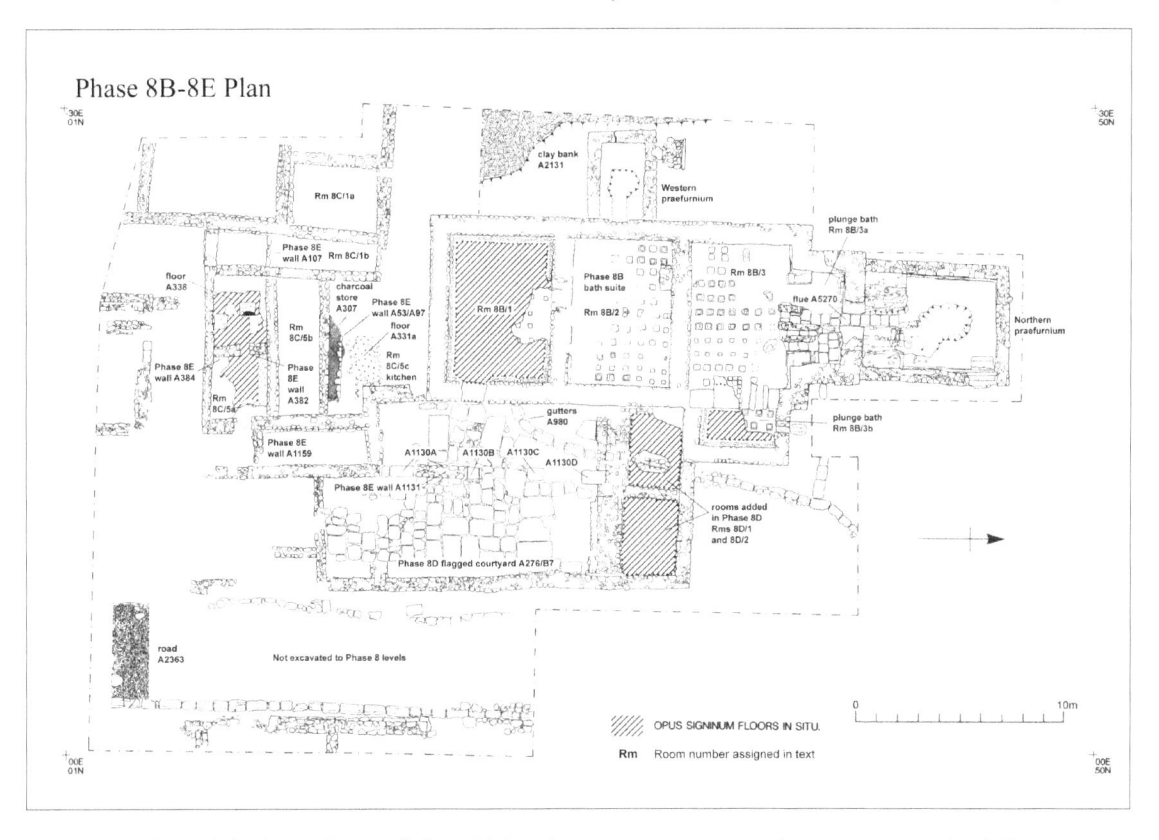

40 Plan of the later phases of the mid-fourth-century stone praetorium, or commandant's house (called Phases 8B–8E in the stratigraphic schema for the 1976–1981 and 1986–1991 excavations).

The construction of the bath building, with its hypocausted rooms and very deep underfloor arrangement, meant that the excavated hole into which the foundations of the building were to be set had to be of considerable size. In fact, the base of this Phase 8B excavation went down far below the level of the natural subsoil itself, and as a result any deposits that can be presumed to have accumulated here between the late first century and the mid-fourth century Phase 8A will have been removed entirely and any pre-Phase 8B features completely destroyed.

The east–west aligned foundation trench along the southern bathhouse wall was examined archaeologically and emptied down to a layer of cobbles and clay. Both inside and outside the building, it was noted that the stone footings of the building, a triple-stepped offset, sat directly on top of the uppermost clay foundation layer. Thirteen courses of stone were recorded in the southern bathhouse wall as exposed in the excavated foundation trench, standing to a height of 1.8 metres (almost 6 feet) above the cobble and clay footings.

Very few finds came from the fills of the foundation trenches. The most unusual find, probably ritually deposited here, was a rough sandstone carving, a rustic sculpture with shallow holes in the surface of the rounded part of the carving, representing eyes. The appearance and form of this anthropomorphic figure is far removed from most other fourth-century sculpture found elsewhere in Roman Britain.

*41 Mid-fourth-century bathhouse foundation trench.*

The Phase 8B bathhouse was a self-contained building unit, in its original plan comprising three major rooms, Rooms 8B/1–8B/3 and one, possibly two, small plunge baths, Rooms 8B/3a–8B/3b, with two related but external praefurnia, or furnace rooms, which will be considered individually below.

The walls were built of cut and faced sandstone blocks generally no different in size and shape from those used in the Phase 8A walls, but the corners of the bathhouse included larger, better cut, quoin stones in their fabric. One of these quoins, at the south-west corner of the building, had a small carving on its southern face. This carving, in low relief, was of an animal, now sadly headless, which was either a representation of a dog or a bull.

There is evidence in only a few places for tile coursing in the main walls, one patch of tiles surviving towards the northern end of the western wall, another near the eastern plunge bath and a third by the doorway into the first room of the baths. A large number of squared putlog holes, to take the ends of wooden beams forming horizontals for scaffolding, were recorded in the bathhouse walls, a series of putlog holes in the southern wall being partly blocked with stone and mortar. Evidence is also here attested for some form of gritty white mortar rendering over the external stone wall surface, but this is largely now destroyed.

The first room of the bath suite, the warm room or tepidarium, had a floor surface of concrete or opus signinum which largely survives intact even today. Access to the room was through a doorway in the eastern wall, towards the southern corner of the

42 Animal carved on the south-western corner of the mid-fourth-century bathhouse.

room. This doorway had an extremely worn flagstone threshold, of which Hooppell noted that 'the threshold of the entrance, a very perfect doorway in all respects, was worn down in remarkable manner, indicative of the continued passage of innumerable feet through a long period of time.'[6] A dowel hole in one of the stones at the side of the door may have taken a wooden fitting while tiles around the doorway may testify to the one-time existence of an arched entrance here. The floor itself goes right up to the lip of the threshold, while over the rest of the room the floor was of a size slightly smaller than the dimensions of the walls, a series of box flue tiles, sixteen along one side and twenty-one along the other, some held in place by T-shaped iron staples or holdfasts, filling the space between the edge of the floor and the inner face of the walls. Evidence for some form of rendering over the face of the box flue tiles survived, but not to the extent indicated by Hooppell when he noted that 'they were plastered over, and the plaster stencilled. Much of the plaster near the floor was in position; and the colours upon it, particularly the red and the green, were very vivid.'[7]

The floor itself was of a pinky-red opus signinum, the colour being created by the numerous red tile chip inclusions in the concrete matrix. Its upper surface was cracked and uneven, and had presumably undergone resurfacing during the Roman period. It had, in places, undergone modern repair. One portion of the floor was missing around the northern central part of the room. A small bronze coin was found stuck into the upper surface of the Roman opus signinum, this being an issue of Constantine II of AD 353-354.

43 Mid-fourth-century bathhouse interior. In situ opus signinum floor and box flue tiles in first hot room, or tepidarium.

In the northern part of the eastern wall was a hole, linked to an outer drain composed of interlinked stone gutters, the lip of the first gutter in the chain being right up against the base of this hole. With reference to this feature, Hooppell commented that 'a hole was roughly made in the front wall of the room above the hypocaust, a flue tile was removed and a drain formed to admit of the outflow of water.'[8] There is a great similarity in the form of this drain outlet with a second one in the north of the building, where an opus signinum-lined channel possibly once held a ceramic or lead water pipe.

The tepidarium had its hypocaust surviving in remarkable condition. Eighty out of a total of eighty-eight pilae tile stacks, which helped support the floor, survived, set into a reddened cement basal floor, the base tile, upon which a stack of sixteen further squared tiles rested, being larger in size. The individual stacks were then topped by two more tiles, the lower larger than those in the stack and the upper, in turn, larger again. Finally, large, thick tiles were placed with one corner resting in the centre of each of four tile stacks and meeting other large tiles on all four sides to form a continuous surface. The concrete of the opus signinum floor was then laid over the top of this tiled surface. The height of the underfloor, from the basal floor to the underside of the largest tiles, was 1.3 metres (just over 4 feet).

Access to the second room, a dry hot room or laconicum, was through a doorway in the western central part of the northern wall. Also in this wall, below floor level, were three arches whose purpose was to link the underfloor of the second room to that of the first.

## BINCHESTER PHASE 8
## BATH SUITE

44 Elevation of wall inside the mid-fourth-century bathhouse.

45 Mid-fourth-century bathhouse interior. Louisa Gidney giving radio interview in underfloor area of first hot room or tepidarium.

46 Mid-fourth-century bathhouse interior. Few remaining pilae stacks of second hot room, or laconicum, and view towards plunge bath.

The internal dimensions of the laconicum were almost exactly the same as those of the tepidarium, but its interior did not survive anywhere near as well as that of the first room. The upper floor did not survive, many of the tile stacks having been completely robbed out, and two disturbances cut through the basal floor itself. The absence of the floor here does, though, afford a good view of the arches in the southern wall and of a fine, large arch in the western wall, all of which originally would have been below floor level. The western and eastern arches in the southern wall survived intact, being built of tile set in mortar and capped by further tiles arranged in a semicircular effect. The third, central, arch did not survive but a very large area, larger than the size of the postulated arch, has been knocked out of the wall here. According to Hooppell, 'tradition says that when the chamber was first found, a couple of generations ago, the bricks were torn from the centre arch to give greater accessibility to the interior to those who hoped to find treasure there.'[9] A number of squared, backfilled, putlog holes were also visible in the face of this wall. Modern bricks from the vaulting that formed an east–west tunnel along the edge of this wall, a feature demolished in 1969, can still be seen in position on the top of the uppermost surviving course of the wall.

But it is in the centre of the western wall that the most interesting feature survived. This is a large, tile-built arch of which Hooppell noted:

*47 Mid-fourth-century bathhouse interior. Flue arch from western praefurnium, or furnace room.*

at a considerable depth beneath the surface of the ground, is a very fine brick archway, giving entrance to a subterranean vestibule, from which access is obtained, through a wall which runs right across the building, into long passage, bounded by that wall on the left, and by the hypocaust arcade on the right. Remains of walls on each side of the archway were discovered.[10]

This arch is merely the eastern face of a longer tile-arched tunnel flue which directly connected the underfloor of the laconicum of the bathhouse to the stokehole of a praefurnium, or furnace room, outside the building to the west. This praefurnium, then, produced heated air that was channelled through the tile-arched tunnel and under the floor of the laconicum, and, in a somewhat cooler form, through the three small tile arches to circulate through the underfloor of the tepidarium. Thus, these two rooms formed a single unit within the bath suite at underfloor level.

Before passing through the doorway at the western end of the northern wall of the laconicum, it is worth noting the existence here of a small stub of wall that juts southwards out from the face of this wall in front of the position of the doorway. This was built of stone, one of the larger blocks in the fabric having a fluted edge and presumably being a reused architectural fragment, with a number of tiles being set into the stub's upper surface. It is probable that this feature was covered by the floor of the room, its surviving height being just below the level of the doorway threshold. Presumably, this is merely an attempt to strengthen the floor at one of its most vulnerable and most-used points, near a doorway, and it may have been added at a later stage of

48 Mid-fourth-century bathhouse interior. Surviving pilae in third hot room, or caldarium, and part of remnant flue to northern praefurnium or furnace room.

the building's history to compensate for structural problems. It certainly does not easily fit in with the conception of the well-built structure, as evidenced by the other walls. Writing of this structural oddity, Hooppell wondered if it had once 'extended right across the room, for the purpose of enclosing a staircase or other arrangement.'[11]

Passing through the southern doorway, indicated today merely by a gap in the wall where the stone courses survived to a lower level, the third room of the bath suite, the steam room or caldarium, was reached. Two small baths projected off the room. This third room was only partly cleared of its backfill in the 1960s/early 1970s excavation campaign and, indeed, the remaining backfill was not cleared out of here until the 1986–1991 seasons of excavation.

As in the laconicum, the floor did not survive here in the caldarium either, though many more of the stacks of pilae tiles forming the underfloor remained in situ, generally standing to a greater height than those in the laconicum. In the southwestern corner of the room the spacing of these stacks was quite irregular, with the stacks being extremely close together, once more possibly representing a later repair to remedy a subsiding or collapsing floor, in an area, perhaps significantly, on the other side of the wall from the inserted stub wall. Three of these added pilae stacks consisted of a basal tile on top of which has been placed what appeared to be a long box flue tile, or one atop another, the central part of the box being filled with opus signinum, poured in in a liquid state, which also partly adhered to the sides of the tiles.

Projecting off the caldarium to the east was a small room. The pink-red opus signinum floor survived over about three quarters of the room, and six box flue tiles remained in situ along the southern wall and eleven along the eastern. The floor was destroyed to the north, while to the west it continued right up to the stepped wall face. The opus signinum also extended partly up the walls and it can be assumed that this was to allow water to be held in this room, hence its identification as a plunge bath, an identification also confirmed by the presence of a drain and a raised step above the adjoining floor level.

The excavators of 1972 noted that 'there survives about a square foot of the floor of the main room attached to the side of the bath,'[12] but this no longer survived when the area was examined in 1977. The plunge bath floor was supported by a hypocaust of which the pilae stacks survived remarkably well. A drain in the northern wall, with a lower channel formed of opus signinum, opened onto a stone gutter system outside the building.

Perhaps the most interesting aspect of this room was the arrangement for access between the caldarium and the plunge bath. Two unusually large and solid stone blocks at either side of the entrance suggest that an arch would have spanned this gap, with two specially strengthened linear blocks of tile taking the extra weight at this point.

A second small room projected off the caldarium to the north. Again, it was hypocausted, being directly linked to the flue arch through which the hot air to heat the third room and the small eastern plunge bath passed from the praefurnium or furnace room outside the building to the north. In the eastern wall of this second small room was another outlet to a stone gutter channel. The praefurnium arch did not survive here, and indeed only a very few tiles at the base of the projected feature testified to its existence.

49 Mid-fourth-century bathhouse interior. Remnant of flue of northern praefurnium or furnace room.

50 Mid-fourth-century bathhouse interior. Remnant of flue of northern praefurnium, or furnace room.

*The Mid- to Late Fourth-Century Praetorium and Bath Suite*

51 Mid-fourth-century bathhouse. Western praefurnium, or furnace room, fully excavated.

Thus, the original plan of the Phase 8B bath suite provided for three large hypocausted rooms, the first two forming a composite unit heated by a single furnace outside the building, the third, and its two small projecting rooms, being serviced by its own external furnace. For roofing the bath suite, it seems most likely that three separate vaults, running east–west, one for each major room, would have been constructed, with two smaller half vaults over the plunge baths. The main material used for the vaulting was a calcareous tufa. Small pieces of this light, vesicular material were found in Phase 8B construction deposits and in Hooppell-derived deposits around the bath building, but by far the greatest amount came from a scatter of stone and tufa rubble lying to the west of the bathhouse. This material represented the collapse of part of a vault, probably the one over the third room, and the upper part of the masonry walling, in the sub-Roman period when the bathhouse had been long out of use. Among this rubble were a number of well-cut and squared tufa blocks, some with opus signinum or mortar adhering to their surfaces, this doubtless having acted as a weatherproof rendering for this easily-eroded and porous material.

Many of the tiles used in the construction of the Phase 8B bathhouse bore the retrograde-stamped legend 'NCON', tiles both in pilae stacks and in the fabric of the large tiled arch. A tile with such a stamp has also been attested from Phase 8A, as related above. The 'N' of the stamp probably stands for 'Numerus' while the 'CON' has been tentatively suggested as being short for Concangium, the Roman name for Chester-le-Street.

52 Mid-fourth-century bathhouse. Northern praefurnium, or furnace room, fully excavated.

There were two praefurnia or furnace rooms servicing the bath suite, a small one to the west of the building, excavated in the 1976–1981 campaign, and a larger one to the north, excavated in the 1986–1991 campaign. The western praefurnium serviced the first two rooms of the bathhouse. The stokehole was sited within a building formed by three walls, the eastern ends of the two east–west running walls being butted onto the outer face of the western wall of the bath building. The floor of the room was of pink-red mortar and survived over about two-thirds of the interior. Dug into the floor was the actual stokehole pit itself, a bowl-shaped feature, perhaps surprisingly small in size. Its sides were composed of a concreted and heavily-burned pinky-red sand. It was backfilled with a number of different deposits, including ash and charcoal. This furnace would presumably have been covered by some form of cowl to direct the heat from the furnace towards the flue. The tile-built arch, whose existence was noted as connecting this praefurnium with the underfloor of the second room inside the main building, had been cut off flush with the outer face of the western wall, whereas two projecting stone stubs inside the praefurnium indicate that the tile arch would originally have formed a tunnel running into the room to the end of these stubs.

Access into this praefurnium, which was a sunken room, its floor being on a level with the interior basal underfloor, was through a doorway in the western end of the northern wall. This doorway had a large, worn flagstone forming the threshold. Related to this entrance was a very elaborate set of stone steps. Excavation allowed only a cursory examination of the foundation trenches of the praefurnium, one of which contained a coin of Magnentius, AD 350–360.

A graded clay bank was related by association to the Phase 8B praefurnium. This clay banking and surfacing would appear to represent a landscaping of the area around the sunken praefurnium.

The northern praefurnium was larger than the western praefurnium, and formed by three walls. Entry was by a doorway in the east wall, reached by a ramp of stone rubble set in mortar and later by a raised threshold formed of four large masonry blocks set in a row on a bed of stone rubble. A large stone block forming a step into the furnace room may also have been a secondary feature. The initial build included a platform in the south-east corner of the room which formed the original base for a large boiler, with another in the south-west corner. The opus signinum floor was cut by the stokehole itself, surrounded by flat stone slabs, and by the tile-lined flue channel. Indentations in the floor surface possibly indicated where lead pipes had been laid to channel water to the copper boiler.

There was evidence for some ongoing minor repair work to the northern praefurnium and the accumulation here of some debris, though both could have taken place at any time in Phases 8B–8D. As might have been expected, the furnace flue contained a significant amount of ash and charcoal debris, probably representing its final firings. At some stage there were to be problems with subsidence at the edge of one side of the boiler platform in the south-east corner of the room, but again these problems cannot be tied with any degree of certainty to any specific phase of the bathhouse's operation.

The area immediately around the northern praefurnium was not excavated, though it can be expected that this structure would again have been approached by

53 Painted wall plaster with part of the leg of a bather or an athlete visible.

sets of stone steps down from the contemporary Roman ground surface and that the clay bank landscaping recorded around the western praefurnium also extended into this area.

It has already been mentioned that there were three outlets for water in the walls of the main bath building, each outlet leading to a system of stone gutter channels. Though this system was in use in Phase 8D it must certainly have been originally conceived in Phase 8B. The outlet from the first hypocausted room, the tepidarium, directly opened out onto stone gutters placed end to end to form a continuous channel that then curved north-eastwards and then ran north–south, where it was met by another stone channel which had brought water from the outlet for the northern extension of the suite and had, in turn, been fed by a channel from the small plunge bath. The main channel outside the Phase 8B building was lined by stone blocks. The gutters were presumably capped or covered, but no evidence of this survived because of the subsequent Phase 8D changes in this area.

Approximately 1,400 sherds of pottery came from this phase, the material again showing a marked functional bias towards tablewares, particularly bowls, and a still rising level of jars, jars being a large component of the overall assemblage. Beaker levels remained low, more or less the same as in Phase 8A. Levels of finewares in general dropped quite considerably again from those in Phase 8A, but nevertheless fineware levels remained quite high. The pottery supply in this phase was no longer dominated by Black Burnished ware (BB1) products. Indeed, Crambeck greyware dominated the coarse pottery assemblage, with Crambeck mortaria being almost exclusive representatives of this vessel type. Nene Valley products made up the bulk of the fineware assemblage. The pottery from this phase included common Crambeck greyware vessels, proto-Huntcliff-type and Huntcliff-type calcite gritted ware jars, the latter clearly post-dating AD 350–5. Late Roman burnished ware was also present, as was Crambeck redware and painted Crambeck parchment ware, again dating after *c.* AD 350–5. Harrold Southern Shell tempered ware also made an appearance, as did Hadham redware and Oxfordshire ware. It may be that the presence of late Roman burnished ware indicates that this phase extended after *c.* AD 370.

Only four glass vessels were represented in Phase 8B: a cast vessel, two wheel-cut cups and a convex jar/jug. One of the wheel-cut conical beakers is elaborately decorated and is without parallel in Britain.

Although the small finds assemblage from this phase was relatively small, there was noted a slight concentration of personal ornaments and equipment in particular, although recreational items such as a die and four gaming counters and military equipment, represented by two horse harness fittings, two plume holders and a mount or boss, were also worthy of note. While fewer jet artefacts were present than in Phase 8A, more waste jet and shale came from Phase 8B than from Phase 8A, again possibly suggesting working of these materials here on site during this period.

A relatively small amount of painted wall plaster was associated with the bath building, most of it, as in Phase 8A, bearing a patchy red paint, though fragments with red bands on a cream ground were also recovered. The most interesting individual fragment, though, was the only piece from the whole site bearing a human figure. On this fragment can be discerned part of the calf and foot of an athlete or runner. Another noteworthy piece from this phase bears a green foliate motif on a cream ground, not unlike the floral motifs found in the Phase 8A house.

The large quantity of ceramic tile from this phase is dominated by those forms of tile needed for the construction of the new, large bath suite, with only a small quantity of roof tiles being present. Most of the relatively small quantity of non-roofing tile recovered from this phase must be assumed to represent breakages from the construction of the new bath suite in this phase.

Two architectural fragments in the bathhouse were recorded in situ: a quoin stone bearing a carving of an animal, either a dog or a horse, and a decorated block. A crude anthropomorphic stone carving came from a foundation trench. Almost 250 kilograms of stone roof tiles came from this phase, including one piece bearing a scratched batch mark or tally. Spatially, most of the stone roof tile was associated with the praefurnia of the bath suite. Tufa appeared in this phase for the first time in small quantities, this material doubtless representing offcuts from the dressing of tufa blocks for the vaults of the bath suite.

54 Charcoal store under excavation in kitchen of altered residential ranges of the mid-fourth-century stone praetorium, or commandant's house.

## PHASE 8C: REPLANNING OF THE RESIDENTIAL RANGES

In this phase we see the first major reorganisation of the plan and the interior of part of the residential range of the original Phase 8A building. Some Phase 8A rooms did, though, remain unchanged and the Phase 8B bath suite continued in use in its original form. Whereas the ground plan of the Phase 8A building had been dominated by the provision of very large rooms, there was an opposite trend in Phase 8C towards the creation of much smaller rooms or units by the insertion of internal dividing walls. For instance, the L-shaped room of Phase 8A was now divided into two separate units by the insertion of a north–south running wall. In the southern range new walls were built to create two new rooms, only parts of which lay within the excavated area.

But the greatest changes in the plan of the building were made to the large, central room known previously as Phase 8A Room 5. Two east–west running walls were now built to divide this once large space into three separate, but unequal, units. A new east–west running wall was also built to close off the northern end of what had been Room 7 in the Phase 8A building. It is not possible to say for certain what happened to the separate, hypocausted Phase 8A eastern range of rooms at this time. The furnace stokehole had certainly gone out of use, and it was also probably at this time that the flue opening was backfilled and blocked with a large, upended flagstone. There was no evidence for any internal refurbishment in this eastern range of rooms, so the basic room plan must have continued in use much as before, even if the rooms themselves were no longer heated.

No other major changes were made to the general ground plan and it must be assumed that as far as the other rooms and areas in the residential ranges were concerned, their functions continued much as before. But, of course, changes now also had to be made with regard to the provision of access to the newly-created rooms and some of the long, narrow spaces now created may have been used as access corridors.

New mortar or concrete opus signinum survived in patches in most of the newly created rooms. One room was provided with two tile hearths. With one exception, though, it was not possible to assign a specific function to any of the rooms. The exception was the new room in the north of the central range whose north wall was formed by the southern wall of the bath building. It would appear that this room was used as a kitchen or service room.

A new floor of yellow mortar with red tile chip inclusions was laid inside the room. Contemporary with this was an elongated, trough-like feature lined with mortar and bounded by a row of stakeholes. It was filled with a deposit of pure black charcoal. This has been interpreted as a charcoal store set against the southern wall of the room, the mortar forming the base of the structure that held the charcoal. The stakeholes were to take the pointed ends of thin, upright poles that probably formed the support struts for a wickerwork fence or screen to hold the fuel in position. Plastering at the base of the fence presumably not only strengthened the structure but stopped any material slipping through holes here. The upper part of the screen may have been rendered with clay.

Finds associated with this phase of replanning of the residential ranges of the praetorium were few. The small group of pottery recovered included Crambeck

*55 Two new rooms added to the east side of the mid-fourth-century bathhouse.*

greywares and Black Burnished ware (BB1), with little calcite gritted ware, and would appear to date before *c.* AD 350–5. Among the twenty or so small finds from this subphase were a die and two gaming counters, whose presence suggests that, as in Phase 8B, leisure activities were important in this period.

A relatively small amount of painted wall plaster came from this phase, most of it bearing a patchy red paint, though fragments with red bands on a cream ground, a green band on cream and a patchy green ground overpainted with stripes were also recovered. The ceramic tile from this phase was dominated by roofing tile, followed by flue tiles, confirming a major reroofing or refurbishment at this time.

## PHASE 8D: THE CREATION OF A GRANDER BATH SUITE

In this phase, the Phase 8B bathhouse was substantially enlarged to turn it into what may best be called a bath complex or bath suite, with most of the new building work taking place on the east side of the original bath building.

Two new rooms were added to the east side of the bathhouse and a large flagged hall was added, again on its east side. To make way for the new rooms, certain parts of the northern and eastern residential ranges of the praetorium required demolition or substantial replanning and renovation.

## The Mid- to Late Fourth-Century Praetorium and Bath Suite

56 Later fourth-century flagged courtyard.

57 Later fourth-century flagged courtyard, with triple-arched entranceway into the extended bath complex.

58 Later fourth-century flagged courtyard, with close-up of one of the pier stones of the triple-arched entranceway into the extended bath complex.

59 Later fourth-century flagged courtyard, looking onto threshold leading into the courtyard off the fort's main road, or via principalis.

The westernmost new room had a pink-red opus signinum floor surviving over most of its interior, a quarter-moulding for this floor surviving only in places. In the south-eastern corner of the room it could be seen that opus signinum went up the wall, presumably as part of the proofing for the room to hold water. Where the floor was broken and collapsed, in the centre of the room, there was visible, underneath, the course of the stone gutter system passing below the floor. Alongside the western side of this room, formed by the pre-existing bathhouse wall, was a structure of tiles bonded together with pink cement that may have acted as a base or support for a statue. The easternmost new room had its floor at a considerably higher level than that of the first room. Again, a solid pink-red floor of opus signinum survived largely intact, with a low quarter-moulding along the walls.

A large paved or flagged hall, created using Binchester Crags stone, was now laid to the south of these new rooms. Hooppell, who lifted a number of the flagstones during the nineteenth-century excavation here, reported that 'memorials of the older worship, ruined and defaced in Roman times, and put to ignominious uses by Roman hands, were found beneath the pavement'. This included a statue of a female deity he identified as Flora,[13] as has been described in Chapter One.

A grandiose triple-arched entrance opening off the main part of the hall was also now built, leading into what would have been a changing room for the bath suite. Four massive arch bases formed of well-cut stone blocks and, in one case, a reused architectural fragment from an earlier structure, survived in situ. At the same time, a new doorway leading into the paved hall and leading off the via principalis was created in the easternmost wall of the praetorium. In front of the doorway, inside the building, were set three large stones which stood slightly above the level of the flagstones, suggesting this was an arched inner porch of some kind.

There were few finds recovered from this phase. Only one of the coins found was of the latter half of the fourth century, this being an issue of the House of Constantine, AD 350–360. A large quantity of stone roof tiles came from this phase, along with a small quantity of tufa, doubtless representing offcuts from the dressing of tufa blocks for extending or repairing the vaults of the bath suite. The ceramic tile from this phase was more or less evenly balanced between roof tiles and tile needed for the construction of the new, large bath suite.

## PHASE 8E: THE STRUCTURE IN DISREPAIR

Probably some considerable time elapsed between the creation of the enlarged, grand bath suite and the final phase of building work and repair recorded as taking place on the praetorium building. At this time further, final changes were made to its ground plan, while in some parts of the residential ranges there was evidence for the structure falling into a state of disrepair and decay.

A number of small partition walls were now built within the residential ranges of the house to further divide some of the rooms into even smaller units, and seemingly to restrict access to some parts of the building. Some of these new dividing walls were very poorly constructed in comparison to the standards of workmanship previously

60 Later fourth-century blocking wall in the residential ranges of the mid-fourth-century stone praetorium, or commandant's house.

seen in this building. In the paved hall some of the arched doorways were now also blocked off, with perhaps only the central archway being open.

Parts of the house now appeared to be in a very poor state of repair, with rubbish deposits being allowed to accumulate inside a number of the formerly residential and well-kept rooms. There was no evidence for any refurbishment of the house during this sub-phase, but rather for a presence that favoured neglect.

It is assumed that the large bath suite still continued in use, but it is apparent that it too was now subject to a cycle of escalating disrepair and repair.

Inside the northern praefurnium or furnace room the total refurbishment of the furnace structure, both the flue and the boiler platform, was recognised during excavation here. This seems to have been a major undertaking, involving the rebuilding of the furnace flue following the robbing-out of the original tile and concrete flue and boiler platform. Clay was used to bond large, irregular stone and concrete blocks, many of them probably from the original structure, among which was a fragment of an inscription. Why mortar was not used is uncertain. Inside the praefurnium there was recorded a building up of deposits at this time, including the dumping here of some large masonry fragments, possibly derived from the original flue build.

The original opus signinum platform for the boiler in the south-west corner of the room was now modified to form a tank or cistern, the works including the building of a

61 Later fourth-century rebuilt furnace in the northern praefurnium, or furnace room, of the bathhouse.

very poor quality mortar wall, the cistern being associated with what has been suggested to be an aqueduct. This cistern was later backfilled. The aqueduct consisted of a bank of clay running along the north and west walls of the furnace room from just short of the doorway to the water tank. It was presumed by the excavator that this represented an attempt to restore the water supply here after the lead pipes associated with the original structure had been removed. After the aqueduct had gone out of use repairs, structural collapse and debris accumulation occurred here, although there was evidence pointing towards the continued firing of the furnace, with the flue being reduced to a much smaller structure than it had originally been by a number of relinings. The flue was full of ash and charcoal, representing the final firing in the stokehole.

The last firing of the furnaces in the western and northern praefurnia could not be dated by either associated coins or pottery. A number of samples of stokehole and flue rakeout material from the northern praefurnium were therefore submitted for carbon 14 dating. The results are discussed below.

Excavation inside the caldarium of the bath suite was limited but important for the light that it shone on the late Roman to sub-Roman use of the building. Unfortunately, most of the interior of the bathhouse had been cleared out prior to the campaigns of work under consideration here having started in 1976. However, there did survive evidence for the repair of the underfloor here, close to the mouth of the flue, with rough stone being used to replace rotted or damaged tile pilae.

62 Inscription naming the Ala Vettonum found in situ in the northern praefurnium, or furnace room, of the bathhouse (courtesy of Simon Clarke).

Few finds came from this phase. The reused fragment of an inscribed sandstone altar found in the northern praefurnium read, '[...] | [...]AVET[...] | [...]MCP[...] | [...]ONIV[...] | [...]VFVS[...] | [...], [I(ovi) O(ptimo) M(aximo) ?] | [al]a Vet[to|nu]m c(ui) p(raeest) [2-3]|[1-2]oniu[s] | [R]ufus[ pr|aefectus) v(otum) s(olvit) l(ibens) m(erito) ?]' ('To Jupiter Best and Greatest, the Cavalry Regiment of Vettones commanded by [ ]onius Rufus, prefect, willingly and deservedly fulfilled its vow').[14] Judging by the other Ala Vettonum altars from the site, this inscription ought to be Severan or a little later in date.

The carbon 14 dates obtained for the final firing of the furnace in the northern praefurnium of the bathhouse were of considerable interest. From various samples of stokehole and flue rakeout material from the northern praefurnium came dates of AD 130–400, AD 130–400, AD 130–390, AD 230–410, AD 20–210, AD 250–430, AD 210–400 and AD 220–420. Leaving aside one apparent outlier, this seems a remarkably consistent set of dates, bearing in mind that the bathhouse construction can be dated by a coin to after AD 350–60. The end of the use of the bathhouse furnaces is estimated by mathematical modelling to have taken place in cal. AD 370–400 with 95 per cent probability, probably placing the actual date towards the end of this range, given that post-AD 350–60 another extensive phase of enlarging and remodelling of the bath complex had taken place.

## THE SIGNIFICANCE OF THE MID- TO LATE FOURTH CENTURY PRAETORIUM

The mid-fourth-century praetorium building was distinguished by the large size of individual rooms in its residential ranges. It was an imposing construction, with plastered and painted walls and opus signinum floors, a hypocausted range in the east and probably a small hypocausted bathhouse range under where subsequently was to be added a grander bath building. As with the two previous praetoria, it fronted onto the fort's via principalis.

The new, grander bathhouse, the structure on display at the site today, comprised three consecutive rooms with a plunge bath leading off the hot-room and a second plunge bath. A small praefurnium on the western side of the building serviced the first two heated rooms, while a larger praefurnium on the northern side serviced the hot room and its associated plunge bath. A securely stratified coin of Magnentius, dated AD 350–360, came from the backfill of the construction trench for the western praefurnium. It is perhaps surprising that such a major replanning of the praetorium and its service facilities should follow so relatively soon after its initial construction. There is an interesting contrast between the grandeur of the new bath building and the artwork with which it was associated, that is the anthropomorphic, possibly phallic or apotropaic, stone carving found in the foundation cut backfill for the bath building, where it had presumably been placed as a ritual offering, and the rather non-committal, amorphous carving of an animal on one of the quoinstones at the south-west corner of the building.

Either at the same time as these changes, or slightly later, alterations were also made within the residential ranges of the house, with a number of the larger rooms being sub-divided by the insertion of new walls. The bathhouse itself was subsequently enlarged by the addition of two new rooms on its eastern side, a large flagged exercise hall or courtyard, and a triple-arched entranceway off the courtyard and into the changing room of the complex, and perhaps an arched entrance off the road into the courtyard. Although the latest coin associated with this sub-phase is again of the period AD 350–360, it is likely that some considerable time had elapsed between the loss and deposition of these two contemporaneously minted coins from the first phase of the bathhouse and from the subsequent phase of its enlargement.

In the residential ranges, repairs and redecoration continued, with there being evidence for the relaying of floors and the replastering of walls. However, the last attested instances of building work here are less easy to understand, in that they comprised the further sub-division of a number of rooms with rough, poorly built, unplastered sandstone rubble walls.

The contemporary continued operation of the bath suite is attested by the evidence of regular repair and maintenance coming from the excavation in the northern praefurnium. Here, the sequence was complex. A major rebuilding of the furnace flue and boiler platform took place, utilising not the tile and well-faced, mortared sandstone blocks of the original structure but rather masonry rubble bonded with clay. This construction itself also bore signs of subsequent repair and renovation. The boiler was now serviced by a roughly constructed aqueduct, which itself seems to have

110 *Vinovia*

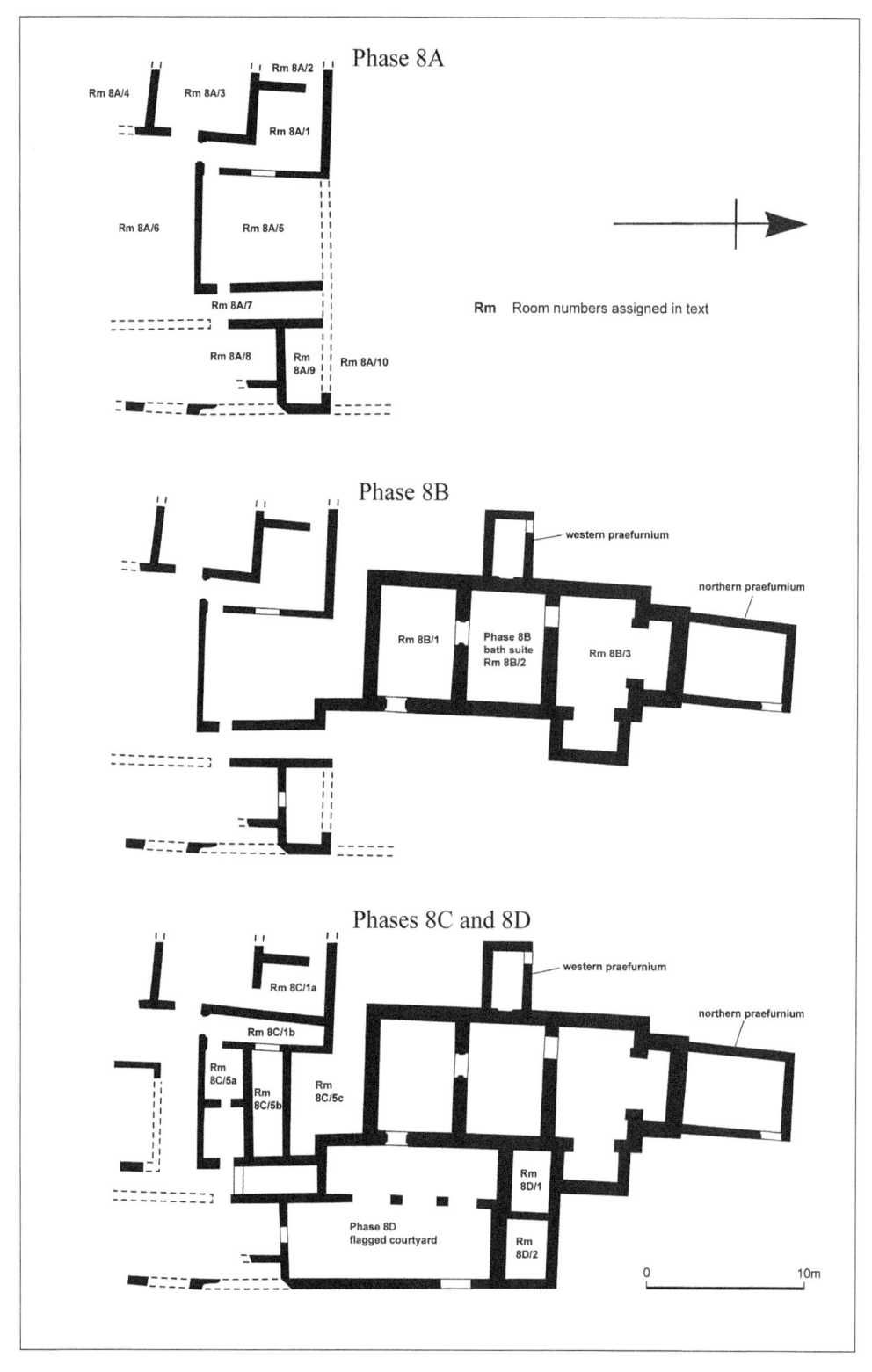

63 Block plans of the mid-fourth-century stone praetorium, or commandant's house, through all phases of its life (called Phases 8A–8E in the stratigraphic schema for the 1976–1981 and 1986–1991 excavations).

gone out of use before the final firing of the furnace. No such sequence was found in the western praefurnium; there, the final firing of the furnace seems to have been followed straightaway by the stripping-off of its roof and the demolition of its walls down to ground level.

In some ways, the changes to the Phase 8 building contradicted each other. The addition of a large, new bathhouse in Phase 8B might be thought to imply a change in status of the occupant of the house or of the house itself at this time. It might imply that the bath suite became a social focus for the operation of the commandant's hospitality, patronage and power or even, as has been suggested, that the bathhouse was a public structure, unlikely though this seems. The residential range of the Phase 8A house was replanned, with many originally large rooms being subdivided in Phase 8C, such subdivision possibly implying a move towards the need for greater privacy. The substantial enlargement of the bath complex in Phase 8D might imply a more important, possibly public, role for this part of the building. Finally, in Phase 8E, further subdivisions were made in the residential range, implying either the need for more privacy here or, conversely, providing evidence of multiple occupancy. Poor quality but numerous repairs were made to the bath suite at this time, implying a continuation of the importance socially, and possibly politically, of bathing.

Although large, well-appointed residences such as the mid-fourth-century house at Binchester are found at many northern sites in the fourth century, such as Piercebridge, Chester-le-Street and South Shields, these comparable buildings were constructed somewhat earlier. All appear to have been designed and equipped in the manner of late Roman private residences throughout the Empire, arranged around a courtyard, with concrete floors and painted walls.[15] Such buildings seem to reflect a common elite culture in the Empire, matching in architectural terms the pattern for the eastern Mediterranean on the basis of written sources.[16] These buildings seem to represent something different from the commandants' houses of earlier periods, and are especially noteworthy at a time when the traditional command arrangements of the Roman army had changed radically. There is clearly reason to believe that the north-east of England was experiencing some new style of organisation towards the end of the third century. At Binchester, the phenomenon represented in the architecture was substantially restated in the mid-fourth century.

If the scale of the house's original construction suggests that it was built for people who saw themselves as part of a wider late Roman elite, its later development raises questions about who lived in it afterwards. The structural sequence shows an evolving use of the house, which maintained its Roman traditions for a considerable period. The various changes all kept intact the style of a late Roman residence, suggesting that the character of its occupants changed little too.

This is significant for addressing another key problem of the period, the definition of military and civilian. The architecture provides no support for substantive changes in the nature of the occupation at Binchester that might reflect change between military and civilian. However, the coin supply could be of relevance here, with only a handful of coins issued after the AD 350s or 360s present on the site. By equating coin supply with military status, we could argue for an end to Binchester's military status at that time. However, there are some later coins, albeit in residual contexts, and they must have reached the site somehow. Perhaps the soldiers of the numerus stationed here in the late period were paid in kind rather than in cash. There are also some key points about the formation processes which created the finds assemblages associated with the house. There are only relatively small assemblages of finds associated with the occupation sequence of the residence because the rooms were kept clean for most of its life. A striking sequence of at least four successive concrete floors inside one room of the house included no finds. Each floor was laid on top of the clean surface of its predecessor or on a levelled spread of clean sand. The sequence represents an intense level of use and activity in the house that left no finds. It suggests, in effect, a negative correlation between periods of use and quantities of finds. Abundant finds on the site came from periods of rubbish dumping, not periods of occupation. This applies as much to coin finds as to pottery and animal bones. The evidence of the end of coin supply is by no means clear-cut, and nor is the nature of the organisation of power at Binchester at this time. The archaeological sequence, in fact, suggests much more continuation than abrupt change for the people living there.

The complex series of alterations and changes to the original house should perhaps be viewed in terms of social and economic changes more generally in the late Roman north, as well as changes in military structure. This fits with the development of the forts as local centres, as demonstrated by the growth of external settlements. It is not only the late date of the third stone praetorium at Binchester that suggests the growing importance of the site as a power centre in the north and occasions interesting chronological contrasts to other northern military sites, but it is also the fact that the bath suite was itself an addition to the original house. It was built at a very late date for northern Britain, no earlier than the second half of the fourth century, some time after AD 350–360. The full extent of its facilities is now clear, as has been described in detail above. The fixing of such an elaborate sequence so late in the Roman period is in itself an important new contribution to knowledge of late Roman Britain. The new evidence on the bath-suite and courtyard house forms the centrepiece to reassessing the role of fourth-century Binchester.

Something about the lives of the inhabitants of the praetorium can be discerned from an examination of the finds from features and contexts of this phase, and to some extent this has been discussed above. Most of the finds came from foundation and levelling deposits, or from the extensive foundation excavation and landscaping associated with the addition of the bathhouse. Towards the end of the life of the house and bath suite, cleanliness apparently started to become less of a priority and finds at this time also come from within the residential ranges of the building.

Where the pottery assemblages from individual sub-phases were large enough to be subjected to functional analysis, it was found that levels of tablewares, particularly dishes, were high and that there were high levels of finewares represented, although this number fell off slightly through time. Glass vessels were few, but interesting, with other contemporary fourth-century vessels also being represented as residual finds in later contexts. A beaker and an unguent bottle were present in Phase 8A, a cast vessel, two wheel-cut cups, one with elaborate decoration and unparalleled in Britain, and a convex jar came from Phase 8B, with two further wheel-cut cups coming from Phase 8C. The pottery and glass vessel evidence therefore largely concurs, with tablewares, finewares and glass drinking beakers or cups attesting to the high-status domestic nature of the building, certainly up to Phase 8E.

Among the small finds from the praetorium, numbers of personal items and objects of adornment, including objects probably attesting to a female presence in the building, were high in Phases 8A–8C. In Phase 8B in particular, but also in Phase 8C, items such as gaming counters and dice, associated with recreation and leisure, were notably present.

The last years of the house in many ways probably mirror the decline of its primary function as a reflection of the status of its occupant to its becoming no more than a building again. A gradually weakening grasp was revealed of the ability of the occupants to maintain the house in the same Roman traditions as previously, or maintaining the house and bath suite in good order was no longer seen as a priority.

The final subdividing of the residential rooms with walls made of rough sandstone blocks in poor mortar again probably reflects a lack of will to do other than maintain the house rather than a loss of Romanised building skills. Yet at the same time the bath suite continued in operation, with regular repair and maintenance being evidenced in the northern praefurnium. The major rebuilding of the furnace flue and boiler platform was needed because of subsidence, not for any other reason, and it was undertaken using masonry rubble bonded with clay, not the mortared tile and well-faced sandstone blocks of the original structure, again a utilitarian repair in a non-public part of the bath complex where neatness of repair was unlikely to have been an issue. The smaller boiler, which was now serviced by a roughly constructed water-channel or aqueduct, again bore signs of subsequent frequent utilitarian renovation. The build-up of layers of ash and clay in the furnace room, both on the floor and inside the flue, probably reflects knowledge of the timetable for the intended abandonment of the bathhouse as a functioning facility. In the western praefurnium, there was no build-up of debris between its final firing and the demolition of the walls; perhaps this had always been an easier, simpler part of the facility to maintain than the northern praefurnium, with its boiler and water supply.

Dating the late Roman sequence, though, has been difficult, as has already been discussed above. Coin assemblages become difficult to interpret as their supply declines towards the end of the fourth century. Coins of the AD 350s and 360s were the latest to be found in Roman or sub-Roman contexts at Binchester. The handful of later coins from the site was recovered from medieval horizons or from the topsoil. The overall coin list suggests change in the nature of coin supply and political organisation in the late fourth century in the area, and could indicate a lack of coin supply to Binchester in the late fourth century, perhaps implying weakened integration into the Roman army command structure. However, there are some curiosities when the stratigraphic position of coin finds is considered. For example, the coins from the AD 350s which date the bathhouse's construction give only a terminus post quem. Had the bathhouse been first built in the 380s or 390s, the coins would have been the same issues. Also, coins minted in the 350s dominated the deposits laid down after the end of the use of the baths.

The same problem applies to the pottery assemblage; there is little pottery that can be safely assigned to a date after the 350s, yet a sherd from an Argonne roller-stamped bowl which dates after AD 370 is present. The scientific dating model based on carbon-14 dates for the final firing of the furnace in the northern praefurnium estimates this to have taken place in cal. AD 370–400 with 95 per cent probability, though it most probably occurred towards the end of this range.

In summary then, the group of large late Roman praetorium houses in northern England, including the mid-fourth-century example at Binchester, seem to represent something different from the commandants' houses of earlier periods and the construction of these buildings is especially noteworthy at a time when the traditional command arrangements of the Roman army had changed radically. There is clearly reason to believe that the north-east of England was experiencing some new style of organisation towards the end of the third century. A clear pattern has emerged of late Roman praetorium residences increasing in size and often dwarfing the principia buildings within forts of this period. These new-style houses shared architectural characteristics and plan forms.[17] Such houses will have reflected the status of the commanders of these late limitaneus units and can be contrasted both with late Roman town houses and villas in southern Britain and with the praetoria of the auxiliary commanders of earlier periods. These later praetoria were the residences of men of considerable power and authority whose patronage needed to be sought by military and civilian alike and whose benevolence or malevolence could affect both the lives of individuals and of the broader regional society.

In its heyday it is tempting to see the mid- to late fourth-century Binchester commandant's house as serving the same kind of purpose in defining power and social relationships as other grand private houses elsewhere in Roman Britain and more widely throughout the Empire at this time. Such private houses of late Roman aristocrats were designed to display the power of their owners to visitors, clients, colleagues, family and friends. They demonstrated the owner's status and helped provide a stage for the drama of forging social and political alliances.[18] Access, or rather the restriction of access to some and the granting of access to others, was a crucial part of the aristocrat's drama of power. One could consider whether the various changes to the Binchester house – opening up and extending the baths while subdividing and restricting access inside the residential ranges – represent just such an exercise in domestic power politics, or potentially in sexual power politics by defining and controlling male space in the bathhouse, and manipulating and maintaining social relationships there.

CHAPTER FIVE

# *From Roman Britain to Anglo-Saxon England and Beyond*

In the last chapter it was seen that the mid- to late fourth-century commandant's house in the centre of Binchester fort had been allowed to decline to a very run-down state and, though the interior was still being used in the late fourth century to early fifth century, no attempt had been made to repair or prevent structural damage. The same gradual decline in the fortunes of the house can also be traced through the next phase of activity but, at the same time, within parts of the house there was a flurry of activity, the nature of this activity being very much out of character with anything that had gone before. This long sequence of activity, traced through the excavations here in 1976–1981 and 1986–1991, ended in the mid-sixth century AD, when an Anglo-Saxon burial took place to the west of the still-standing shell of the bathhouse building. This highly important sequence, unique in the Roman north, will now be summarised and its significance discussed.

## THE LATE TO SUB-ROMAN HOUSE

Evidence for continued structural decay was found both inside and outside the mid- to late fourth-century building, with waste deposits and what appeared to be demolition rubble in some places now being allowed to accumulate over the floors in some of the residential rooms, in the two rooms later added to the bathhouse and over the flagged courtyard outside the bathhouse. However, in a number of other rooms in the residential range there was recorded a high level of activity associated in one part of the house with metalworking, and in another with the operation of a slaughterhouse. Clearly a dramatic change in the use of the building had taken place.

The metalworking took place inside one of the rooms in what had been the western residential range of the house. Here were excavated a number of furnaces, the largest consisting initially of a large hole, widest at its western end and rounded at both ends, dug to a depth of over 1 metre (just over 3 feet). The sides of the hole were generally vertical, apart from those at the western end which gradually sloped in, forming a shelf. The base of the hole was lined with a dirty mottled silt and, to the west, lined by two layers of flat stone slabs. The furnace had evidently been

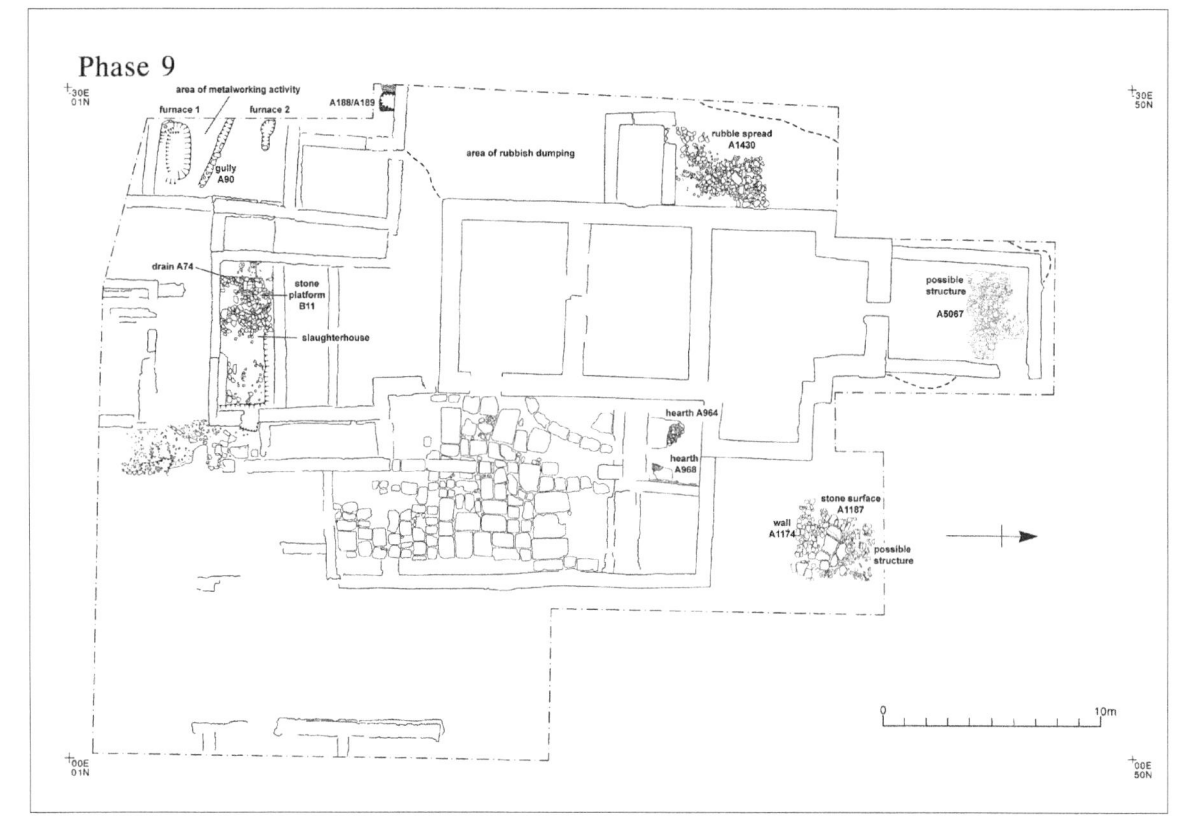

64 Plan of late Roman to sub-Roman activity (called Phase 9 in the stratigraphic schema for the 1976–1981 and 1986–1991 excavations).

fired on a number of occasions as there was evidence for it having been raked out and relined at least four times. In the north-west of the room was located a second, similar feature, being well-cut and shaped, in the form of a keyhole with a flattened base. The vertical sides were lined with a heavy clay fired to a bright red colour, with the occasional stone inclusions. A thin smear of charcoal covered the clay, in places. There was no evidence here for any relining or rebuilding. Between the two furnaces was a narrow and shallow straight-sided gully with a rounded channel in its base, aligned roughly north-west–south-east. It was backfilled with grey-brown mixed clay and a mass of iron slag.

To the north and west of the keyhole furnace was a bowl-shaped hole, lined with plaster and backfilled with a deposit of pure black charcoal. A square, shallow hole was linked to the bowl cut, and was filled with a mass of soft, sticky, white lime with inclusions of charcoal and organic material, including straw. The upper surface of this material was absolutely solid, like the surface of a floor, and had a small hole cut into it, the lime around the edges of the hole being raised to form a narrow circular ridge.

Between and around the two furnaces and the gully were spreads of burned soil and charcoal-rich deposits containing iron slags and other metalworking residues. In all, a total of almost 3.5 kilograms of iron-smithing slag was found within this room,

65 Late Roman to sub-Roman metalworking furnace fully excavated.

attesting to intense activity associated with the working and smithing of iron inside this room after it ceased to have a residential function. The numerous repairs to the largest furnace perhaps testify to the longevity of the industrial activity here.

Another feature possibly associated with metalworking was found in one of the two rooms added to the bathhouse later in its life. In the central northern part of the room, overlying the opus signinum floor, was a semi-circular patch of mixed red, yellow and orange clay silts with pebbles and charcoal, and around the feature were patchy spreads of red-brown clay loam, charcoal and slag, almost half a kilogram of slag being associated with these deposits.

Inside another residential room a rough stone oven was constructed, while inside the northern praefurnium, for a short period after the rebuilt furnace structure had itself gone out of use, a number of small ovens built of clay and stone were in operation here at a time when the praefurnium walls and roof were presumably still intact.

Even more extraordinary was the turning over of part of the former southern residential range to use as a slaughterhouse. Here during excavation was encountered a number of most unusual layers and features. A thick deposit of very aerated green silt was spread across the southern part of one room and the eastern part of another. A number of articulated cattle bones, showing signs of butchery, were found within this soil, which lay around a number of stone-built structures. The largest of these consisted of a great number of stone blocks arranged as a flat platform surface over

*66 Above:* Late Roman to sub-Roman slaughterhouse, looking onto stone platform and rough stone wall.

*67 Left:* Late Roman to sub-Roman slaughterhouse, showing close up of stone platform and animal bones in situ close to platform.

a layer of smaller stones and masonry rubble acting as a foundation base. The upper surface of this feature showed signs of wear indicative of great use. To the west of this platform was a roughly north–south aligned row of stone blocks forming a possible drain.

It is suggested that, taken together, all the above could be evidence for a slaughterhouse or abattoir. Certainly the presence of a number of articulated or butchered bones here could point towards this. The ubiquitous green silt deposit could have been derived from dried manure. The stone platform could have been the surface onto which cattle or other animals were herded before being slaughtered, and, if indeed this was a slaughterhouse, then a drain channelling running water would have been something of a necessity.

But confirmation of this identification came from the excavation and examination of deposits dumped some 10 metres (about 33 feet) or so away to the north, on the west of the bath suite. Here, the interior of the now-derelict and unroofed western praefurnium was used for dumping, as was the area directly around it and to the north, to a height level with the top of the clay bank which acted as landscaping around the bathhouse. The now-levelled northern praefurnium was also subsequently infilled with dumped spoil as well. These dumps, consisting of numerous individual deposits of soil, included many deposits of brown-green silt loam containing a mass of finds, particularly animal bones and small dumps of broken-up opus signinum flooring, stone rubble, cobbles, tiles and mortar.

It cannot be stressed too much that these deposits were packed with finds. During their excavation large numbers of overflowing finds trays were regularly brought into the finds hut throughout the day, periodically followed by wheelbarrow-loads of tiles or animal bones; in over thirty years of archaeological fieldwork I have never encountered horizons quite like this. It is the uniqueness of these deposits that stands out even now; there were thousands of pottery sherds, tens of thousands of pieces of animal bone, many with marks of butchery, and, most interestingly, a number of pole-axed cattle skulls and some articulated cattle limb bones. The smell of this deposit, when originally laid down, must have been disgusting and it is likely that it acted as a magnet for flies, rodents and carrion birds. Canine coprolites recovered from some of the dump deposits attest to dogs scavenging around this area and gnawing on discarded bones. There were also numerous coins and small finds in the dump. Less easy to explain was the presence in two dumped deposits of two human skulls.

An on-site examination of the deposits indicated that it was quite probable that they were derived from mainly organic material, probably cess. This dump therefore must represent the point of disposal for the waste from the activities taking place at the same time in nearby residential rooms and from a possible bone-working area close by. The similar nature of the green dump soils and the green soil around the stone slaughtering platform also suggests a direct link between, and thr contemporaneity of, these activities.

The uppermost surface of the midden was subsequently levelled, both former praefurnia now being completely buried. There may have been a time-lapse between the levelling and the next recorded events in this area, the churned-up upper horizon of the levelled midden suggesting that plant root action and worm

68 Late Roman to sub-Roman stone flagged antler working area to north of Roman bathhouse.

activity were responsible for this distinctive horizon recorded in section. Overlying the green-hued deposits were extensive spreads of large masonry rubble fragments, including one huge stone block, and many tufa blocks in mortar, some of them well-cut and squared-off and still retaining their opus signinum weatherproof coating, representing material which had collapsed off the roof and upper walls of the bath building.

There was also evidence for dumping to the east of the bathhouse and to the north of the rooms added to the bath suite in its later phases. These deposits were once more full of finds, especially of pottery and animal bones, including some articulated bones from the forelimb of a dog. Though this was also probably another rubbish tip, it was of a very different nature to the one in the west and did not appear to have contained the huge amounts of organic waste that coloured many of the western deposits green.

A working floor was subsequently laid over the now-level top of the dump that had infilled and perhaps covered some of the walls of the former northern praefurnium. This consisted of rough stone paving slabs laid to cover an area around 3 metres by 4 metres (about 10 feet by 13 feet), possibly utilising the Roman wall stubs as part of the floor. Partially disturbed by later intrusions, including Hooppell trenching, it may once have continued further east. Two possible post holes were associated with the floor and testified to there having been some kind of protective structure here. The structure obviously had some degree of longevity, in that a number of episodes of subsidence of the floor into the soft backfill deposits below were repaired by three successive dumps of river cobbles. Offcuts of worked antler and other articulated animal bones remained in situ on the flagged floor. A second such building, of a similar size and build, lay to the east but there was no evidence for antler working associated with this second structure.

Inside the third, northernmost room of the bath suite, extensive tips of broken tiles were recorded, indicating that the stripping out of good, intact tiles for reuse elsewhere was now taking place. Later still, a robber trench was dug to help facilitate the removal of the tile arch here. Two large postholes for a possible winch structure were also recorded.

As already noted, the finds assemblages from this phase of industrial activity, slaughtering, butchery and rubbish dumping were enormous and of great interest.

The 141 coins recovered were mostly mid-fourth century in date, with the latest coins being of the period AD 350–360, and therefore were all much earlier in date than the horizons from which they came.

There were approximately 4,500 sherds of pottery recovered, among which there was a marked functional bias towards tablewares, both bowls and dishes, and a high level of jars, jars now being percentage-wise the largest component of the overall assemblage. Beaker levels were low and fineware levels quite high. The assemblage was dominated by East Yorkshire calcite gritted wares, followed by Crambeck greywares and parchment wares. Nene Valley finewares continued to be the principal type of these vessels represented. Interestingly, small quantities of southern shell-tempered ware and Hadham ware were present. The most noteworthy imported ware was a bowl in Argonne roller-stamped ware.

*69 Late Roman to sub-Roman activity. Robbed-out archway in the northern praefurnium, or furnace room.*

While there was a substantial amount of vessel glass in this phase, only three vessels were represented, a facet-cut beaker, a beaker with horizontal cordons, and a jar. A convex cup from this horizon is without parallel in Roman Britain. One piece of glass-manufacturing waste was also recovered.

The assemblage of 126 small finds represents the most significant single period assemblage from the 1976–1981 and 1986–1991 excavations at Binchester. Functionally there was a marked concentration of personal ornaments and equipment in particular, although tools and craft items and fixtures and fittings were also well represented. Tools and craft items included twelve iron knives, knife blades and knife or tool handles, six hones, four querns, three crucibles, four spindle whorls, three bobbins and two needles. There was a noticeable increase in the number of jet and especially bone and antler artefacts in this phase, and the presence of sixteen pieces of jet/shale waste, sawn shale and unworked shale and sixteen pieces of antler-working waste confirms working of these materials here on site during this period. Five pieces of decorated jet inlay, seven bone or antler tool handles, one certainly unfinished, and three bobbins might also represent items manufactured here at this time. It is possible that not only bone or antler handles and bobbins were being made in this phase but also bone pins and gaming counters.

Along with the smithing slag recovered, tapped smelting slag was also present in significant quantities.

A single fragment of ceramic tile stamped 'VIV', of the Sixth Legion, came from this phase, along with 12 kilograms of stone roof tiles, including one piece bearing a scratched batch mark, or tally. Tufa appeared in the upper levels of the rubbish dumps in quite large quantities, this material doubtless representing material robbed from, or collapsed from, the vaults of the bath suite. The very large ceramic tile assemblage from this phase, over 400 kilograms, was the largest single assemblage of tile from the entire site and was larger than the combined weights of the retained tile from all the earlier phases added together.

The animal bone assemblage from this phase was again the most substantial assemblage from any period on the site and consisted of approximately 10,500 bones and bone fragments, including over 250 bird bones. As might be expected, cattle, pigs and sheep were the best represented species, in that order, with many other species being present to a much lesser extent, including horse, red deer, roe deer, hare, badger, otter, fox, and possibly wolf. Cat and dog were also present and, as already mentioned, dog coprolites were recovered from six separate deposits within the huge rubbish dump to the west of the now-decaying bathhouse.

Bird bones present included those of domestic fowl, duck, goose, white-tailed eagle, golden eagle, raven, rook, carrion crow, lapwing, plover and song thrush. The twenty-one raven bones, representing a minimum of six individual birds, all came from one context. Over fifty bones of white-tailed eagle were also recovered. Of the five eagle proximal humeri present, one had a knife mark across the proximal articulation, and others had been chopped off either across or just below the proximal articulation.[1]

Once more, dating this phase of activity was difficult. The only piece of pottery from the phase which has an intrinsically later date than the other mid-fourth-century material recovered was the Argonne roller-stamped bowl, dated after *c*. AD 370. The coins suggested very weak occupation on the site after *c*. AD 364, yet the structural evidence and the ceramics do not accord well with this. Recourse to scientific dating was again deemed to be the only possible way to adequately date these horizons. Carbon 14 dates were recovered from a number of samples from different activities grouped above as belonging this phase. These activities were not necessarily contemporary; indeed, it can be demonstrated stratigraphically that some were sequential.

From samples from contexts forming part of the major rubbish dump in and around the former western praefurnium came dates of AD 230–420, AD 240–430, AD 210–410, AD 230–380 and AD 340–550; and AD 250–540, AD 260–420, AD 130–420, AD 255–420 and AD 210–410. From samples associated with the structure in which bone and antler working took place came dates of AD 230–420, AD 260–540, AD 330–550 and AD 340–540.

It would appear, therefore, that the rubbish dumping could have taken place around AD 410 or later and the antler working some time later, perhaps even in the sixth century.

It would be all too easy to denigrate the activity of this phase at Binchester as representing some sort of decline at the site, following the construction and use of the grand praetorium and bath suite at its peak as an elite residence. What happened at Binchester at this time would appear to have been rather more, though, than glorified squatter occupation. It was centrally organised and managed activity, though it could

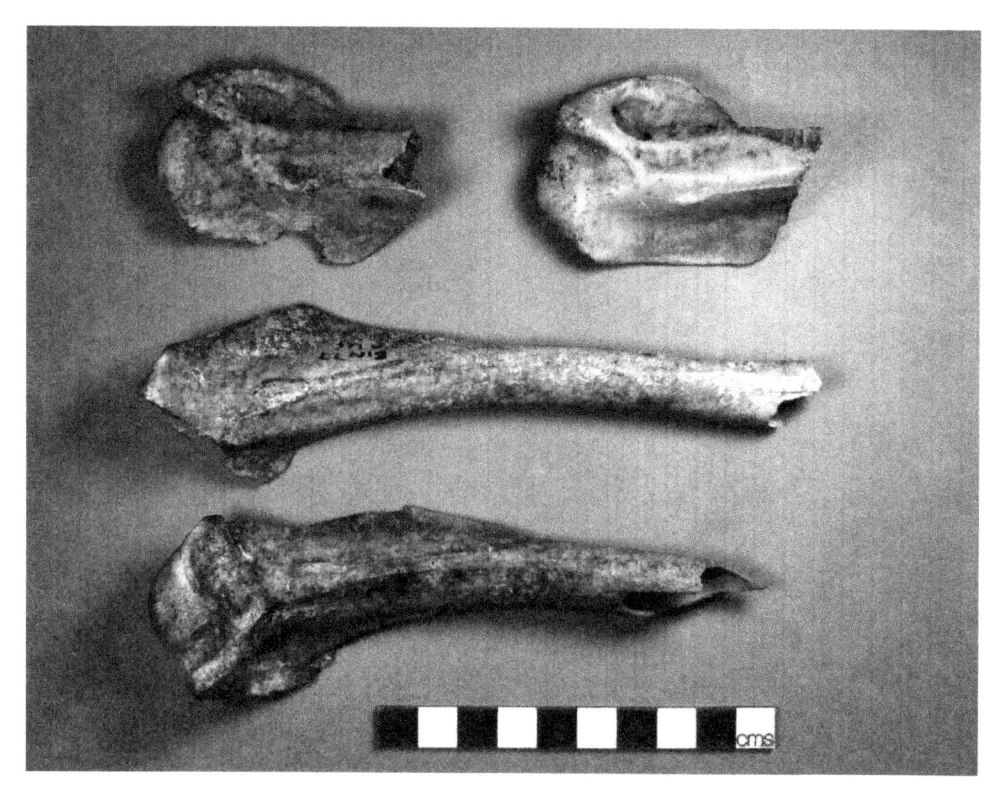

70 Butchery marks on a white tailed sea eagle bone.

not be defined as having been in any way military in character. When these events took place, the site was no longer a fort as such.

There are no direct parallels for the massive rubbish dumps at Binchester, though the phenomenon of the unrestricted disposal of rubbish at certain sites at certain times in the fourth century in Roman Britain may be similar. The kinds of public locations taken over for rubbish disposal at this time included parts of the fortress baths at Caerleon, streets adjacent to the forum in Caerwent and the principia in York, inside one of the horrea at Birdoswald, in the Marlowe car park baths in Canterbury and inside a large courtyard house in Cirencester.[2]

## ANGLO-SAXON BINCHESTER

A number of Anglo-Saxon objects were found during the 1976–1981 excavations, including a copper alloy short long brooch and an iron Francisca throwing axe, both of which might have been derived from disturbed burials, though both were residual or redeposited in later contexts.

More significantly, in 1978, to the west of the fourth-century bath suite and to the north of where its western praefurnium had stood, only a few centimetres below the present-day ground surface, was found a human skeleton accompanied by Anglo-Saxon grave goods. There was no evidence for the body having been buried in a formal grave or a coffin, but rather the skeleton lay in a shallow scoop, its position respecting a scatter of building material and tufa that had fallen off the upper part of the walls and the roof of the Roman bath building. This indicates that the bathhouse was in a perilous state of repair when the burial was made.

The body was laid on its back in a crouched position with the left arm folded across the chest, and the knees drawn up. It was aligned roughly north–south. The skull was represented only by bone fragments, having been largely destroyed by a modern intrusion whose backfill included a sherd of willow-pattern pottery. The right arm had also been disturbed and all that remained of this were the distal quarter of the right humerus, the radial head and the lower two-thirds of radius and ulna.

The skeleton was that of a female whose probable age at death was at least 20–30 years. A number of artefacts were found in association with the skeleton, the most interesting of which was, undoubtedly, a reversed S-shaped copper alloy brooch with birds' head terminals found near the shoulder. The brooch was of a type which was common on the continent, but rare in Britain, being represented by only eleven parallel examples. This brooch type has been broadly dated to the late fifth and early sixth centuries AD, examples from Lakenheath in Suffolk and Sleaford in Lincolnshire perhaps being of the mid-sixth century. A string of beads was also found with the Binchester burial, comprising twenty-six beads, most of them found in the same area as the brooch, though one or two had been displaced. Eighteen of the beads were of amber, eight having been worked while the rest were of an irregular, natural shape. There were also seven glass beads, five of which were reused Roman beads.

71 Anglo-Saxon female skeleton buried with grave goods.

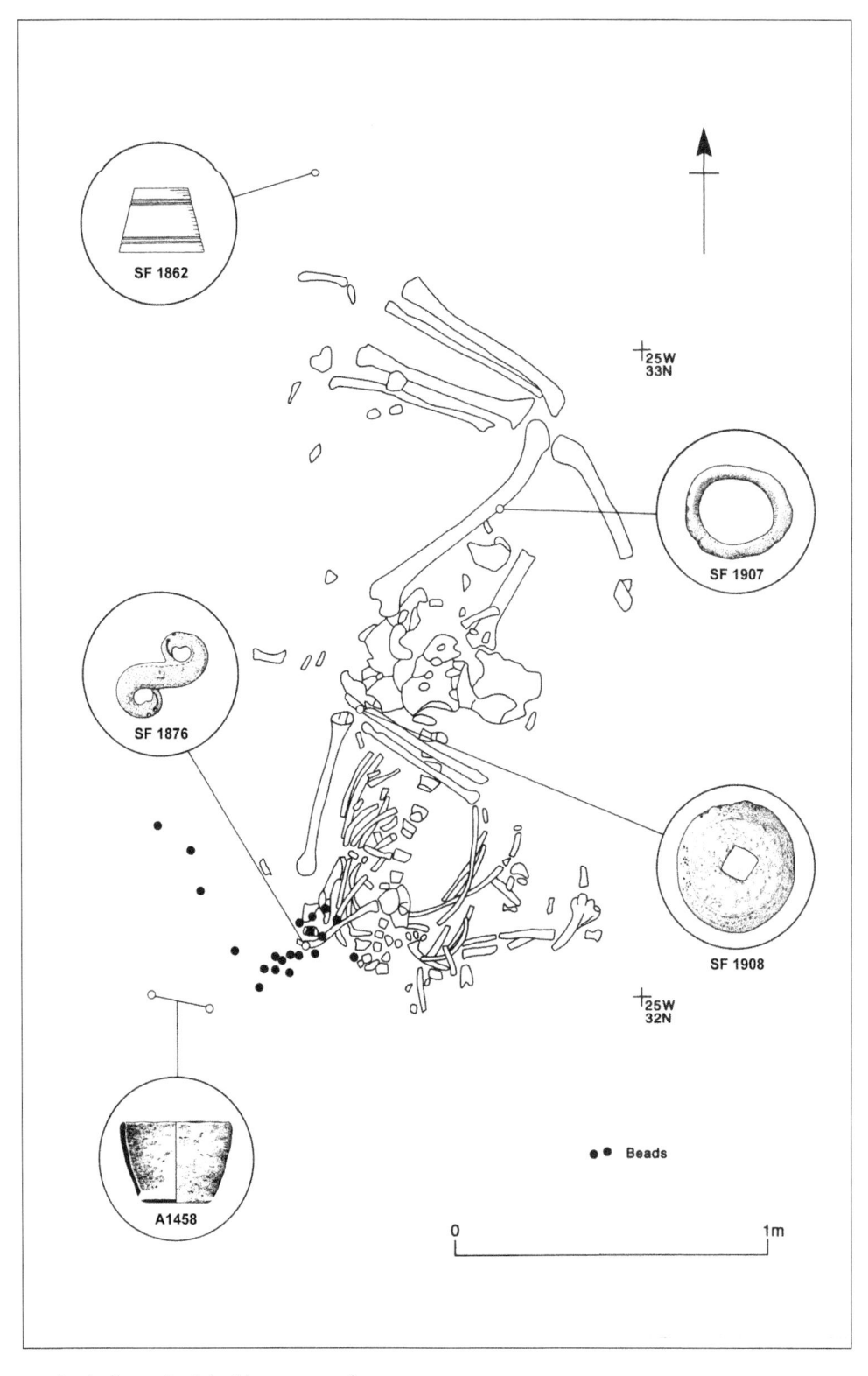

72 Anglo-Saxon burial with grave goods.

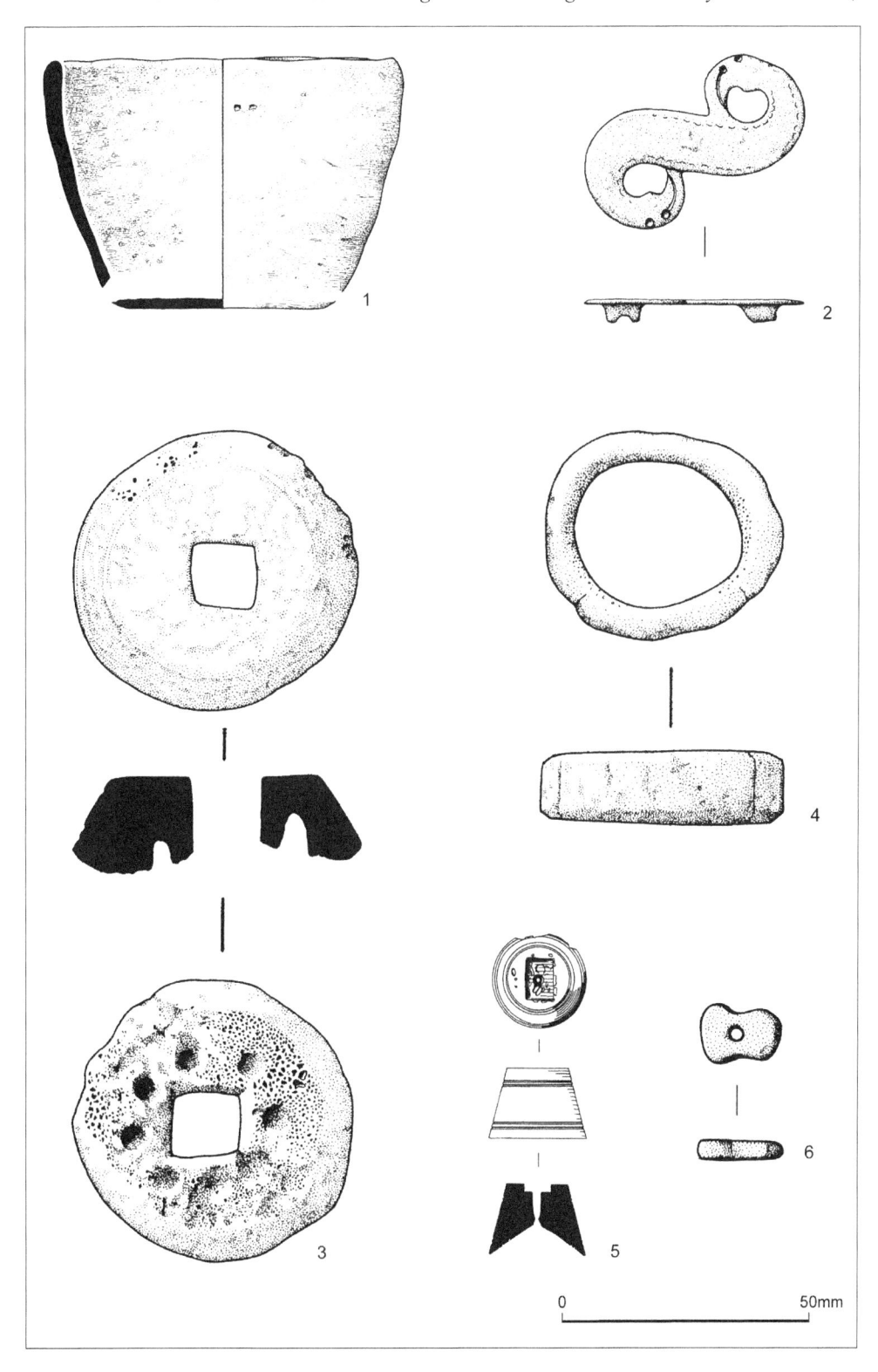

*From Roman Britain to Anglo-Saxon England and Beyond* 127

73 Anglo-Saxon grave goods from burial.

To the left of the remains of the skull were found parts of a very coarse, heavily gritted, dark fabric, hand-made, flat-based pot. Above the pelvic bone of the skeleton was a domed antler disc, pierced in the centre by a square hole. It appeared to have been lathe-turned and polished. The fibrous underside bore eight small holes. Below the left femur was an oval ring of antler with polished and rounded edges. Also found in association with the burial was a circular-sectioned, turned and polished, cannel coal object in the shape of a truncated cone with a rough upper surface.

The female skeleton was radiocarbon dated to AD 400–580 and the antler objects with the burial in one case to AD 600–900 and AD 340–540 and in the other to AD 380–540. Certainly this burial raised very interesting questions about the continuity of occupation at Binchester and the transition in the region to part of Anglo-Saxon England.

The finding and dating of the female burial led to a re-evaluation of the contexts of discovery of other human remains at the site. In his *Vinovia* book, Hooppell records how a woman's skull was found 'some years ago' on the hillside by the Binchester Plantation Woods and goes on to relate that:

> Almost whenever and wherever the ground is disturbed, human bones are met with. These cannot have been Roman burials, for the bones are found above the level of the Roman rooms, above the level of the Roman Street, within and without the Roman ramparts. They can hardly, either, have been interments in some old, consecrated burial ground, for there is neither tradition nor indication of any such having ever existed there. Some of them may have been interments of inhabitants of the Mansion Houses which for centuries succeeded one another on the historic site ... (or be) ... remains of victims or assailants slain in attacks or forays.[3]

A large number of human skeletons, none with grave goods, were discovered during the 1971 excavation carried out ahead of the extension of what was then Binchester Hall Hotel, though at the time these too, like Hooppell's finds, had been thought to date to the sixteenth century or later.[4] Further burials, again without grave goods to help date them, were found during the excavation of a trial trench dug in 1978 to the north of the bathhouse, within what was then the derelict walled garden of the Binchester Hall Hotel.[5] Given the firm dating of the female burial by both analysis of her grave goods and by carbon 14 dating, it was decided to submit human bone samples from the 1971 burials for dating and, at the same time, to have dating done on samples from the trial trench excavation of 1978, whose burials were now suspected of being Anglo-Saxon in date as well.

The results obtained from both groups of bones were highly significant and very important in terms of helping us to understand the nature of activity here at Binchester in the post-Roman period. Carbon-dated human bone samples from the 1971 excavation were variously dated, in sample order, to AD 610–980, AD 590–800, AD 660–1000, AD 640–950, AD 680–1040, AD 770–1170, AD 620–780, AD 650–780 and AD 650–780. One carbon 14 date was returned for a human bone sample from the 1978 trial trench, this being AD 650–960. All the samples submitted, therefore, can be seen to have returned dates that placed them in the Anglo-Saxon period, though later than the isolated female burial with grave goods, thus indicating that there was an extensive later Anglo-Saxon cemetery sited here within the bounds of the former Roman fort.

Indeed, represented among the Anglo-Saxon skeletal material so far recovered from Binchester are around fifty individuals and four juveniles from the 1971 excavations and the 1978 trial trench, along with the female with grave goods from the excavated area to the south. Further, probably Anglo-Saxon skeletons, mainly heavily disturbed, were found at the site in 1989, 1990, 1995, 1996 and 2005, confirming the location here of a significant and extensive Anglo-Saxon inhumation cemetery.

Despite the fragmented nature of much of the skeletal material from 1971 and 1978, analysis turned up some extremely important information on the health of the Anglo-Saxon population here. Potentially most significant was a juvenile individual aged approximately 6–10 years with extensive new bone formation as a result of inflammation in several areas of the skeleton, congenital syphilis being the suggested diagnosis. Such an early pre-Columbian identification of this condition is more-or-less unprecedented. There is also evidence of a possible case of tuberculosis in the material, and this makes this group particularly interesting. This is based on the presence of visceral surface lesions on the ribs and focal destructive lesions in the vertebrae. Rib lesions are very common in people who are known to have died of tuberculosis, and vertebral lesions are also characteristic of tuberculosis infection. Analysis of the animal bones from Binchester has also isolated a number of cattle bones with infective lesions in ribs and vertebrae. Cattle bones with infective lesions in ribs and vertebrae associated with possible human cases have been found at the Spong Hill Anglo-Saxon site in Norfolk, although there the human bone material was mostly cremated. As both human and non-human tuberculosis was represented in the Binchester material, it provided a unique opportunity to integrate human and non-human palaeopathology.

There is no doubt that the Anglo-Saxon presence within the fort at Binchester is of considerable importance in understanding the evolution of the post-Roman north. Unfortunately, the picture that has emerged of the Anglo-Saxon period at Binchester is somewhat compromised by the fact that so little of the Anglo-Saxon horizon has been investigated. The picture at present would seem to be that there is an isolated female burial with grave goods of the mid-sixth century positioned on the west side of what must by then have been the still substantially intact shell of the late Roman bathhouse. To the north of this burial was later laid out an inhumation cemetery of at least 1.5 hectares (just over 3.5 acres) in area, containing probably hundreds of burials and dating to the seventh to eleventh centuries.

The question must be asked as to whether the early female burial here was of someone of high status in the locality whose burial site was somehow marked on the ground and acted as the focus for the location of a later cemetery. It is otherwise difficult to explain the location of the later burials here if the site was not already known as an earlier burial location. This female burial may have been of some importance in terms of encapsulating cultural memory and may have retained an emotional currency into the later Anglo-Saxon period which led to further burials taking place at the site. Again, cultural memory embodied in this link with Binchester may account for the use of robbed stone from the fort being incorporated into the

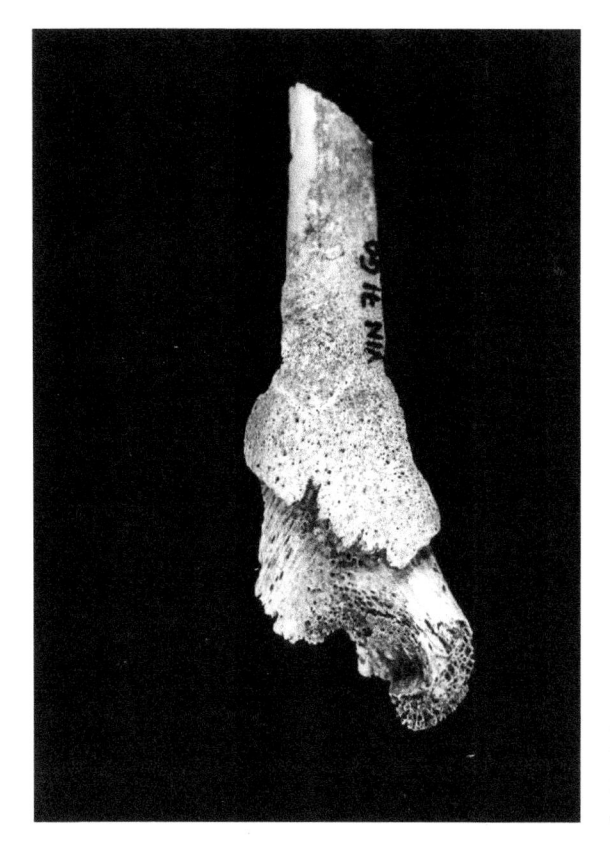

74 Human bone. Sheath of new bone on left humerus of an Anglo-Saxon skeleton, probably the result of congenital syphilis.

building of nearby Escomb church in the seventh century.[6] Monumentality was perhaps here part of an enchainment of memory linking Escomb to Binchester and to the site of this important female burial, albeit not a Christian burial. This very neatly contrasts and resonates with the inclusion of some Roman beads among the grave goods that accompanied the female Anglo-Saxon burial. It has been suggested that those northern fourth-century fort sites with present-day place names ending in -chester or -caster, of which there are ten examples, reflect through their naming an Anglo-Saxon recognition of their significance, though only at six out of these ten sites are Anglo-Saxon finds recorded to date.[7]

Evidence for Anglo-Saxon burials in what was the kingdom of Bernicia is scarce.[8] Former Roman fort sites in the north[9] where burial and non-burial evidence for Anglo-Saxon activity is present include Benwell, Binchester, Carvoran, Chesterholm, Chesters, Housesteads, Manchester, Piercebridge and Ribchester. As has been pointed out by a number of authorities,[10] in general there is little evidence for Anglo-Saxon settlements and cemeteries in the north before the mid-sixth century, though settlement in the Tees Valley south into the kingdom of Deira is attested. By the late sixth century Anglo-Saxon expansion had led to a political geography defined by rapid change and Bernicia may have been founded as a breakaway kingdom from Deira.

As there was an Anglo-Saxon cemetery at Binchester, so it would be expected that there would be a settlement associated with it or sited nearby. However, at present we have no idea as to where this settlement focus is located. If a lease of the tenth or early

75 Escomb church.

eleventh century recorded in the *Historia de Sancto Cuthberto* is to be taken at face value, it would appear that Bynceastre was one of a number of northern estates owned by the Community of St Cuthbert and leased at that time to Earl Northman by Bishop Aldhun.[11] Although the evidence for this period therefore remains slight and full of frustrating gaps, Binchester has nevertheless provided important new evidence about the interplay between the sub-Roman to Anglo-Saxon settlements in central Durham at Escomb, Bishop Auckland and West Auckland.

The Anglo-Saxon church building at Escomb, about 2.5 kilometres (about 1.5 miles) to the west of Bishop Auckland, survives today in a remarkably original form, set within its circular churchyard. The church is thought to date to AD 670–675. The reuse of some Roman stone to build the church is not disputed, given the presence here of a number of inscribed stones built into the walls, along with other stones thought to exhibit typical Roman mason's tooling marks, and a chancel arch of a typical Roman form. Little altered, though heavily restored between 1875 and 1880, the church has therefore been deemed to be linked to Binchester/Vinovia, given the relative proximity of the two sites. It was indeed the Revd Hooppell who recorded the inscribed stones here at Escomb during the Victorian restoration, the most significant and convincing of which, set upside down high up on the exterior of the north wall, bears the words 'Leg(io) VI' ('The Sixth Legion [built this]').[12]

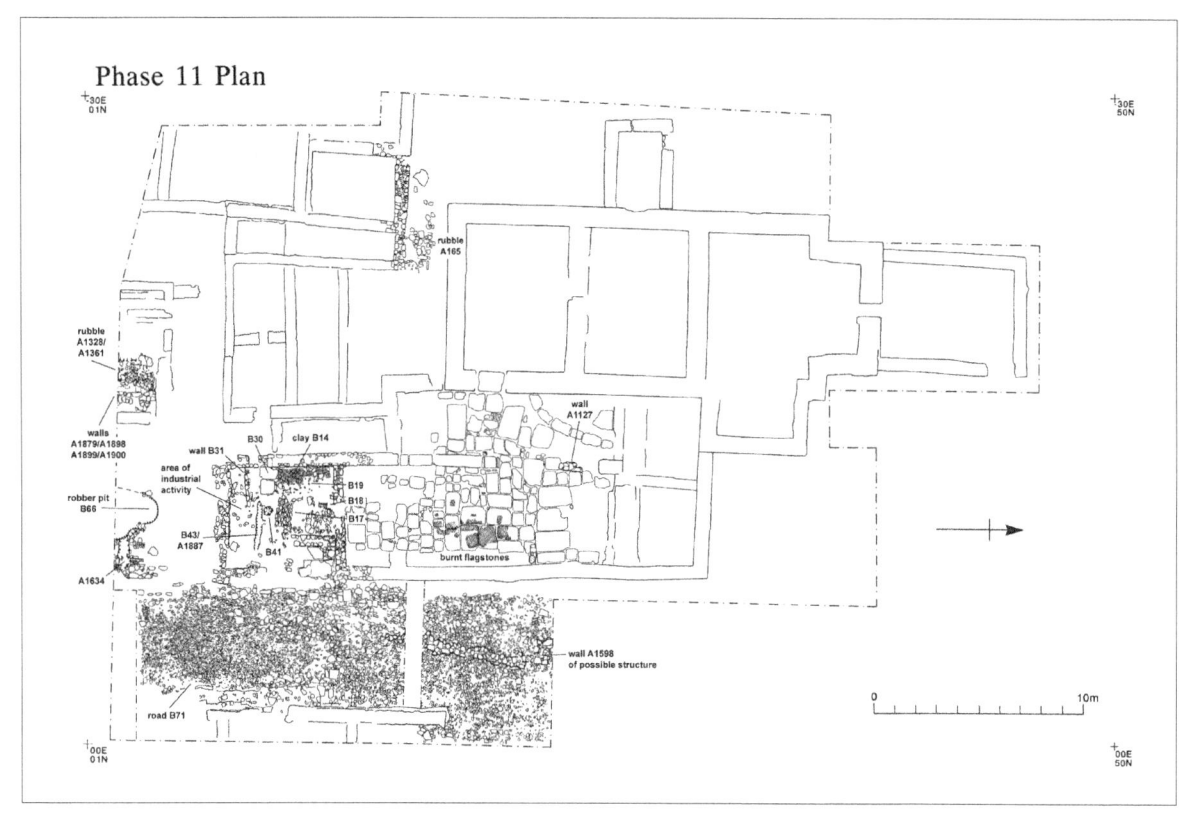

76 Plan of medieval features (called Phase 11 in the stratigraphic schema for the 1976-1981 and 1986-1991 excavations).

## MEDIEVAL ACTIVITY

Evidence for medieval activity was found in a number of places within the area excavated between 1976 and 1981, though the medieval users of the site generally avoided the reuse of that part of the mid- to late fourth-century building's residential range which boasted the greatest density of standing or partly standing walls. The reason for this is probably that by the onset of the medieval period the Roman house was still partially standing but was in a somewhat decayed state and its walls dangerously perilous. Thus medieval activity tended to be concentrated in the more open area directly to the west of the line of the Roman road, and indeed over the line of that road itself. This activity took a number of forms: industrial activity, construction and stone robbing.

Over the top of the final Roman surface in the area directly to the south of the later fourth-century paved courtyard was spread a thick deposit of cobbles and pebbles, tile chunks and mortar, the deposit containing a number of sherds of green-glazed medieval pottery and a small quantity of iron-smithing slag. This surface provided a level working surface and a good base for a number of stone-built features, including a rectangle of squared stone blocks set on their sides in parallel alignment to form a level surface, just standing proud of the ground surface and possibly acting as the

77 Medieval beam trench and posthole.

support for a water tank, and, to the north, a small rectangular feature resembling a box, the sides and the flat base being formed by thin stone slabs which may be reused Roman stone roof tiles and which may again have been intended to hold water or metalworking scrap and offcuts. Both features were associated with quantities of iron-smithing slag. Contemporary with these was a number of cut features including a stakehole, postholes and a beam trench, indicating that there was a makeshift timber structure located here, possibly a lean-to of some sort braced against one of the rebuilt walls of the shell of the former Roman building that formed the structure's western limit. To the south-west were the remains of a slight wall butted up against the base of this rebuilt Roman wall.

A number of successive, roughly built stone walls over the line of the former Roman via principalis would appear to mark the position of other light timber structures located here on a firm foundation and away from the main part of the crumbling shell of the Roman building to the west.

The nature of both the features and the finds suggest that this activity represents the remains and detritus of some form of workshop activity, probably connected to iron smithing. Over 7 kilograms of iron-smithing slag and other residues were recovered from features and deposits of this phase. This activity may have involved the reworking of iron used in the construction of the Roman buildings and robbed out at this time, such as the massive iron beams known to have been used in bathhouse construction.

At the same time, extensive stone and tile robbing of the Roman building on the site was taking place, represented by a number of robber pits and robber trenches, the largest of these being a massive circular pit in the south of the site. The pottery from these horizons dates this phase of activity to the thirteenth–fifteenth centuries, probably making the people present here inhabitants of the 'poore villag' at Binchester seen by John Leland in 1540.[13]

Similar medieval activity, again involving the reuse of Roman structures, the robbing of stone and tile and metalworking, would appear to be represented in the area of the new excavations started in 2009.

Two hundred and thirty sherds of medieval pottery were recovered from more than a hundred separate deposits during the 1976–1981 excavations. The assemblage was a typical later medieval domestic assemblage of almost exclusively local or regional wares,[14] with a higher than average number of two-handled jars. The medieval pottery almost exclusively dated to the thirteenth–fifteenth centuries. There were only three later stratified pottery sherds found. The only closely diagnostic medieval small find on the site, a brooch fragment, was also coincidentally of the thirteenth–fifteenth centuries.

The slag from medieval deposits, much of it concentrated in specific areas, can probably be thought to represent waste from contemporary activity. There was evidence for both smithing and smelting, although the quantity of smelting slag was small. The characteristic smelting slag, the tap slag recovered, showed an unusual microstructure which indicates that the smelting operation which produced it was extremely inefficient.

## THE POST-MEDIEVAL PERIOD

Activity of the fifteenth to nineteenth centuries was also recorded during excavations in the centre of the fort. A number of robber trenches along the line of Roman walls and some large robber pits in the area of former hypocausted rooms contained post-medieval pottery in their backfills and indicated the ongoing process of robbing out of stone and tile from the Roman buildings that had first started in the Anglo-Saxon period, continued in medieval times, and which unfortunately did not end until the nineteenth century.

It is likely that extensive landscaping across parts of the fort took place under the auspices of the various inhabitants of Binchester Hall, which lay within the curtilage of the former Roman fort. There is no evidence at present as to whether the medieval lords of Bynchestre resided at the site and, indeed, there are few records relating to the workings of the manor of which it was a part. It was not indeed until after 1570, when the confiscated estate that included Binchester was sold by the Crown to William Wrenne, that we can be sure that the land's owners took up residence here. The estate was to remain in the Wren family, ancestors of Sir Christopher Wren, for over 200 years until the death of Farrer Wren in 1794, when it passed to his daughter, who had married into the Lyon family. The Lyons sold the estate to Bishop van Mildert in 1832 and by court order were forced to give up possession of Binchester Hall and its grounds.[15] Most of the estate has remained the property of the Church Commissioners up to the present day.

The hall, described by Hutchinson in 1794 as 'a fine old building of the style used in Queen Elizabeth's time, composed of a centre and two wings, the south wing having a noble semi-circular window projected from a bracket, the north wing is modernized',[16] though probably actually early seventeenth-century in date, was depicted by Buck in 1723.[17] This hall building was demolished in 1835 and a less grand edifice was erected as the new Binchester Hall, with some of the stone and brick being used to build the nearby farmhouse. Binchester Plantation Woods were created at this time, as was the large walled garden whose northern wall originally bisected the Roman bath building. This new hall would eventually go on to become the Binchester Hall Hotel and the Binchester Hall Nursing Home in the second half of the twentieth century. It is now sadly derelict.

CHAPTER SIX

# *Object and Economy, Religion and Ritual*

As at many sites of the Roman period, excavations at Binchester over the years have produced huge quantities of finds, both artefacts, principally pottery, glass, coins, so-called small finds of metal, bone and antler, jet and stone, and what are often termed ecofacts, that is human bone and animal bone in this case. For example, the 1976–1981 and 1986–1991 excavations together recovered approximately 22,500 Roman pot sherds, 2,000 medieval pot sherds, 2,300 fragments of Roman glass, 500 Roman coins, 1,600 small finds, 4,300 iron nails, 140 kilograms of ironworking residues or slags, human bones from possibly fifty individual adult burials and four juveniles, 21,600 animal bones, and 750 shells, in addition to tons of ceramic and stone tiles, two dozen or so stone architectural fragments, and a few hundred fragments of painted wall plaster.

While the study of finds from archaeological excavations can often answer many of the most basic questions about the date of a particular site or structure on a site and its place in its contemporary world, other, more nuanced questions can sometimes also be asked of this artefactual and ecofactual material which contribute towards the writing of a history of daily life on a site at any particular period. At Binchester, study of the finds from 1976–1981 and 1986–1991 has added in particular to an understanding of the Roman military community here as both producers and consumers of material at different times, and of the economic basis of the site from the Roman to medieval periods. Chronological patterns of the use of particular classes of object have emerged through the comparison of finds assemblages from different phases of the fort at Binchester between the first and fifth centuries. The fact that much of the work to date has focused on the excavation of the fourth-century commandant's house, or praetorium, and its associated bath suite means that quite a detailed reconstruction of life in this building has emerged through the study of contemporary artefacts from this particular building. An insight can also be gained into religious beliefs at the site in the Roman period through the study of specifically religious inscriptions on stone, religious statuary and other small votive artefacts, and through the identification of religious or ritual practices mediated through the use of certain items as part of the ritual process. Each of these aspects will now be discussed in turn.

78 Part of a decorated South Gaulish samian bowl of the late first or early second century. Alongside gladiators appear figures tossed by a bull and a sacrificer.

## THE ROMAN ARMY AT BINCHESTER AS PRODUCERS AND CONSUMERS

A study of the finds assemblages from the 1976–1981 and 1986–1991 excavations at Binchester has revealed a great deal about the mechanisms of Roman army supply between the first and fourth centuries, and particularly about the exploitation of local raw materials and resources and the on-site production of artefacts and materials. Of especial importance is the evidence for industrial-scale metalworking at the site in the second century AD. Evidence from the study of the pottery, ceramic tiles, glass, small finds, ironworking residues and animal bones will now be considered separately.

The pottery assemblage associated with the first-century timber praetorium building in the first fort, in both its construction phase and during the life of the building, is dominated either by pottery from York, south-east England and the Midlands, or by imported finewares, many of which were Gallic, or South Gaulish samian. Some local pottery, in the form of an Iron Age-tradition gritted ware, was associated with this phase. In the second century phases, pottery from York became increasingly less important and locally produced wares became more significant. The first appearance of Black Burnished ware pottery came towards the end of the industrial and dumping phase, perhaps in the early AD 120s. Up to then South Gaul had been the most significant source for the site's samian pottery, with only small numbers of Central Gaulish vessels being present.

By the end of the life of the first stone praetorium on the site in the later third century the coarse pottery supply to Binchester was dominated by Black Burnished wares, with finewares from the Nene Valley and Rhenish ware, along with samian, being significant. Mortaria now mainly came from Mancetter in the Midlands and were no longer represented by continental imports, and amphorae were more numerous, with the first appearance now of Gallic wine amphorae. The picture was much the same during the life of the second stone praetorium, though the dominance of mortaria supply by the Mancetter potteries was now being challenged by Catterick and Oxfordshire mortaria, while the quantities of amphorae started to fall away. The samian by now was mainly Central Gaulish in origin and present in much smaller quantities. It would appear that small quantities of East Gaulish ware were reaching the site from the start of the Antonine period, mostly from Rheinzabern, and the import of samian probably came into its own in the third century after the cessation of the Central Gaulish potteries. A small quantity of third-century vessels was present and these must have remained in use alongside carefully preserved Central Gaulish bowls throughout much of the third century.

Pottery found associated with the third stone praetorium, the large mid- to late fourth-century house, started by being dominated still by Black Burnished wares. Importation of samian had now stopped. However, in the phase associated with the addition of a large new bathhouse the pottery assemblage was dominated by Crambeck greywares, with Crambeck mortaria being the almost exclusive representative of this vessel type. Finewares were most significantly dominated by Nene Valley vessels. In the very latest Roman or perhaps sub-Roman levels, after the significant change of use of the third praetorium and its partial demolition, the pottery assemblage recovered, which must be partially if not mostly residual, was dominated by East Yorkshire and Crambeck pottery and Nene Valley finewares, though small numbers of southern shell-tempered ware and Hadham ware were of interest, as was a sherd of imported Argonne roller stamped ware, dated after AD 370.

Local pottery production, on site or nearby, is not proven for any period represented within the area excavated in 1976–1981 and 1986–1991, though at one stage it was thought that a number of items of kiln furniture were among the Hooppell finds collection, but these are now identified as being spacer bobbins, possibly used in building work. There is some evidence for local pottery production in the Flavian period, but it is in the last part of the second-century industrial and dumping phase that large numbers of locally produced vessels really first appeared; whether this means that pottery was being produced at the site solely for on-site consumption or whether pottery was being produced in sufficiently large quantities to be distributed to other military sites in the area at this time cannot be answered because of the lack of good Trajanic pottery groups for comparison in the region. By the Trajanic period, if not actually earlier, there is evidence at Binchester for links to the east coast trade, suggesting that there were viable and active water transport links up the River Wear for pottery, and presumably for other goods perhaps less visible in the archaeological record. Evidence of this trade was still apparent in the make-up of the later fourth-century assemblage. This raises interesting questions about the use made of the River Wear by river traffic linking with the coastal ports.

Ceramic tiles would almost certainly have been manufactured on site, as was standard Roman army practice, and it is interesting to consider if a tile from Binchester inscribed with check lists of at least twenty-six names of individual soldiers, discussed in more detail below, represents evidence for the kind of work detachment cohort attested on some of the Vindolanda tablets,[1] in this case relating to work at a military tilery. Stamped tiles of the Sixth Legion and the Numerus Concangiensium attest to workgroups from these units producing tiles used in the fourth-century buildings. Perhaps light relief was provided for one member of the tilery work party in inscribing a graffito caricature, perhaps of an officer or fellow soldier, on a wet tile that was subsequently fired and used in the building at Binchester.

The Binchester glass assemblage is among the largest groups of glass from north-eastern England, comparable in size with assemblages from South Shields and Piercebridge. Glass vessels were in use at the site throughout its occupation, and much of the assemblage was chronologically and spatially pinpointed. As most of the material being discussed here came from the high-status early timber building and from the three successive stone praetoria, it has been possible to interpret some of the material in the light of the official and personal activities of a high-status official within a northern military context by typological analysis and comparison with material from buildings of similar and different status at South Shields, Housesteads, Birdoswald, Catterick and elsewhere in the Roman north. A glass assemblage of this size inevitably included a high degree of fragments of individual importance. At

79 Graffito list of names on tile, probably a detail of men working at a military tilery.

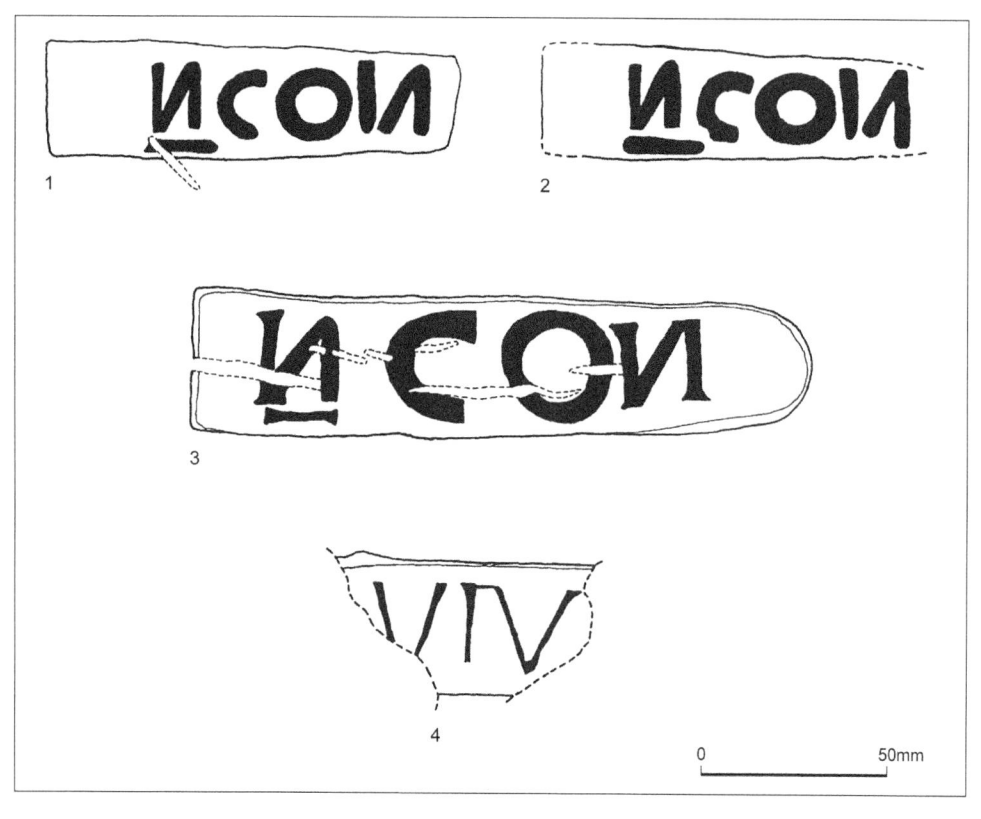

80 Ceramic tile stamps; the NCON stamp and the VIV stamp.

Binchester a number of cast facet-cut and mould-blown vessels fell into this category, including fragments of vessels currently unique in Britain.

In the early phases, a small group of early imperial mould-blown glass included a vessel with a Greek inscription which is unparalleled in Roman Britain and a series of Flavian mould-blown beakers which have extended knowledge of these vessels in the province. The quantity of glass from the first phases of activity, up to *c*. AD 120, was remarkable, and contrasts with assemblages from other northern fort sites such as Ribchester, where little early material was securely stratified.

The analysis of the glass from the various phases of the mid-fourth-century praetorium was particularly valuable to Roman glass studies. The mid-fourth century was a period of development and transition for many vessel forms and the close-dating potential of this material has allowed the introduction of later fourth-century forms to be more closely refined. The assemblage included glass of the very late Roman period, and is important in assessing the degree of continuation of certain forms into the fifth century. Window glass was noticeably present in this phase. Some rooms in the commandant's house and the bath suite almost certainly contained glass windows. Glass manufacturing was represented by one fragment of manufacturing waste from the first stone building and one from the third stone house.

Again, the Roman small finds assemblage from Binchester represents one of the largest and best documented such assemblages from northern Britain. Its study has

*Object and Economy, Religion and Ritual*

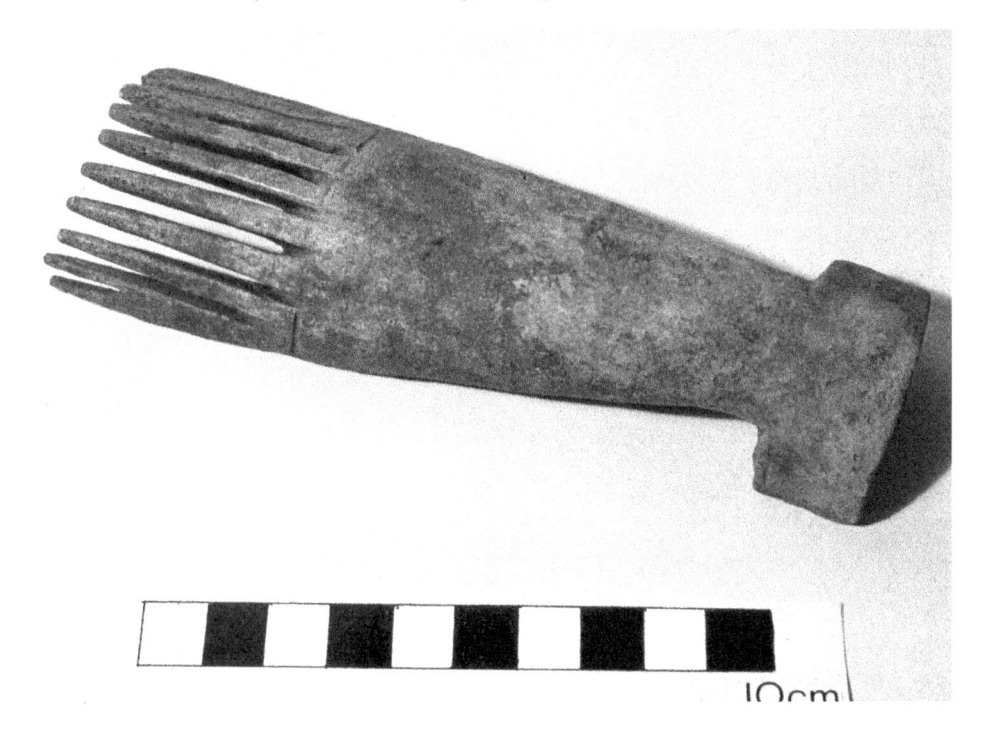

81 A bone weaving comb.

told us much about issues relating to site function, about manufacture and supply, and about taste and aesthetics. The small finds have also been used to explore the exploitation of raw materials on a local basis. The identified craft and industrial activity on the site, that is bone working and jet or shale working in the mid-fourth century, and bone and antler working in the late Roman to sub-Roman period, has also added an extra dimension to research. The demonstrated early exploitation of local stone resources at Binchester Crags is also of great interest.

Among the small finds there is quite a lot of evidence for on-site industrial and craft production at Binchester at different times during the fort's occupation. Small amounts of bone and antler waste came from a number of phases, with large-scale bone and antler working being attested in the late Roman to sub-Roman dumping phase. Small amounts of jet and shale waste and unworked jet or shale came from five of the pre-fourth-century phases, with large-scale jet working again being attested in the mid-fourth century and in the late Roman to sub-Roman period.

Textile production and repair at craft level was represented by a bone weaving comb in a second-century context, in the mid- to late fourth century by two needles and three spindle whorls, and in the late Roman to sub-Roman period by three bone bobbins, seven spindle whorls and two needles. Another bone weaving comb was recovered from the 1978 trial trench to the north of the bathhouse.

Knives and hones or whetstones need not necessarily have been domestic items and their presence at Binchester in the Roman period could have been related to craft activity rather than utilitarian usage. Two hones came from first- to second-century contexts, two from second-century contexts, four from fourth-century contexts and six from late Roman to sub-Roman horizons. One knife came from a first- to second-century context, one from a second-century context, five from fourth-century contexts and five from late Roman to sub-Roman horizons. One knife handle came from a first- to second-century context, one from a second-century context, one from a late third-century context and seven from late Roman to sub-Roman horizons. A bone point, possibly an awl, came from a mid- to late fourth-century layer.

The analysis of the Binchester stone, that is building stone in the form of cut blocks for wall building and flat slabs for flooring or roofing, as well as stone artefacts or small finds, has allowed a picture to emerge of the chronology of exploitation of the most locally available stone, from outcrops at nearby Binchester Crags which contain sandstones, siltstones and thin coal bands. Hones and roof tiles in Binchester Crags stone first appeared in the first-century timber building phase, with use of this resource increasing up to the time when the first stone building was constructed on the site in this local stone. Both the second and third stone buildings were again of Binchester Crags stone. The calcareous tufa used in the construction of the vault of the mid-fourth-century bath suite could also have come from relatively local deposits of magnesium limestone.

The identification of a major episode of smithing at Binchester occurred during the excavation of the early to mid-second-century levels in the centre of the fort. The recovery of large quantities of metalworking residues from this horizon was linked to the physical presence and operation at this time of a considerable number of smithing hearths. Hammerscale was also recovered from this horizon, confirming the occurrence of on-site iron smithing in this period. Metallurgical analysis of the metalworking residues and slags has provided significant information on the nature of the metalworking processes undertaken at the site at this time, suggesting that it was a highly controlled and technically precise and consistent operation.

Evidence for extensive smithing activity has previously been recognised at a number of other Roman forts, for example at Ribchester and Newstead,[2] but the nature and extent of the activity there has not been satisfactorily defined. Binchester has offered the opportunity to analyse smithing activity carried out during the earliest phase of the fort's occupation, both in the central zone and in an area excavated in 1971 to the north, and indeed probably over the whole zone between the two sites, and to analyse the way in which at least part of the site in this period may have functioned as a military works or supply depot.

It is suggested that the second-century metalworking at Binchester is an example of goods beyond the needs of the unit stationed at the site being produced.[3] Binchester may not have been a military works depot as such at this time, like Holt, but nevertheless the evidence of a very large part of the retentura of the fort here having been turned over to industrial-scale smithing of iron suggests a substantial commitment to controlling large-scale materials production here. Some parallels for this metalworking have been cited above, and at other forts and military-controlled areas outside of forts specific areas may also have been turned over to the intensive production of other goods, such as leather at Catterick and Brithdir, north Wales, and possibly wooden artefacts at Carlisle.[4]

Analysis of the combined animal bone assemblages from the second-century dumping and industrial horizons has yielded much useful information on both the food supply to the fort, butchery practices and animal husbandry at this time, and the assemblage was comparable to animal bone assemblages from other sites in northern England such as South Shields, Carlisle, Piercebridge, Catterick and York.

The species present in these phases at Binchester were fairly typical for this type of site, with the major domestic livestock species dominant, with a small presence of other domesticates such as horse and dog, as well as wild species like Red and Roe deer. Cattle were the principal economic animal represented, followed in abundance by sheep, then pig. Cattle butchery patterns fitted almost exactly with those recorded at South Shields,[5] where the butchery appeared to have been carried out by someone with little knowledge of anatomy, creating joints of beef of equal size, perhaps to be fairly divided between soldiers or groups of soldiers.

A particular type of scapula butchery observed at both Binchester and South Shields was also noted at the General Accident site in York,[6] where it was thought to be indicative of curing or smoking, with holes pierced through the scapula allowing it to be hung by a hook during its processing. Another practice common at both Binchester and York was the chopping-up of the epiphyses of long bones, this material representing the waste products from the production of marrow, fats, and possibly leather dressing, cosmetics and soap.[7]

## LIFE IN THE LATE ROMAN COMMANDANT'S HOUSE

A certain amount of information about life in the commandants' houses or praetoria at Binchester, and in particular about diet, comes from an examination of the animal bones and shells found associated with each of the houses. In the first- to second-century timber praetorium bones of Red Deer were present, along with the regular triumvirate of cattle, sheep and pig. Mussel and oyster shells were also found. A dog represented by bones in the assemblage may have been a hunting dog, a guard dog or even a pet. In the first stone commandant's house, along with cattle, sheep and pig bones were found dog and horse bones, along with those of an unidentified small mammal and three birds, again not identified to a specific species. Mussels, oysters, winkles and cockles were recovered here too. From the second stone house came just the standard cattle, sheep and pig bones, along with shells from mussels, oysters, winkles and limpets.

In the third, mid- to late fourth-century commandant's house were found cattle, sheep and pig bones, along with four birds, including domestic fowl. Bones from a cat and three dogs were also recovered. Shells of mussels, oysters, winkles, cockles and limpets were present.

Therefore it can be seen that during all phases when a commandant's house stood on the site at Binchester, cattle, sheep and pig were the predominant meat animals represented in order of magnitude of numbers of bones found, with there being little enhancement of this beyond the appearance at one stage of hunted Red Deer meat and at another of domestic fowl meat. Seafood appears to have been part of the expected table of food, probably being brought here in barrels or tanks of seawater.

Pottery amphorae, in their different, very specific forms, can also provide some information about foodstuffs present at the site in different periods. From the first to

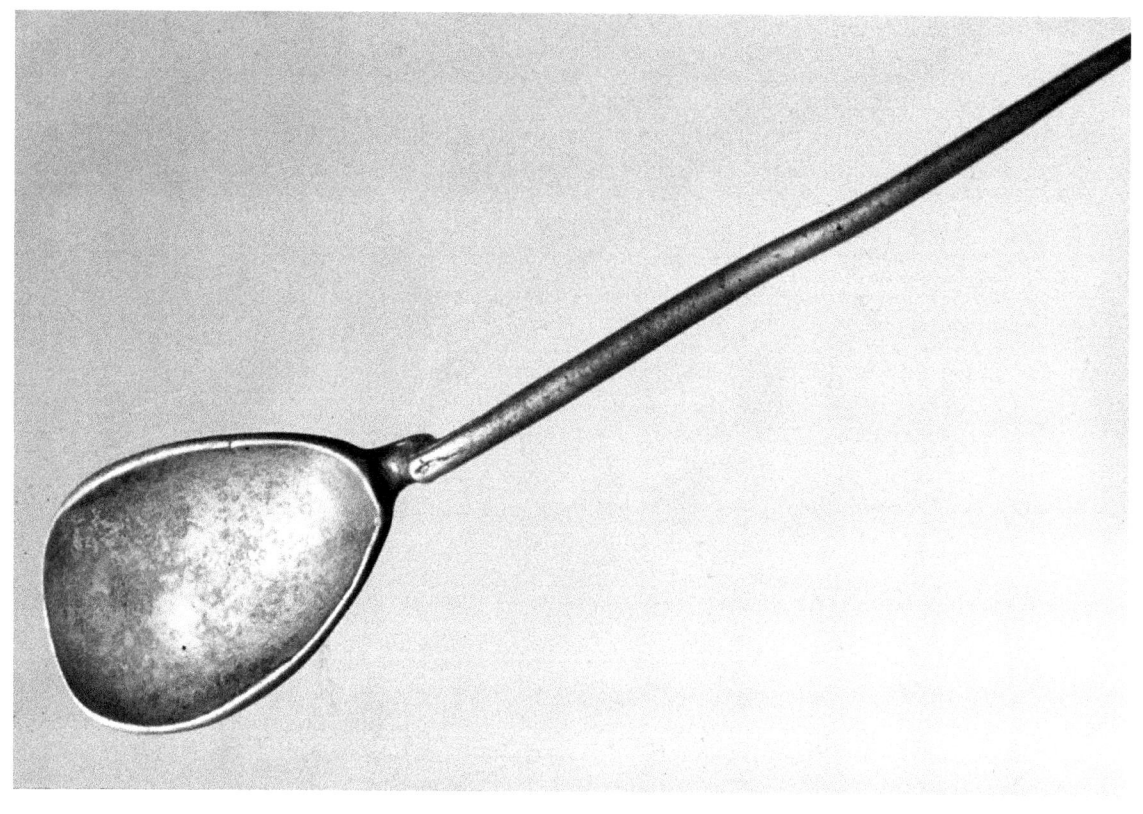

82 A silver spoon, probably in use in the fourth-century praetorium, or commandant's house.

mid-second-century horizons came the common Dressel 20 olive oil amphorae, along with a few Gallic wine amphorae, a garum or fish sauce container, and a rare North African olive oil container. Later phases contained mostly wine amphorae, though not in great numbers. It is likely, therefore, that for all periods most wine imported into Binchester came in barrels, either from the Rhineland or from northern Gaul.

An insight into what kind of information about the food supply to the high-status residents of a military praetorium is potentially missing from the archaeological record at Binchester and at most other military sites in the north can be gained from a reading of some of the Vindolanda tablets, which give a unique insight into the status and symbolism of diet in the Roman army at the time.[8] Caution must be taken not to assume that the Vindolanda praetorium diet can be accepted as a universal commander's diet, given both the specificity of the date of the tablets and the ethnic origins of the units based at Vindolanda. Firstly, both wine and beer were regularly provided for the praetorium at Vindolanda, not just wine, as might have been expected, and there was a bias in meat preferences towards pig, chicken and game, alongside the common staples of grain, bacon and beans. Fish sauce was regularly used in food preparation and dressing and herbs and spices from a wide area were consumed, pepper and cumin being the commonest spices in the recipes of Apicius. Olive oil, also essential for an Apician cuisine, was sometimes available, although perhaps not always. The tablets have also revealed something about the social networks and power networks

*Object and Economy, Religion and Ritual*  145

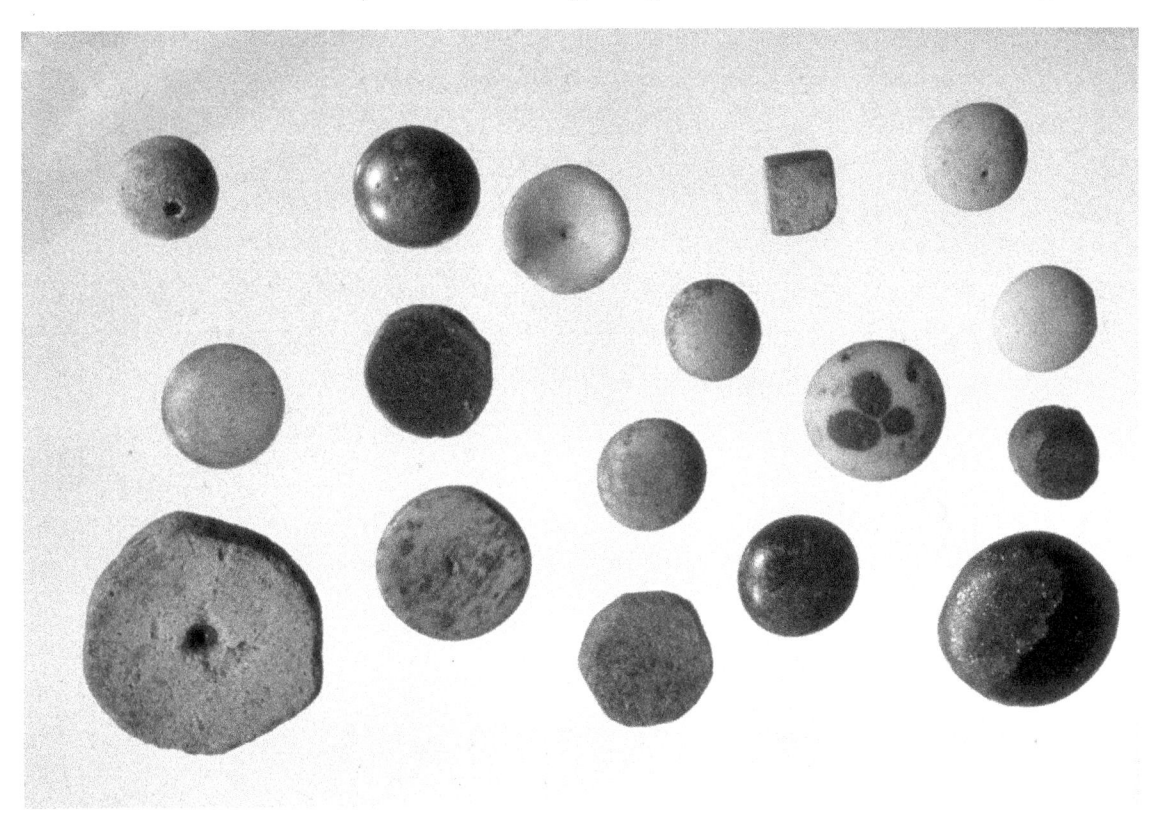

83 A selection of glass, stone, ceramic and bone gaming counters and a bone die, probably used for gaming in the fourth-century praetorium, or commandant's house, and its bath suite.

into which a northern military commander connected, with links to the provincial governor, as well as to those locals who sought their patronage. The convivium culture of the praetorium was a highly important part of status enhancement and the display of power for the military commander.

One potentially very interesting avenue of research relates to the identification of the presence of women and children inside Roman forts and other military establishments and how this presence might be proven through the analysis of small finds in particular.[9] The presence of women, both family and female servants or slaves, might be expected in a praetorium building in a permanent fort. Though there are problems in 'sexing' small finds,[10] that is assigning a gender to the ownership and use of particular items of material culture, it is likely that many categories of jewellery in Roman Britain were almost exclusively female items and these, then, might be used to detect a female presence inside the Binchester praetorium at a particular period.

If one accepts that hair pins are more likely to be female-related items than male[11] and that jet, encompassing all so-called shiny black materials used for jewellery manufacture in Roman Britain, was a material particularly favoured by Romano-British women, then some trends might emerge from the Binchester data relating to hair pins and jet jewellery and personal possessions. In the first- and second-century phases sixteen hair pins were found, in the phases encompassing the first two stone

84 A selection of bone pins.

praetoria twelve pins, in the mid- to late fourth-century house twenty-six pins and in the late Roman to sub-Roman period fifteen pins. In other words, hair pins were found in all Roman phases, peaking in the mid- to late fourth century. As to jet and shale items, these were virtually absent from the pre-fourth-century phases, and quite well represented in the mid- to late fourth-century phases and late Roman to sub-Roman phase by nineteen and fifteen items respectively. However, of the nineteen jet and shale items of the mid- to late fourth-century, fifteen were items of jewellery beads, finger rings, pins and bracelets – and of those in the later phase only six jewellery items were represented, all bracelets. So once more, it looks as if a female presence was more marked in the mid- to late fourth century than in any other phase on the site. Perhaps the presence of the commandant's wife in the praetorium was important in terms of the enhancement of the social rituals played out here to define his power and status.

As might, though, be expected at a Roman fort, there are no inscriptions from the site naming any women present here, as dedicatees of altars for instance, yet there is a significant bias towards the dedication of altars at Binchester to female deities and other female-related religious items are also present on the site, as will be discussed shortly. However, one woman's name – Armea – does appear twice, scratched as a graffito on two tiles from the site, one found by Proud and Hooppell in the nineteenth century[12] and the other, more complete, example being found during the 1976–1981 excavations. The fuller graffito, inscribed in well-formed capitals, reads, 'ARMEAMEDOCVITRECTE

85 Armea graffito on a tile.

| BIDICERECVNCTIS', 'Armea me docuit "Recte (ti)bi" dicere cunctis' ('Armea has taught me to say "No, thank you" to everyone [else]').[13]

This is a hexameter line from an otherwise unknown poem obviously dedicated to a woman called Armea or Ar(...)mea. Whether she was real or fictional we do not know, though the appearance of her name twice on tiles at Binchester, and within what appears to be the same formula of a poem repeated both times, suggests she was a fictional object of some soldiers' desire.

## ROMAN RELIGIOUS BELIEFS AND RITUAL PRACTICES

No temples, shrines or other buildings with religious or ritual affiliations have yet been found at Binchester, either in the fort or in the vicus. Rather, evidence for religious and ritual practice at Roman Binchester comes in the form of inscribed altars to specific deities, votive statuary, and other smaller votive items in metal, bone or jet whose links to certain gods and goddesses seem certain. The majority of these items testify in most instances to personal belief rather than to communal worship, though this, of course, is perhaps to make a distinction that did not necessarily exist in the ancient world.

Many of the pagan gods and goddesses of the Roman pantheon are represented here, including Jupiter, Mercury, Venus and Bacchus, as might be expected. There is no evidence for Christianity on the site, though this would scarcely be expected to be found in a Roman military context in any case.

As was standard practice, 'Jupiter, Best and Greatest' was invoked on a decorated altar found at Binchester in 1891, although in this case the dedicatee, Pomponius Donatus, the beneficiarius of the governor, also called upon the Matres Ollototae or Mother Goddesses Ollototae, that is 'of Other Peoples'. This represents one of the most intriguing religious affiliations between soldiers at Binchester and the gods and goddesses of the Roman world, as no fewer than five stone altars dedicated to these Matres have been found at the site and it is highly likely that a temple to the Matres existed here. It is interesting that the dedications to the Mother Goddesses found at Binchester are all made by men. Perhaps it is no coincidence that Venus figurines have also been found at the site, as will be discussed below, and that some sculptural representations of Mother Goddesses from other sites depict her with her hound, perhaps once more of significance in terms of a jet dog knife handle found at Binchester which, again, will be discussed later in the chapter.

Interestingly, there is only one other dedication to the Matres Ollototae from Roman Britain, from the site of Heronbridge in Cheshire. An altar found here was jointly set up by Julius Secundus and Aelia Augustina, demonstrating that the cult of these particular Matres could be of appeal to both men and women at the same time.[14]

Mention has already been made in Chapter One of the discovery of a dedication slab depicting the healing god Aesculapius and his daughter Salus and of a statue perhaps of Flora, both found during the Proud and Hooppell excavations in the later nineteenth century, and of a relief perhaps of a faun and a carved stone bearing an image of Priapus, both finds reported on by earlier antiquarians and now sadly lost.

In the Roman world personal affiliations with individual gods and goddesses were often demonstrated by the commissioning or purchase of items either bearing representations of the deities, sometimes with their animal or artefactual attributes, or of those animal or artefactual attributes on their own, or in some instances by pictorial allusion to a particular deity. Thus at Binchester, from the 1976-1981 excavations came: a copper alloy key handle bearing the figure of a panther emerging from the cover of an acanthus leaf, both the feline and acanthus being linked to the god Bacchus; a bone hairpin decorated at the head with a small cockerel, this bird being commonly associated with the god Mercury; and part of a square-bodied glass vessel known today as a Mercury flask because of the common depiction of the god on the base of such vessels, though that part of the vessel is not present at Binchester. The eighteenth-century antiquarian John Cade makes mention of a bronze image of Bacchus from the site in the form of some kind of pendant. From McIntyre's pit excavations in the vicus in 1929 comes part of a pipeclay so-called Venus figurine, part of a second Venus figurine being found inside the fort during the more recent 2009 season of excavation. Also there in 2009 was found a leaded copper alloy cast figurine of a goat which is probably of Roman date, and, if so, probably linked once more to Mercury, who often was depicted in the company of both a goat and a cockerel. A small cast copper alloy eagle with a panther's head found in the banks of the River Wear, below the fort, in the late 1970s may have been linked to Jupiter or, it

86 Carved intaglio or gemstone in an iron ring (photo by Robert Wilkins).

has been suggested, to Taranis. A second copper alloy eagle found by metal detecting over the one-time ploughed field to the east of the fort may once more allude to the god Jupiter[15].

Five intaglios or carved gemstones originally set into finger rings have been found on the site, the earliest reported on by antiquarian commentators, the latest coming from the 2010 excavation. These intaglios were each engraved with scenes which were probably of some personal significance to their owners, particularly with regard to their religious beliefs and affiliations, or those of their families or loved ones if the rings were gifts. Unfortunately, three of the five intaglios from Binchester are now lost and our knowledge of them comes only from descriptions and drawings of them made soon after their discovery. These three comprise: a cornelian engraved with the figure of Bacchus with a thyrsus, the Bacchic wand of power; a red jasper engraved with a so-called Janus face, that is a mask of a bearded man thought to be Silenus, companion of Bacchus, and a young Pan with what have been described as 'incipient horns'; and another red jasper stone engraved with a cockerel facing a serpent, a design that might initially be thought to be less overtly religious in subject than the designs cut into the other two gemstones but which could provide an allusion to Mercury in the form of his companion animal, the cockerel, and to potent chthonic underworld powers as represented by the snake.[16] The fourth intaglio was found in the 1976–1981 campaign of excavations and dates stylistically to the late first or early second century. The intaglio is a niccolo, that is an onyx with an upper blue layer on a dark ground, and is engraved with an eagle standing on an altar and engaged in using its beak to tear apart a hare that it holds in its talons. The close connection between the Roman army, particularly the legions, and the eagle, the bird symbolically associated with the god Jupiter, is well attested in Roman Britain and in the wider Roman world. The fifth intaglio, a purple cut stone, was found in 2009 but was too damaged for any carving on it to be identified.

Perhaps, though, one of the most aesthetically pleasing finds from the site which probably had a personal link to an individual's devotion to a particular deity is a small Roman carved jet dog recovered during excavations in 1971 within the fort, in the vicinity of what was then Binchester Hall Hotel, to the north of the praetorium.[17] As this is such an interesting individual object and it has not yet been described in any archaeological publication, it will be described in detail here and then discussed in terms of parallels for the object from elsewhere in Roman Britain and beyond. The possible symbolic meaning of the image of the dog more broadly in Romano-British art and life will also be considered.

Largely complete, though with some damage to the right-hand side of the object in particular, this 62 millimetre (2.5 inch) long carved jet dog is an extremely well-modelled, three-dimensional piece. The dog's pose is quite striking, partly naturalistic, partly stylised. Quite alert, the beast sits up on its haunches, its back legs tucked up underneath it. Its front legs are straight and angled down, probably with its front paws resting on the ground, though the lower parts of the legs are either missing, as in the case of the right front leg, or damaged, as in the case of the left. When viewed from the front the dog can be seen to be gracile, with a thin, tapering face and alert, open eyes. Its back and neck are modelled almost in a single, graceful, though flattened, curve when viewed from the side, the neck long and slender, the ears held flat against the head and the mouth partially open. The smooth finish on the dog's body, head and legs implies that it is of a breed with a smooth, glossy coat. The dog sits on a rectangular pedestal or plinth that forms the base of the object. The base is pierced by a now-empty, circular socket hole into which something would have been affixed, possibly with lead solder.

The breed of dog represented is most closely comparable to a present-day greyhound or lurcher. Examples of greyhound-like dogs represented in Roman art include the so-called Townley Greyhounds, marble dogs of the first to second century AD from Lanuvio, Italy,[18] and from Roman Britain the now-fragmentary stone statue of a dog from the temple site at Pagans Hill, Somerset.[19]

While the Binchester carved jet dog could possibly have been a decorative finial of some sort, adorning a piece of furniture perhaps, this seems unlikely. A more probable identification is that it was a handle of some kind, probably from a tanged knife or a medical instrument.

Jet in the Roman world was a material which was deemed to be imbued with magical properties, and in Roman Britain was a material which was often used for the manufacture of items of apotropaic value.[20] The most obvious source for the jet from which the Binchester dog is made is the relatively close North Yorkshire coast at and around Whitby. Jet workshops are known to have operated in Roman York[21] and possibly also at South Shields, and jet working is attested on site at Binchester

87 A jet dog, possibly a knife handle, found during excavations in 1971.

fort, particularly in the mid- to late fourth and into the fifth century, with working waste also being present in a number of other phases. However, it is likely that this object was made off-site and that it reached the fort as a finished item. The date of the Binchester jet dog is uncertain, though the horizon in which it was found has been dated to the third or fourth century.

There are no direct parallels for the Binchester jet dog. However, jet handles in the form of other types of animal are known from Roman Britain and the Rhineland, figures of dogs do appear on bone and antler handles, and images of dogs were commonly used in other media in Britain and in the Roman world more widely, often to convey abstract concepts or religious ideas.

It is likely that at Binchester the selection of the image of the dog to adorn the handle of a knife or medical instrument represented a deliberate reflection of some aspect or aspects of the owner's character or religious beliefs and that the marrying of this image with the chosen raw material of jet was seen to be appropriate for a knife that was in all probability to be used for a non-utilitarian, perhaps ritual or religious, purpose of some kind, perhaps connected to the worship of Aesculapius or the Mother Goddesses.

Dogs in the art of Roman Britain appear in a number of media and come from sites of different dates and different functions. They range from sculptures such as the Pagans Hill dog and portions of statues of dogs reported as having been found at Lydney Park temple, Gloucestershire, but now lost, to smaller, probably votive figures of dogs in copper alloy.[22] Dogs also appear on mosaic pavements, pottery and glass vessels, on brooches, and on more utilitarian items such as patera handles and knife handles.

In terms of the complexity of identities potentially encoded in its image, the dog in the Roman world and in Roman Britain probably had as many potential layers of meaning to its viewers as did the lion and other felines,[23] dependant on the contexts in which the images appeared. While some of the small bronze figurines of dogs from Roman Britain might portray pet dogs and had been commissioned for that very purpose by proud and devoted owners, most are, in fact, likely to represent votive figurines of some sort.

The so-called Lydney dog, a small copper alloy figurine of a dog from the temple site at Lydney Park, Gloucestershire,[24] has a long muzzle and patterned coat, probably identifying it as being an Irish wolfhound.[25] But this is only one of ten bronze or copper alloy images of different breeds and sizes of dogs known from the site, along with six images in stone. One of the copper alloy items comprises a sheet metal figure of a possible dog with a human face and another is in the form of an inscribed copper alloy plaque bearing a depiction of a small dog. The Lydney temple and its residing god, Nodens, were inextricably linked to the process of healing of pilgrims to the site, with perhaps real dogs also being present on the site in addition to images of dogs, the healing power of their saliva being one of the physical elements of the healing process here. As well as being linked to Nodens, dogs were also linked in mythology to the healing god Aesculapius, who would also have been deemed to have been present at the temple.

Images of dogs were not only often associated with specialised healing shrines, with Aesculapius and Nodens, and with other types of temples where the presiding deity may have held healing attributes among its other powers, but often with specific deities and mythological figures including Mother Goddesses, the goddess Diana, male hunter deities, Hercules, and eastern figures such as Mithras and Orpheus.

A lapdog appears on a relief of three Mother Goddesses from Cirencester.[26] The goddesses sit together on a bench of some kind with three children. The right-hand figure nurses a small dog on her lap. A dog, fish and fruits also appear with Mother Goddesses on a relief from Ancaster, Lincolnshire.[27] In both cases the figures of the dogs appear as attributes of Mother Goddesses who were both of the underworld and of this world as the source of its fertility,[28] linking the dogs both to concepts of healing, birth, and fertility, and to death and the afterlife, just as they were when featuring as attributes of Aesculapius, the healing god who also, most probably, had chthonian powers. As noted above, from Binchester there comes both a dedication slab to Aesculapius and Salus, dedicated by a medicus with the Ala Vettonum at the fort, and no fewer than five dedications to the Mother Goddesses Ollotatae or to the Mother Goddesses.

Hunting became a defining elite male leisure activity in the later Roman Empire. A mounted, hunting aristocrat appears alongside his two hunting dogs, their elaborately portrayed shaggy coats marking them out as Irish wolfhounds, on the late Roman etched glass bowl from Wint Hill, Somerset, driving their prey, a sprinting hare, into a catch-net set up in a lightly-wooded landscape.[29] In the late Roman period such an activity would have been the preserve of not only the aristocratic landowner but also of senior bureaucrats and military officers. Indeed, it is likely that the three altars dedicated to Vinotonus and other altar fragments found in the shrine to the god on Scargill Moor, Bowes, County Durham,[30] were dedicated by senior military commanders hunting there, probably principally officers from nearby Bowes Fort but also possibly officers from other Roman forts in the region, possibly indeed also including Binchester.

Thus, while images of dogs could have been utilised in Romano-British art on occasions for purely decorative purposes or in commemoration of a patron's beloved pet or hunting dog, in most instances where a canine image was used a deeper, more subtle, even nuanced, meaning could have been intended. Hunting was both a highly symbolic metaphor for a human's life and in late antiquity a status-enhancing activity for the upper echelons of society and the military, and possibly also by then a metaphor linked to concepts of salvation. The dog could also act as an apotropaic symbol, much like the lion, guarding both property and an individual's life. The dog's link to the underworld and to concepts of death and salvation meant that it was also linked to gods and forces of healing and to healing shrines. Specific links to Mother Goddesses, to Aesculapius, to Diana, and to a number of eastern deities and figures such as Atys, Mithras, Danubian Rider-Gods and Orpheus mean that images of dogs cannot necessarily be taken at face value in Roman Britain.

The carved jet dog handle from Binchester Roman fort is without doubt one of the most accomplished examples of carving in this material from Roman Britain. That the dog may have been a deliberately commissioned to reflect some aspect or aspects of the eventual owner's character or religious beliefs and that the image and the raw material from which it was wrought were specifically chosen as appropriate to adorn a knife used for a non-utilitarian, perhaps ritual or religious purpose, seems certain. The possibility exists that the jet handle could have come from a ritual knife or a medical instrument, and that the image of the dog was intended to evoke in the knowledgeable contemporary viewer in Binchester Roman fort thoughts of either the healing god Aesculapius or the Mother Goddesses.

Other items which are often found associated with religious practice, indeed often placed in burials as grave goods, are so-called facepots and headpots, a number of which were found during the Proud and Hooppell campaign, though only one of these, a headpot, was subsequently published in Hooppell's *Vinovia*. Fragments from seven further facepots found in the Hooppell archive were published in the 2010 Binchester monograph because of their inherent significance. Unfortunately, there are no records of where specifically within the fort or vicus any of these latter pots were found.

Also related to Roman religious practice is the ritual dedication of certain items by their burial in specific, regulated contexts. At Binchester such ritual deposition is mainly, though not exclusively, connected to the foundation of a particular building or the start of a new phase of activity, or indeed to the demolition of a building or the end of a phase of activity in a so-called closing deposit. The following such dedicatory ritual deposits were identified during the 1976–1981 excavations: the deposition of organic material, a number of whole pots, including a buff flagon and a rustic ware vessel, part of a lamp chimney, a quantity of samian ware and a copper alloy

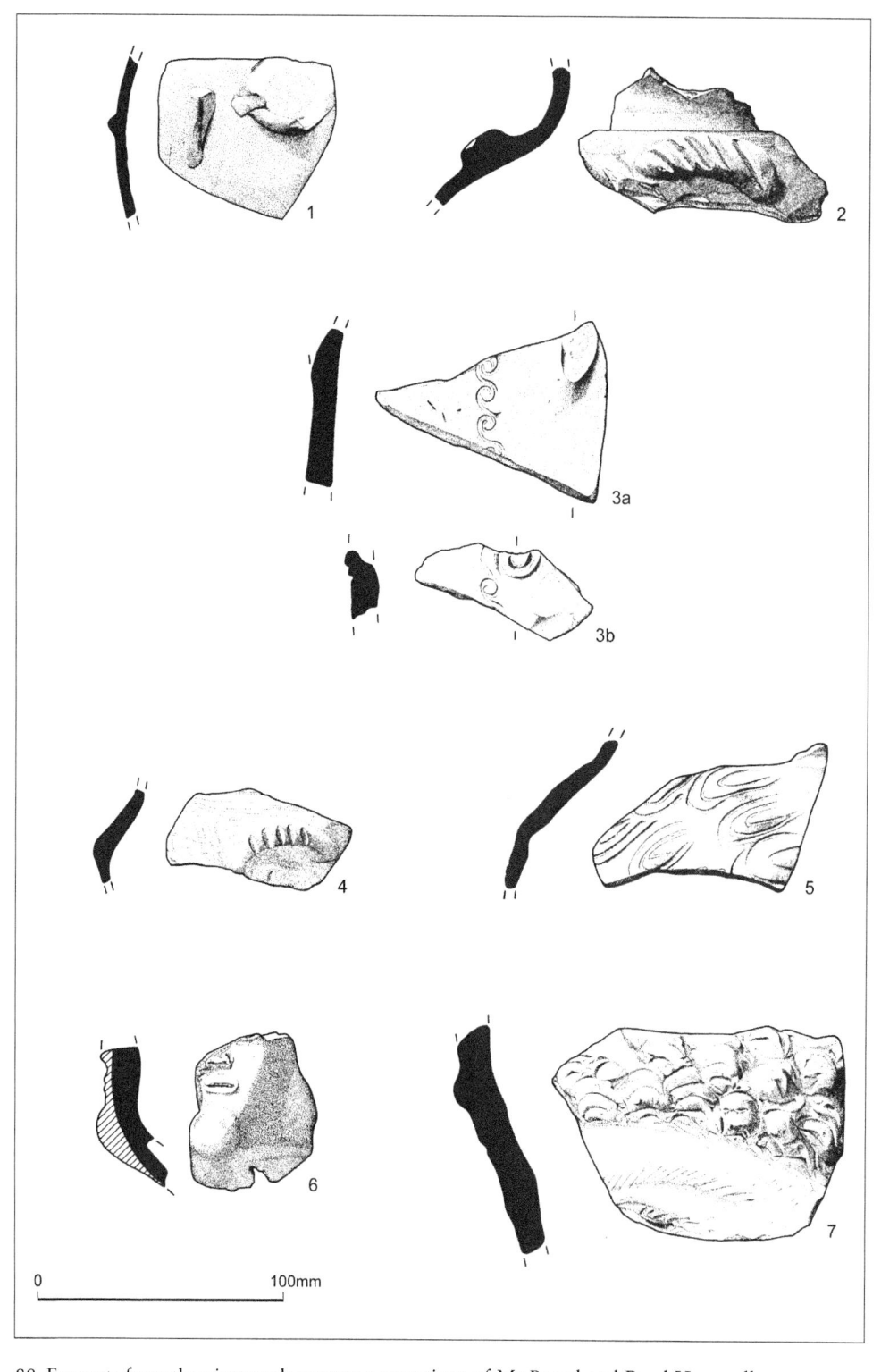

88 Facepots from the nineteenth-century excavations of Mr Proud and Revd Hooppell.

89 Graffito on one of a pair of ritually deposited pots.

seal box in a pit inside one of the rooms of the first-century timber commandant's house or praetorium; the disposal of a more or less complete mortaria and three very large decorated samian bowls and the forming of a closing deposit at the end of the second-century industrial and dumping phase; the placing upside down of two pots, one with a stone stopper in its mouth and a graffito inscription on its shoulder, in clay-lined holes in the foundation trench for one of the walls of the mid-fourth-century commandant's house or praetorium (indeed, one of these vessels may have been dug up from an earlier phase, curated and then reburied); and, finally, the burial of a rough anthropomorphic stone head in the foundation trench for the large new bath suite added to the mid-fourth-century commandant's house, or praetorium, perhaps in c. AD 350–60.

Two further unusual occurrences identified by the study of the bird bones from the 1976–1981 excavations are the specific use and structured disposal of the remains, in one instance, of a number of ravens and, in another, of a number of white-tailed eagles, both in the late Roman to sub-Roman period. Twenty-one bones from at least six ravens were found together in a single deposit, suggesting some very specific event having taken place here at this time rather than the birds simply having been killed for food. Forty-one bones from at least three white-tailed eagles were found, over half of

90 Anthropomorphic stone figure from the foundation trench of the mid-fourth-century bathhouse.

these bones deriving from the birds' wings, and butchery marks on some of the other bones suggest removal of the wings was the main motive in their dismemberment. A parallel for the occurrence of white-tailed eagle bones in Roman contexts was found at South Shields Roman fort, where they are reported as having been found in the commandant's house, it being suggested that the wings might have been used as brushes or the feathers as arrow flights.

A more formal type of Roman ritual was the burial and commemoration of the dead, as represented by burials themselves, burial structures and funerary memorials. Urned cremation burials of the Roman period were reported as being found in the Bishop's Park in the nineteenth century, some distance away from Vinovia, so the exact relationship of these to the fort at Binchester is uncertain. Stray finds of human remains within the bounds of the fort have been made for many years and it is now seen as likely that most of these represent disturbed burials from the large Anglo-Saxon cemetery known to have been sited here over the northern part of the fort.

A tombstone reported as having been found in a causeway leading to a footbridge over the Bell Burn, about a quarter of a mile to the north of Binchester[31] but presumably dug up outside the fort, was dedicated to Nemonius Montanus, a decurion at the fort who died aged forty, by his brother Nemonius Sanctus and his joint heirs. The stone, like so many of the recorded carved and sculpted stones from Binchester,

91 Excavation of a mausoleum in the civilian settlement, or vicus, by *Time Team* in 2007 (copyright Wessex Archaeology).

is now lost. Part of a second possible military tombstone, again now lost, is reported on by Hooppell in his *Vinovia* book and took the form of a carved stone on which are represented the lower parts, leg and lower body of a male figure, presumably a soldier.[32]

A row of stone-built mausolea was identified in the Binchester vicus in 2007, during the *Time Team* investigation there that year. Part of an inhumation burial with pottery grave goods was encountered in one mausoleum, but no tombstones or other inscribed dedicatory slabs were found.[33]

CHAPTER SEVEN

# A Military Base, a Centre of Power

Well-known to antiquarians since the sixteenth century, as has been discussed in Chapter One, Binchester Roman fort has acted as a magnet for visitors interested in the history and archaeology of northern Roman Britain right up to the present day. After excavation work spread over more than a hundred years at the site, we are now in a position to start to understand how Binchester fort developed and changed its character over a period of many centuries. Founded during the governorship of Agricola, around AD 80, the fort had a long and complex history that extended into the fifth century and beyond into the Anglo-Saxon and medieval periods, as has been described in detail in Chapters Two to Five. Most important in that process was the substantial continuity of activities from the late Roman to sub-Roman periods, as evidenced by the excavations centred on the large stone praetorium, or commandant's house, and bath suite in the centre of the fort in 1976–1981 and 1986–1991. The main importance of these discoveries is to have brought about a new understanding of the processes of transition from Roman to medieval in the northern frontier zone of the Roman Empire. Analysis of events at Binchester, along with those at other sites such as Birdoswald and South Shields, replaces the once-postulated idea of catastrophic change with a picture of a more gradual evolution from one type of society to another in northern England. Indeed, Binchester and Birdoswald probably now represent the two most important sites in northern England for providing evidence of this once-shadowy period.[1]

However, study of Binchester now contributes as much towards a social and economic interpretation of the Roman north of Britain as it does to a military history. The economic role of Binchester as both a consumer and producer at different times was highly significant, as was made clear in Chapter Six.

The study of change over time at Binchester has been possible through the existence here of an unusually detailed excavated sequence and accompanying finds assemblages in the centre of the fort. The site had suffered relatively little disturbance in the post-Roman period. Limited medieval activity had meant that most of the earlier levels had been affected only by the occasional episode of stone robbing. The substantial survival of the late Roman walls protected the interiors of the rooms they defined and thereby also what lay beneath their floors. More recent ploughing had had no chance to penetrate deep into the archaeological deposits. Ironically, most damage to the later Roman horizons within the areas excavated in 1976–1981 and 1986–1991 had been done by the trenching of the nineteenth-century excavators Proud and Hooppell. This combination of factors produced generally excellent preservation of the stratigraphic record, allowing an important new understanding of many issues relating to Binchester's history.

In this final chapter consideration will firstly be given to Binchester fort's place in the overall framework of the history of the Roman army in Britain, in terms of who the communities of soldiers here were between the late first century and the late fourth century and what we know about the identities of individual soldiers here at different times. The second theme to be pursued in this chapter is how we can perhaps understand the ending of Roman Britain in AD 410, or perhaps rather the transition from Roman Britain to Anglo-Saxon England in the north.

## BINCHESTER AND THE ROMAN ARMY

Throughout this book, Binchester has been analysed as both a settlement site and as a military establishment by focusing on the definition of the social and economic character of the settlement and fort both at specific periods of time and over the extended period of time represented by the exceptionally high quality archaeological record.

For many reasons, it is presently highly unfashionable to study the Roman north, implying as that does the Roman military north, or the Roman army in general. Maybe the last few generations of Roman military archaeologists only have themselves to blame for this situation and for the witty mocking of one fellow academic who has encapsulated their concerns as intellectually amounting to the need to know: 'Was cohors IV Martianorum in garrison at Great Chesterheads during Wall Period III?'[2] More recently, though, the intellectual tide has been turning and the newly defined focus on studying the Roman army as a community of soldiers is already humanising the study of the army and move it away from the simplistic definition of 'war machine'.[3]

Fortresses, forts and camps are still probably the most commonly investigated types of Roman-period sites in Britain, though the research emphasis in Romano-British archaeology has certainly shifted away from this category of site, perhaps too far away. Traditionally, Romano-British military sites have been seen as holding the keys to understanding the histories of the military campaigns which have so preoccupied the minds of many of the archaeologists of Roman Britain. As a result, there is a very large set of excavation reports which have mostly been concerned with identifying structures related to the perceived historical sequence of political and military events. This has tended to discredit the study of military sites in the eyes of those more interested in broader issues of social and economic processes in Roman Britain, a tendency reinforced by the view that Roman forts all broadly conform to the same standard plan. However, to dismiss Roman forts in this way grossly undervalues the real importance of the Roman army as both an agent of change and a catalyst for

92 Excavations underway on a fourth-century stone barrack block in 2010.

change in the newly-conquered province, and as the predominant institution in those frontier regions where there was a permanent military presence. To approach the issues of the role of the army and its forts in their regional environment, research has to be carried out on a wider plane than the traditional obsession with campaign histories. This is what has been attempted in studying Binchester.

Binchester, therefore, has more general lessons to offer for proto-historical archaeology. As already noted, the only way to begin to understand the site's complexities has been to approach it like a settlement rather than a piece of military history, trying to establish the nature of activity at each stage rather than to perceive the hand of some general or emperor. However, this is not to be in denial about the fact that Binchester was a fort, that its foundation and subsequent history was largely dictated by external military and political factors and that the soldiers in the fort at various periods were part of a broader community of soldiers.[4] Discussion will therefore now be turned to the fort itself, to its garrisons and to a number of other military-related issues.

Binchester was the site of a Roman fort, or, more correctly, forts, which formed part of a dense network of Roman military sites in northern England, in the geographical zone which eventually linked the legionary fortress at York with the frontier system of Hadrian's Wall. Its history and fortunes, therefore, were inextricably linked to the history and fortunes of the extended frontier system itself, though that system in the second and third centuries was very different indeed from the system in the fourth century, shown by the changed nature of the Roman army itself between these periods. The very fact that this system of forts and garrisons existed for so many hundreds of years attests to the potential volatility of the region, and perhaps its vulnerability at the fringes of the province.

Present evidence points towards the foundation of the first fort at Binchester taking place under Agricola during his campaigning in the north, though there still remains the possibility, yet to be proved, that the foundation of the fort, or at least the establishment here of a temporary marching camp, could have taken place a few years earlier, under Petillius Cerialis.

Before the present excavations, it was thought that both Binchester and Ebchester were unoccupied at some stage in the second century, possibly under Hadrian, possibly *c.* AD 140, and that this marked the period of construction of the fort at Lanchester in their stead.[5] Again, received wisdom dated the reoccupation of both forts to *c.* AD 160. Evidence from the 1976–1981 and 1986–1991 excavation campaigns has indeed identified a hiatus in activity in the central area of the fort between the end of the industrial and dumping phase in *c.* AD 125 and the building of the first stone commandant's house within the second, stone fort in the Antonine period. An Antonine horizon was, however, identified in the 1971 excavation area to the north. Interestingly, the possible Antonine abandonment horizon again was not identified during small-scale excavation elsewhere in the fort in 1996.[6]

The size of the first fort at Binchester is unknown but can be guessed at, and it is suggested by geophysical survey that it was likely to have been larger than the second fort. The second fort, whose ramparts survive as upstanding earthworks in places today, is known to be about 3.6 hectares (9 acres) in area, a large size for the region. If the size of this fort is compared to the sizes of other Roman forts and their known garrisons, it might be possible to attempt to correlate fort size to garrison type at Binchester too. Binchester falls into a relatively rare group of forts which, it has been concluded, utilising evidence from inscriptions, were mainly garrisoned by ala quingenaria units, that is, they were built to house 500 auxiliary cavalry, although the British examples in this group were generally smaller than the continental ones.[7] There may therefore be some significance in the size of the second Binchester fort, though it must be borne in mind that there is, however, no provable or firm correlation between the size of a fort and its garrison.

Attested units stationed at Binchester include the Ala Vettonum from Spain; a cohort of Frisians, the Cuneus Frisiorum, from the Low Countries; the locally recruited Numerus Concangiensium, attested on numerous stamped tiles; and possibly a detachment of the Sixth Legion, attested on a stamped tile at Binchester and an inscribed stone in Escomb church. If the site of Morbio listed in the late Roman document the *Notitia Dignitatum*[8] is indeed Binchester, then the equites catafractariorum would also have been here, though opinion would now consider Piercebridge to be a better candidate to have been Morbium.[9] The analysis of ceramic evidence has led to the suggestion that a Gallic auxiliary unit was stationed at Binchester at one time, and that in the earliest phases the presence of men from the Ninth Legion, Hispana, is also likely. If it is accepted that the so-called list tile from Binchester inscribed with columns of soldiers' names is arranged by legionary cohort,

93 The fort rampart at the north-east corner, with a culvert, as recorded by Mr Proud and Revd Hooppell in the nineteenth century. Drawing by W. Heatlie (from R. E. Hooppell's 1891 *Vinovia*).

as has been suggested, then this is further confirmation of a legionary presence on the site at some time in the fourth century. Mention should also be made here of an altar from the fort at Bowes recording the restoration of the bathhouse there, following its destruction by fire.[10] The restoration work was attributed to Virius Lupus, imperial praetorian legate with the First Cohort of Thracians, under the charge of Valerius Fronto, cavalry prefect of the Cavalry Squadron of Vettonians, probably the same Ala Vettonum stationed at Binchester and presumably seconded to carry out this work. Virius Lupus was governor from AD 197 to *c.* AD 202.

In addition to the known units on the site, inscriptions and graffiti also record the names of a number of individual officers and soldiers stationed at Binchester. Attested individuals at Binchester include: Marcus Aurelius [...]ocomas, a doctor with the Ala Vettonum; Marcus Valerius Fulvianus, prefect of cavalry; Pomponius Donatus, beneficiarius of the governor; Tiberius Claudius Quintianus, beneficiarius of the governor; Gemellus; a tribune; Nemonius Montanus, decurion, and Nemonius Sanctus his brother; Julius Victorinus; the Celtic-sounding Cunovendus and Catugnavus and their eight fellow-soldiers Matutinus, Virilis, Marinus, Bellicus, Cupitus, Solinus, Senicianus and Lucillianus (men with names popular in Celtic-speaking provinces because they incorporated Celtic name-elements, and who would seem to have formed a tilery work detachment recorded for posterity by a graffito on a tile in the fourth century); []atoverus is recorded in a tile graffito, and other graffiti on pot sherds record the property of Candidus, possibly of Selius and probably also of Suttonis; finally, an

94 Reused fragment of an inscribed altar naming the Ala Vettonum from the northern fourth-century praefurnium or furnace room.

unnamed soldier or officer, possibly an overseer with the tilery detachment mentioned above, is recorded in the form of a graffito caricature on a piece of fourth-century tile from the site.

Finally, in terms of finds evidence relating to the military and to individual soldiers or groups of soldiers, a small amount of military equipment was recovered during the excavation in the centre of the fort, along with some items that attest to the more bureaucratic aspects of army routine that might have been expected to be associated with fort life. Military equipment recovered included an iron spear, part of an iron shield boss, iron bolt heads, copper alloy scabbard chapes, and other copper alloy items, including a scabbard runner, helmet plume holders, a helmet handle, a belt stiffener, harness clips and junction loops, and possible stone ballista balls or artillery shot, along with numerous other copper alloy fittings, including buckles, mounts, terminals, pendants and plates, probably also from military equipment. A lead seal stamped with the letters PBI, standing for Provincia Britanniae Inferioris, provides evidence for official outside communication with the fort and its residents. Other evidence for such record-keeping and communication takes the form of copper alloy and iron writing styli and copper alloy seal-boxes.

## BINCHESTER AND THE ENDING OF ROMAN BRITAIN

The old vision of the end of the Roman frontier as being a single, simple event, with soldiers leaving the forts and heading south or just disappearing back into rural communities in the northern region, is no longer considered acceptable. Understanding the changes on the frontier is critical to wider interpretations of the Roman administration in Britain and of the processes by which cultural and power relations were transformed over the Roman Empire as a whole. The idea that change in northern Britain was not a sudden catastrophic withdrawal, a year zero event, has long been accepted.

Binchester is of particular importance for contributing information on the late Roman transition in the north because it does not lie on the Roman frontier line of Hadrian's Wall. The area enclosed by its defences was larger than most such forts in the hinterland of the Hadrian's Wall frontier line, until it was matched in the later Roman period by Piercebridge on the River Tees to the south, and this perhaps underlines its prominence in the Roman frontier system. The campaigns of excavation at Binchester in 1976–1981 and 1986–1991 add another substantial investigation to a set of such north-eastern sites, particularly Piercebridge, South Shields, Greta Bridge and Chester-le-Street.[11] Results from these sites complement each other to provide a comprehensive new view of the northern frontier that was unimagined when these excavations began.

The development of Binchester throughout and beyond the Roman period shows the changing frontier conditions and functions of the fort sites. Binchester's earliest phases appear to be typical of first-century military bases. However, the subsequent turning over of so much of the fort interior to industrial production in the second century represents something quite different. It is certainly outside the conventional interpretations of contemporary military sites, but is not unparalleled.[12] Another contemporary example of very extensive industrial activity is found at Newstead, north of Hadrian's Wall, and on an even larger scale than at Binchester.[13] This phenomenon is now of wider significance than the specific activities at particular sites. It suggests that what are normally labelled frontier forts in the second century were very often committed to substantial industrial production, at the expense of space for barracks and presumably therefore at the expense of garrison troops. The involvement of what appeared to remain military bases in such production systems forces reconsideration of the dynamics of what the Roman army was doing in Britain in the second century.

At Binchester the large pottery and animal bone assemblages associated with this industrial phase give another dimension to the economic role of the site. The assemblages are of major significance for studying the early stages of army supply, as is the remarkable glass assemblage from this period. Few other sources match the information available here on how meat provision was organised in the first generations of Roman occupation in northern England.

The apparent vitality of Binchester in the late Roman period helps to explain the continuation of importance of the site into the fifth century, as carbon 14 dating now confirms. The best parallels to the Binchester sequence come from Birdoswald.[14] In both cases, careful excavation of well-preserved stratification has shown the continuing use of fort sites into the sub-Roman period. Binchester allows the reconstruction of a strong stratigraphic sequence that is ended by a terminus ante quem from a burial dated by a brooch to the mid-sixth century. In that sequence, the bath-suite's main furnace plinth was reconstructed to function as a boiler, but when the knowledge to make mortar to bond the stone had been lost or when the impetus to make long-lasting repairs had been lost. The inference to be drawn could be that the population still sought to continue using their traditional facilities such as the bath suite, but that economic and technological support was failing. However, the present writer would favour the idea that the use of the bathhouse ended because the Romanised traditions inherent in bathing became of little or no importance to those who controlled the site in the early fifth century. Whatever status had been accrued from bathing and from participating in the convivium culture of the praetorium was now invested in other acts and other types of material culture that reflected a new idea of status enhancement. The indications that Binchester gives of strong survival of traditions into the fifth century does, however, deny the old idea of a sudden abandonment of the Roman north.

Dating the late sequence at Binchester has been problematic, as has been explained above in Chapter Five. This is a familiar problem for those trying to date activities suspected to have happened in the very late fourth or fifth centuries. Whether at Birdoswald, Bath, Wroxeter or perhaps Verulamium, the structural sequence may be secure in suggesting activity into the fifth century, but the recognisably dateable finds were left over from the fourth century.[15] Finding AD 410 in the archaeological record remains problematic.[16]

At Binchester the abundance of pottery and coins came to an end with the fourth century. After that, there were few firm chronological indicators until the appearance of green-glazed pottery in the later medieval period. However, there were deposits including what is probably material of fourth-century origin redumped in the fifth century.

The terminus post quem for the third stone commandant's house or praetorium in the mid-fourth century is only the beginning of the long stratigraphic sequence of activities. This includes the continuing elaboration of the building by the addition of its bath suite, built at a very late date for northern Britain, and substantial extensions to that suite, followed by a period when the building was still in use while knowledge of various aspects of Roman technology, or the will to further invest in this technology, fell away. Even when the buildings were at least partially ruined, significant activity was still occurring at the site. This included the phase of cattle butchery and metalworking, rubbish dumping, the extraction of the metal fittings from the bathhouse, presumably for re-use, and the systematic removal of the arch stones from the bath suite. All these activities suggest that there was still a well-organised community present in the area, rather than it simply representing disparate, unrelated phases of sporadic robbing. All these activities, except the removal of the arch, are dated before a burial of the mid-sixth century. This places them most probably in a period best labelled sub-Roman.

The radiocarbon dating programme has provided the following chronology for the late-Roman and sub-Roman phases at Binchester, based on the mathematical modelling

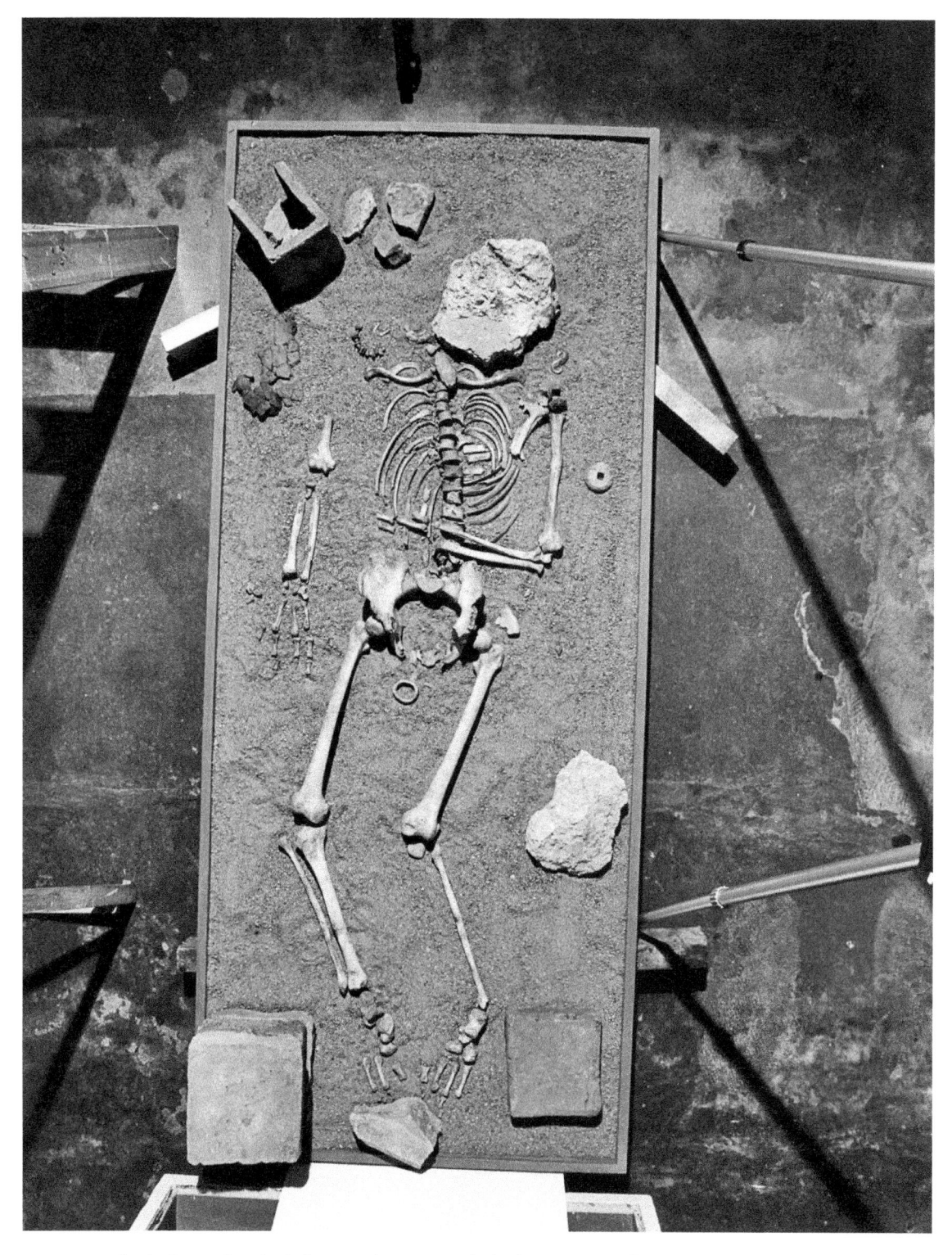

95 Anglo-Saxon female skeleton and grave goods laid out in a sand tray at the Bowes Museum, Barnard Castle.

of the individual carbon dates: the end of the use of the third stone praetorium's bathhouse furnaces and the start of the major rubbish dumping is estimated to have taken place in cal. AD 370–400 (95 per cent probability); the end of the dumping is estimated to have taken place in cal. AD 370–410 (95 per cent probability) and probably cal. AD 380–400 (68 per cent probability); the laying of a flagstone floor above the midden deposits over the northern praefurnium or furnace room took place after cal. AD 370–410 (95 per cent probability); the use of the structure as a bone and antler workshop had ended by cal. AD 380–450 (95 per cent probability) and probably by cal. AD 390–430 (68 per cent probability); masonry collapse on the west side of the bathhouse is estimated to have occurred in cal. AD 380–460 (95 per cent probability) and probably in cal. AD 380–420 (68 per cent probability); the Anglo-Saxon female burial at the end of the archaeological sequence is estimated to date to cal. AD 400–540 (95 per cent probability). However, if individual dates are examined: the final firing of the bathhouse furnaces could have occurred as late as *c.* AD 420–430; the dumping could have gone on as late as *c.* AD 420–430, or, less likely, even into the sixth century, as two dates suggest; the bone and antler workshop could have dated to as late as *c.* AD 420, or even to the sixth century, as three dates suggest. Grave goods dated to the mid-sixth century provide confirmation that the Anglo-Saxon burial dates to very late on the carbon 14 date range scale for samples from the burial.

The military organisation on the northern frontier in the late Roman period is a complex topic. Although Binchester was a hinterland fort in the frontier system, nevertheless it can be expected that the implications of army reorganisation in the late Roman period would have a similar political and social impact on Binchester as on Birdoswald and the other forts in the northern frontier command. This is probably why very late Roman occupation is now being recognised on a group of sites that includes Catterick, Binchester, Birdoswald, Piercebridge, Malton and South Shields, all sites with a substantial civilian settlement linked to a fort and perhaps elements of the field army.[17] The army reforms had led to a situation where, by the third century, locally recruited troops were forming the auxiliary units in Roman Britain and ethnically and culturally these troops were probably indistinguishable from the local inhabitants in settlements outside and around the forts in the frontier zone.[18] Locally recruited garrisons may have remained in situ at such sites, their economic maintenance being aided, if not actually controlled, by the local civilian elite.

Although there is only sparse evidence for what was going on in the rest of the Binchester site while changes were happening in the mid- to late fourth-century praetorium, the scale of external settlement and hints of its late vitality suggest that Binchester was an important part of the local social and economic landscape. The combination of evidence from the north-eastern sites demands the rejection of any notions that the late Roman northern frontier was moribund. It is more positive to see these changes as part of social and economic changes more generally in the late Roman north, with forts acting as local centres, closely related to their regions. Unfortunately the regional settlement evidence is too sparse to provide any convincing context for Binchester at the moment, though a programme of field survey over the next few years, to be undertaken as part of the new research project centred on the site which began in 2009, may help to solve this problem.

96 A circular hypocausted room forming part of a building in the vicus, as recorded by Mr Proud and Revd Hooppell in the nineteenth century. Drawing by W. Heatlie (from R. E. Hooppell's 1891 *Vinovia*).

In northern Britain in the late Roman period the elite was a military elite, unlike the civilian elite whose interests dominated the affairs of the non-militarised part of the province to the south.[19] This probably accounted for the apparent importance of many northern military sites as local centres and the appearance of late Roman to sub-Roman sequences on military sites in the north, but on civilian sites in the south and south-west of England. In many ways a similar point was made about Binchester serving as a local centre almost forty years ago; the well-known reference by the geographer Ptolemy to Vinovium as being a 'city' of the Brigantes begs the question as to whether Binchester had at this time had some degree of special importance in the administration of the region.[20]

Another, more recent theory, that there was a fifth- or sixth-century reoccupation and redefence of Hadrian's Wall,[21] also requires some brief consideration here. While the present author does not subscribe to this idea, it is nevertheless an interesting hypothesis. Where, perhaps, the thesis falls down is in the assumption that every fort was a similar establishment to the other forts in the region and that the military units stationed at each fort were still part of a homogeneous army, with an overarching command structure. Perhaps local factors and the structure of the late Roman army, with its barbarian units and limitanei, had eroded away such certainties. Certainly there are enough differences in the form of late Roman forts and their buildings and layout in the north, and thus probably their strategic function, discernible in the archaeological record at sites such as South Shields, Housesteads and Birdoswald.[22]

Whatever the situation in the late Roman north, it seems more than likely that fort commanders would have possessed the requisite authority to maintain their establishments and soldiers in a partially autonomous way that would have been unthinkable in earlier centuries, and thus maintain and enhance their own individual power.[23] It is therefore easier to understand Binchester if it is regarded not simply as a Roman fort and a long-term settlement but also as a regional power centre at this time. As has already been noted, at the present time the relationships between Binchester and the neighbouring native population remain largely unknown. However, by the late Roman period the extent and intensity of the settlement outside the fort suggest that Binchester had become an important focus for settlement for the lower Wear Valley and lowland Durham in general, with at least some urban functions. The blurring of the boundaries between fort and vicus may have been further exacerbated by the Diocletianic army reforms which allowed soldiers' families to live with them inside forts.[24] Such communities may well have been experiencing declines in population and prosperity, but can hardly be expected to have faded away before the end of the fourth century. Indeed, it may well have been difficult to distinguish in the fourth century between what we call forts, like Binchester and Piercebridge, and what we call small towns, certainly those in Yorkshire like Catterick or Malton-Norton, or even those further south. Binchester would certainly appear to have retained some of that importance into the post-Roman period.

Though when it was first founded around *c*. AD 80, the soldiers at the fort at Binchester would have been markedly different from the local native population of the area in terms of their cultural and or ethnic affinities, their economic status, their dress and appearance, their language or languages, their diet, their material culture and their religious beliefs, by the fourth century these differences would have been eroded away and it is likely that the soldiers at Binchester were firmly part of a broader military and civilian community there.

The pattern at Binchester, then, appears to be one of a gradually declining level of activity into the fifth century, but with some residual importance retained. If the mid- to late Roman stone praetorium and its bath suite was allowed to decline and eventually go out of use, then this may have been the result of a redefinition of the relationship between power and status at this time and how material culture was used to negotiate and demonstrate elite status. Timber halls in use at Birdoswald and Wroxeter in this period demonstrate just such a process of renegotiation in action. Could there have been a timber hall building at Binchester outside the area excavated in 1976–1981 and 1986–1991, away from the crumbling walls and collapsing masonry of the former Romanised elite dwelling that was the fourth-century praetorium? The recognition of a cemetery dated to the Middle Saxon period by radiocarbon dating underlines this possibility. Although the regional evidence for settlements and cemeteries in this period remains slight,[25] Binchester has provided important new evidence about the interplay between the sub-Roman to Anglo-Saxon settlements in central Durham at Escomb, Bishop Auckland, and West Auckland.

The group of late Roman residences located in the forts of north-east England on the frontier, of which Binchester is a distinctive example, has surprising similarities to buildings in the Mediterranean, raising questions about the nature of society on

97 The arches leading to the underfloor of the first room of the mid-fourth-century bathhouse, as recorded by Mr Proud and Revd Hooppell in the nineteenth century. Drawing by W. Heatlie (from R. E. Hooppell's 1891 *Vinovia*).

98 The mid- to late fourth-century praetorium house at its grandest.

the fourth-century frontier, and so about cultural integration across the Empire. Binchester's picture of gradual change into the sub-Roman period denies catastrophic change at the end of the political organisation of the Roman Empire, implying that a strongly rooted, locally Romanised culture had been established, one that had to change its power structures and elite organisation, reflected in its material culture, to tackle continuity and transition from the late Roman period into the sub-Roman and earlier medieval periods.

Rather than external agents or factors remaining predominant in influencing Binchester, this situation gradually changed as local factors came to dominate. The scale of the last stone praetorium house at Binchester suggests an occupant of high status in residence at the fort. Its development and maintenance implies a continuation of such status beyond the time when it can have been legitimated by the direct authority of the Empire. The best explanation seems to be that Binchester's importance came to depend increasingly on locally based power structures. In this way, it offers a parallel in the north to the kind of transformation of a local elite apparent at Wroxeter.[26] Like Birdoswald, Binchester now forms a northern example of an evolving occupation and material culture across the sub-Roman period. Binchester and Birdoswald match Wroxeter in showing the retention of importance at Roman centres within what became British kingdoms.

When I first came to work at Binchester in 1977 it never, of course, occurred to me that thirty-three years later I would still somehow be involved in the study of the archaeology of the site. Then, the site was little known outside the north and seldom mentioned in publications on Roman Britain. Binchester's great value to Romano-British studies has now been realised, with the major excavations of 1976–1981 and 1986–1991 having been fully published in 2010, and with the appearance of this book. Research has demonstrated that the beautiful rooms of the late Roman house at Binchester were not empty immediately after AD 410, nor possibly for many more years after that. They continued to resonate with the sound of eating and drinking, talking and singing, laughter and tears, much as they had before. Recognising this has led to the reconfiguration of our understanding of the rhythm and pattern of change in power, material culture and society in the late Roman to sub-Roman north.

# Notes

Many of the issues raised in this book in summary form are discussed in greater detail in Iain Ferris 2010 *The Beautiful Rooms Are Empty: Excavations at Binchester Roman Fort, County Durham 1976-1981 and 1986-1991*, to which interested readers are first directed. Where reference is made in the notes below to other books or articles listed in the Binchester bibliography and the 'Roman North' bibliography at the end of this book, only a short reference to the cited work will be given, e.g. 'Hooppell 1891', with specific page numbers where relevant. All other books referred to here in the notes but not in the two bibliographies will be cited in full.

## PREFACE

1. On the Vinovia/Vinovium place name see A. L. F. Rivet and C. Smith 1979 *The Place-Names of Roman Britain*, Batsford, London, 504–505.
2. J. K. St Joseph 1951 'Air Reconnaissance in North Britain.' *Journal of Roman Studies* 41, 53.
3. St Joseph 1951 op. cit., 53 and D. P. Dymond 1961 'Roman Bridges in County Durham.' *Archaeological Journal* 118, 138–139.
4. On the background to the taking of the bath suite into county council guardianship see Fawcett 2003.
5. These academic aims and objectives were formulated and developed with Rick Jones in Ferris and Jones 1996, 59–60.

## CHAPTER ONE: ANTIQUARIES AND EARLY ARCHAEOLOGISTS AT VINOVIA

1. Leland 1540.
2. Camden 1586, 738.
3. Horsley 1732, 295 and 399.
4. Hutchinson 1794, 346–349.
5. Hutchinson 1794, 348.
6. Hodgson 1915, 208.
7. Nathaniel Buck 1728 *The South-East View of Bishop-Aukland-Palace, in the Bishoprick of Durham*.
8. Samuel Hieronymous Grimm 1778 *A General View, in Outline, of the Country Near Binchester, in the Parish of St. Andrew Auckland*.
9. Peter Fair, quoted in Surtees 1922, 20.

10 RIB 1032. This and all subsequently quoted translations of inscriptions (using RIB numbers) come from R. G. Collingwood and R. P. Wright 1965 *The Roman Inscriptions of Britain. I Inscriptions on Stone*. Clarendon Press, Oxford. Full bibliographic references to each inscription will also be found there.
11 RIB 1031.
12 RIB 1033.
13 RIB 1037.
14 RIB 1035.
15 RIB 1036.
16 RIB 1039.
17 RIB 1029.
18 Cade 1785, 161.
19 Quoted in Surtees 1922 op. cit., 28–29 and J. Oxberry 1938 'Dr Thomas Sherwood of Snow Hall. A Helper of Surtees.' *Proceedings of the Society of Antiquaries of Newcastle-upon-Tyne* 4.8, 208 respectively.
20 Raine 1852, 4 Note 1.
21 Roach Smith 1854, 132.
22 Hooppell 1891, 6 and 26.
23 Roach Smith 1854, 131–136.
24 Hooppell 1887.
25 Hooppell 1879.
26 Hooppell 1891.
27 Hooppell 1891, 10–12 and Plate 2 U.
28 RIB 1028.
29 RIB 1034.
30 RIB 1040.
31 Hooppell 1891, 39.
32 RIB 1030.
33 Hooppell 1879, 43.

## CHAPTER TWO: THE FIRST-CENTURY FORT

1 On the invasion and its extended aftermath see, for example, M. Millett 1990 *The Romanization of Britain: An Essay in Archaeological Interpretation*. Cambridge University Press, Cambridge, 40–64. On the invasion and subsequent events in the north, see particularly Hanson 1987 and Hanson and Campbell 1986.
2 http://www.channel4.com/history/microsites/T/timeteam/2008/binchester
3 A. S. Esmonde Cleary and I. M. Ferris 1996 *Excavations at the New Cemetery, Rocester, Staffordshire 1985–1987*. Staffordshire Archaeological and Historical Society Transactions Volume XXXV Monograph, Stafford.
4 A. Johnson 1983 *Roman Forts*. Adam and Charles Black, London. And P. Bidwell 1997 *Roman Forts in Britain*. Batsford, London.
5 Johnson 1983 op. cit., 135 Fig. 101.
6 Johnson 1983 op. cit., 129 Fig. 98.
7 Johnson 1983 op. cit., 138 Fig. 104.
8 Rainbird 1971a, 1971b, and 1972; Ferris 2010, 542–543 and Ferris Forthcoming d.
9 D. Starley 2000, 'Metalworking Debris'. In K. Buxton and C. Howard-Davis 2000 *Bremetenacum: Excavations at Roman Ribchester 1980, 1989–1990*. Lancaster University Archaeological Unit, 346.
10 Allason-Jones 2001, 822.
11 G. B. D. Jones 1974 *Roman Manchester*. Manchester University Press, Manchester, 67–75.

## CHAPTER THREE: THE SECOND FORT AND TWO SUCCESSIVE PRAETORIA

1 On the history of the northern frontiers from *c.* AD 120/130 up to the fourth century, see principally Breeze 1993 and 2007 and Breeze and Dobson 2000.
2 Hooppell 1891, 7–9; Steer 1937 and in Ferris 2010, 540–541; Ferris 2010, 107–110.
3 Dobson and Jarrett 1957.
4 On the 1995 evaluation see Northern Archaeological Associates 1997; on the 1996 evaluation see Durham County HER; and on the 2005 evaluation see Archaeological Services, Durham University 2005.
5 On vici in general in Roman Britain see S. Sommer 1984 *The Military Vici in Roman Britain*. BAR British Series 129, Oxford.
6 For the most extensive geophysical surveys see Geoquest Associates 2004 and Geophysical Surveys of Bradford 2007.

## CHAPTER FOUR: THE MID- TO LATE FOURTH-CENTURY PRAETORIUM AND BATH SUITE

1 On historical events in the fourth to fifth centuries in the north, see in particular the relevant sections of Breeze 1993 and 2007 and of Breeze and Dobson 1985. See also the volume of collected papers on the late Roman transition in the north, Wilmott and Wilson (eds.) 2000, especially the papers by Dark 2000, 8–88 and Esmonde Cleary 2000, 89–94. The reorganised late military command in the north is well described in detail in Wilmott 1997, 219–220 and 224–230. The best general book on the period is still A. S. Esmonde Cleary 1989 *The Ending of Roman Britain*. Batsford, London.
2 D. Mattingly 2006 *An Imperial Possession: Britain in the Roman Empire*. London, 530.
3 Hooppell 1879, 32.
4 Fawcett 2003.
5 Fawcett and Rainbird 1973.
6 Hooppell 1891, 18.
7 Hooppell 1891, 15.
8 Hooppell 1891, 17.
9 Hooppell 1891, 14.
10 Hooppell 1891, 17.
11 Hooppell 1891, 16.
12 Fawcett and Rainbird 1973, 5.
13 Hooppell 1891, 38–39.
14 R. Tomlin in Ferris 2010, 240–241.
15 S. J. Ellis 1988 'The End of the Roman House'. *American Journal of Archaeology* 92, 565–576.
16 P. Brown 1992 *Power and Persuasion in Late Antiquity*. University of Wisconsin Press, Madison.
17 A. S. Esmonde Cleary 2000 'Summing Up.' In Wilmott and Wilson (eds.) 2000, 90.
18 S. J. Ellis 1991 'Power, Architecture and Décor: How the Late Roman Aristocrat Appeared to His Guests.' In E. K. Gazda (ed.) 1991 *Roman Art in the Private Sphere: New Perspectives on the Architecture and Décor of the Domus, Villa, and Insula*. University of Michigan Press, Ann Arbor, 117–119.

## CHAPTER FIVE: FROM ROMAN BRITAIN TO ANGLO-SAXON ENGLAND AND BEYOND

1 A. Gardner 2007 *An Archaeology of Identity. Soldiers and Society in Late Roman Britain*. Left Coast Press, Walnut Creek, California, 175.

# Notes

2. A bone of this quite rare bird first appeared on the site in a dumped deposit of this phase. All the other sea eagle bones occurred in what was first thought to be a medieval deposit, as it also contained a single small sherd of medieval pottery. It is now thought that the pot sherd is intrusive and that the deposit in fact is part of the late-sub-Roman activity here.
3. Hooppell 1891, 54–55.
4. Rainbird 1971a, 1971b, and 1972; Ferris 2010, 542–543.
5. Ferris 2010, 105–106.
6. M. Pocock and H. Wheeler 1971 'Excavations at Escomb Church, County Durham'. *Journal of the British Archaeological Association* Third Series XXIV, 11–29.
7. K. Dark 1992 'A Sub-Roman Re-Defence of Hadrian's Wall?' *Britannia* 23, 118.
8. R. Miket 1980 'A Re-Statement of Evidence for Bernician Anglo-Saxon Burials'. In P. Rahtz, T. Dickinson and L. Watts (eds.) 1980 *Anglo-Saxon Cemeteries. The Fourth Anglo-Saxon Symposium at Oxford, 1979*. BAR British Series 82, Oxford, 289–305.
9. Dark 1992 op. cit., 111–120.
10. R. J. Cramp 1983 'Anglo-Saxon Settlement'. In J. C. Chapman and H. Mytum (eds.) 1983 *Settlement in North Britain 1000 B.C.-1000 A.D.* BAR British Series 118, Oxford, 263–297; N. J. Higham 1986 *The Northern Counties to AD 1000*. Longman, London, 250–335; M. R. McCarthy 2002 *Roman Carlisle and the Lands of the Solway*. Tempus, Stroud, 132–154.
11. T. J. South (ed.) 2002 *Historia de Sancto Cuthberto: A History of St Cuthbert and a Record of His Patrimony*. Anglo-Saxon Texts No. 3. D. S. Brewer, Cambridge, 66–69.
12. RIB 1038.
13. Leland, as above, Chapter One Note 1.
14. Ferris and Rátkai Forthcoming.
15. Surtees 1922, 17–22; Thompson 1902; Herdman 1923.
16. Hutchinson 1794, 349.
17. Nathaniel Buck, as above, Chapter One Note 7.

## CHAPTER SIX: OBJECT AND ECONOMY, RELIGION AND RITUAL

1. On work parties being assigned to specific tasks at Vindolanda see text of Tablet 155 in A. Bowman and D. Thomas 1983 *Vindolanda: the Latin Writing Tablets*. Society for the Promotion of Roman Studies, London, 98–100.
2. On Ribchester and Newstead compared see K. Buxton and C. Howard-Davis 2000 op. cit., 337–347.
3. R. F. J. Jones 1990 'Natives and the Roman Army - Three Model Relationships'. In H. Vetters and M. Kandler (eds.) 1990 *Akten des 14. Internationalen Limeskongresses 1986*. Vienna, 99–110.
4. P. R. Wilson 2002 *Cataractonium: Roman Catterick and Its Hinterland: Excavations and Research, 1958-1997*. CBA Research Reports 128 and 129. York, 455; Jones 1990 op. cit., 104; M. R. McCarthy 2005 'Social Dynamics on the Northern Frontier of Roman Britain'. *Oxford Journal of Archaeology* 24/1, 60.
5. P. R. G. Stokes 2000 'A Cut Above the Rest? Officers and Men at South Shields Roman Fort'. In P. Rowley-Conwy (ed.) 2000 *Animal Bones, Human Societies*. Oxbow Books, Oxford, 145–151.
6. T. P. O'Connor 1988 *Bones from the General Accident Site, Tanner Row*. The Archaeology of York. The Animal Bones 15/2. CBA, London.
7. P. R. G. Stokes 2000, 'The Butchery, the Cook and the Archaeologist'. In J. P. Huntley and S. M. Stallibrass (eds.) 2000, *Taphonomy and Interpretation. Symposia of the Association for Environmental Archaeology No. 14*. Oxbow Books, Oxford, 69.
8. J. Pearce 2001 'Food as Substance and Symbol in the Roman Army: A Case Study from Roman Vindolanda'. In P. Freeman, J. Bennett, Z. T. Fiemm and B. Hoffman (eds.) 2001 *Limes XVIII. Proceedings of the XVIIIth International Limes Congress, Amman, Jordan*. BAR International Series S1084, Oxford, 931–944.

9   L. Allason-Jones 1995 'Sexing Small Finds'. In P. Rush (ed.) 1995 *Theoretical Roman Archaeology: Second Conference Proceedings*. Cruithne Press, Glasgow, 22–32; C. van Driel Murray 1995 'Gender in Question'. In P. Rush (ed.) 1995 op. cit., 3–21; P. Allison 2008 'Measuring Women's Influence on Roman Military Life: Using GIS on Published Excavation Reports from the German Frontier'. *Internet Archaeology* 24.
10  Allason-Jones 1995 op. cit.
11  Allason-Jones 1995 op. cit., 28–29.
12  Hooppell 1891, 40–41.
13  R.Tomlin in Ferris 2010, 244.
14  RIB 574.
15  On the Bacchic item see Cade 1785, 161; on the McIntyre Venus figurine see Ferris Forthcoming c; on the first copper alloy eagle see Allason-Jones 1980; the second copper alloy eagle was seen on site by the author but its present location is unknown.
16  M. Henig 1974 and 1978 *A Corpus of Roman Engraved Gemstones from British Sites*. BAR British Series, Oxford, 20 No.101, 54 No. 375, and 90 No. 684.
17  Ferris Forthcoming a.
18  C. Johns 2008 *Dogs: History, Myth, Art*. British Museum Press, London, 120.
19  G. Boon 1989 'A Roman Sculpture Rehabilitated: the Pagans Hill Dog'. *Britannia* XX, 201–217.
20  L. Allason-Jones 1996 *Roman Jet in the Yorkshire Museum*. The Yorkshire Museum, York, 5, 8–9, 15–17.
21  L. Allason-Jones 1996 op. cit., 11–12.
22  J. M. C. Toynbee 1964 *Art in Britain Under the Romans*. Clarendon Press, Oxford, 126–127.
23  I. M. Ferris 1990 'The Lion Motif in Romano-British Art'. *Transactions of the South Staffordshire Archaeological and Historical Society* XXX, 1–17.
24  R. E. M. Wheeler and T. V. Wheeler 1932 *Report on the Excavation of the Prehistoric, Roman, and Post-Roman Site in Lydney Park, Gloucestershire*. Reports of the Research Committee of the Society of Antiquaries of London No. IX, 41, 88–89 and Plates XXV, XXVI and XXXIV.
25  J. M. C. Toynbee 1973 *Animals in Roman Life and Art*. Thames and Hudson, London, 104–105, 119 Plate 47.
26  J. M. C. Toynbee 1962 *Art in Roman Britain*. Phaidon, London, 154–155 No. 72 and Plate 76.
27  M. J. Green 1976 *The Religions of Civilian Roman Britain*. BAR British Series 24, Oxford, 167.
28  J. M. C. Toynbee 1973 op. cit., 123.
29  M. Henig 1995 *The Art of Roman Britain*. Batsford, London, 143, 147 Plate 87; J. M. C. Toynbee 1962 op. cit., 185–186 No. 142 and Plate 161.
30  RIB 732, 733 and 737 and probably also more fragmentary RIB 735, 736 and 738 from the site but without mention of the god's name being present on the pieces recovered.
31  RIB 1039.
32  Hooppell 1891, 38.
33  http://www.channel4.com/history/microsites/T/timeteam/2008/binchester

## CHAPTER SEVEN: A MILITARY BASE, A CENTRE OF POWER

1  On Birdoswald, see Wilmott 1995, 1997, 2000 and 2001.
2  Esmonde Cleary 2000, 89.
3  A. Goldsworthy and I. Haynes (eds.) 1999 *The Roman Army as a Community*. Journal of Roman Archaeology Supplementary Series 34; S. James 1999 'The Community of Soldiers; a Major Identity and Centre of Power in the Roman Empire'. In P. Baker, C. Forcey, S. Jundi, and R. Witcher (eds.) 1999 *TRAC 98 Proceedings of the Eighth Annual Theoretical Roman Archaeology Conference*. Oxbow Books, Oxford, 14–25.; S. James

2001 'Soldiers and Civilians: Identity and Interaction in Roman Britain'. In S. James and M. Millett (eds.) 2001 *Britons and Romans: Advancing an Archaeological Agenda*. CBA Research Report 125. English Heritage and Council for British Archaeology, York, 77–89; and S. James 2002 'Writing the Legions; the Development and Future of Roman Military Studies in Britain'. *Archaeological Journal* 159, 1–58.
4   A. Goldsworthy and I. Haynes (eds.) 1999 op. cit. and S. James 1999 op. cit.
5   Dobson 1970, 34.
6   Buxton 2008.
7   J. Bennett 1986 'Fort Sizes as a Guide to Garrison Type: A Preliminary Study of Selected Forts in the European Provinces'. In *Studien zu den Militargrenzen Roms III. Forschungen und Berichte zur Vor-und-Fruhgeschichte in Baden Wurttemburg 20. Limes 13. Internationaler Limeskongress Aalen 1983*, 707–716.
8   *Not. Dig. Occ.* XL; Dobson 1970, 35; A.L.F. Rivet and C. Smith op. cit., 220, 420.
9   Rivet and Smith 1979 op. cit., 261–262, 420.
10  RIB 730.
11  J. Evans, R. F. J. Jones and P. Turnbull 1991 'Excavations at Chester-le-Street, County Durham 1978–9'. *Durham Archaeological Journal* 7, 5–48; R. F. J. Jones 1981 'Change on the Frontier: Northern Britain in the Third Century'. In A. King and M. Henig (eds.) 1981 *The Roman West in the Third Century. Contributions from Archaeology and History*. BAR British Series, Oxford, 393–414; R. F. J. Jones 1984 'Settlement and Society in North-East England in the Third Century A.D.' In P. R. Wilson, R. F. J. Jones and J. Evans (eds.) 1984 *Settlement and Society in the Roman North*. University of Bradford, Bradford, 39–42.
12  R. F. J. Jones 1990 'Natives and the Roman Army - Three Model Relationships'. In H. Vetters and M. Kandler (eds.) 1990 *Akten des 14. Internationalen Limeskongresses 1986*. Vienna, 99–110.
13  R. F. J. Jones 1995 'The Frontier of Contact: Romans and Natives at the Edge of the Empire'. In B. Kuhle (ed.) 1995 *The Archaeology of Contact*. University of Calgary, Calgary; R. F. J. Jones, P. Cheetham, K. Clark, S. Clarke and J. Dent 1991 *The Newstead Research Project, 1991 Field Season, Preliminary Report*. University of Bradford, Bradford.
14  Wilmott 1995.
15  On Birdoswald, see Wilmott 1997 and 2001; on Bath, see B. Cunliffe and Davenport 1985 *The Temple of Sulis Minerva at Bath*. Oxford Committee for Archaeology Monograph 7, Oxford; on Wroxeter, see P. A. Barker, R. White, K. Pretty, H. Bird and M. Corbishley 1997 *The Baths Basilica, Wroxeter: Excavations 1966–90*. English Heritage Archaeological Reports 8, London; on Verulamium, see S. S. Frere 1983 *Verulamium Excavations, Volume II*. Research Reports of the Society of Antiquaries of London 41 and D. Neal 2003 'Building 2, Insula XXVII from Verulamium; a Reinterpretation of the Evidence'. In P. R. Wilson (ed.) 2003 *The Archaeology of Roman Towns*. Oxbow Books, Oxford, 195–202.
16  Esmonde Cleary 2000, 91.
17  P. R. Wilson op. cit. 2002, 474.
18  Wilmott 1997, 219.
19  Esmonde Cleary 2000, 92.
20  Dobson 1970, 36.
21  K. Dark op. cit. 1992.
22  R. Reece 1997 *The Future of Roman Military Archaeology. The Tenth Annual Caerleon Lecture*. National Museums and Galleries of Wales, Cardiff, 9.
23  R. Collins 2004 'Before 'the End': Hadrian's Wall in the Fourth Century and After'. In R. Collins and J. Gerrard (eds.) 2004 *Debating Late Antiquity in Britain AD 300-700*. BAR British Series 365, Oxford, 131.
24  C. M. Daniels 1980 'Excavations at Wallsend and the Fourth Century Barracks on Hadrian's Wall'. In W. S. Hanson and L. J. F. Keppie (eds.) 1980 *Roman Frontier Studies. 12th International Congress of Roman Frontier Studies*. BAR International Series 71 Volume 1, Oxford, 189–190.

25 R. J. Cramp op. cit. 1983; R. J. Cramp 1996 'The Funerary Evidence'. In P. R. Wilson, P. Carwell, R. J. Cramp, J. Evans, R. H. Taylor-Wilson, A. Thompson, and S. Wacher 1996 *Early Anglian Catterick and Catraeth*. Medieval Archaeology Volume 40, 29–30; M. L. Faull 1984 'Settlement and Society in North East England in the Fifth Century'. In P. R. Wilson et al. (eds.) 1984 op. cit.; N. J. Higham 1986 op. cit.; N. J. Higham 2004 'From Sub-Roman to Anglo-Saxon England: Debating the Insular Dark Age'. *History Compass* 2 [2004] B1 085, 1–29; R. Miket 1979 op. cit.

26 Barker et al. op. cit. 1997.

# *Bibliography*

A highly detailed description of the excavations in the centre of the fort at Binchester, including full analysis of the finds and broader contextual discussion, will be found in Iain Ferris 2010 *The Beautiful Rooms Are Empty: Excavations at Binchester Roman Fort, County Durham 1976–1981 and 1986–1991*. This short bibliography is intended to provide interested readers with a comprehensive list of sources for Vinovia/Binchester specifically, including a number of examples of so-called 'grey literature', that is, unpublished client reports prepared by archaeological contractors, and a general list of sources for the archaeology and history of the Roman north more broadly. Copies of all grey literature reports are held by the Durham County Council Historic Environment Record (HER). Further individual references appear in the Notes, being cited in relation to specific issues raised in the main narrative text.

## BINCHESTER ROMAN FORT

Allason-Jones, L. 1980 'Two Roman Bronzes from County Durham'. In *Transactions of the Architectural and Archaeological Society of Durham and Northumberland* 5, 47–49.
Archaeological Services University of Durham 2005 *Binchester Hall, Bishop Auckland, County Durham. Archaeological Evaluation*. ASUD Client Report.
Archaeological Services University of Durham 2007 *Binchester Hall Farm, Bishop Auckland, County Durham. Archaeological Monitoring*. ASUD Client Report.
Archaeological Services University of Durham 2010 *The Binchester International Field School Interim Report 2009–2010*. ASUD Report.
Bidwell, P. and Hodgson, N. 2009 *The Roman Army in Northern England*. Arbeia Society for XXIst International Limes Congress, Newcastle Upon Tyne, 151–155.
Bowman, A. 1989 *A Study of the Roman Brick and Tile from Binchester and Chester-le-Street Roman Forts*. University of Durham. Unpublished BA dissertation.
Bowman, A. 1991 'Brick and Tile Roman Style-An Analysis of Roman Tile from Binchester and Chester-le-Street Roman Forts'. *Durham Archaeological Journal* 7, 49–56.
Buxton, K. 2008 *Binchester Hall Farm, Binchester Roman Fort, County Durham. Excavation for a Sheep Dip in 1996*. English Heritage Research Department Report Series 84-2008.
Cade, J. 1785 'Conjectures On the Name of the Roman Station Vinovium or Binchester'. *Archaeologia* 7, 160–163.
Camden, W. 1607 *Britannia*.
Clarke, S. 1989 *Archaeological Observation at the Binchester Hall Hotel in 1989*. Typescript in Binchester archive.
Clarke, S. 1996 *Binchester Commander's Bath House Excavations 1986 to 1990*. Typescript in Binchester archive.

Coggins, D., Ferris, I. M., and Gidney, L. 1981 *Binchester Roman Fort*. Durham County Council and the Binchester Trust.

Detsicas, A. 1962 'An Unusual Samian Vessel From Binchester'. *Antiquaries Journal* XLII, 248–250.

Dobson, B. and Jarrett, M. G. 1957 'Excavations at Binchester, 1955'. *Transactions of the Architectural and Archaeological Society of Durham and Northumberland* 11, 115–124.

Dockrill, S. 1980 'Binchester Geophysical Survey 1979'. In Ferris, I. M. and Jones, R. F. J. 1980, 249–253.

Durham County Council 1993 *Binchester Roman Fort*. Durham County Council.

Durham County Council 2009 *Binchester Roman Fort Guide Book*. Durham County Council.

Fawcett, W. C. 1971 *The Binchester Hypocaust 1968–1970 Excavations*. Unpublished manuscript. The Bishop Auckland Archaeological Research Group.

Fawcett, W. C. 2001 *The 1972–73 Excavations at Binchester*. Unpublished manuscript. The Bishop Auckland Archaeological Research Group.

Fawcett, W. C. 2003 'The Bishop Auckland Archaeological Research Group and the Rescue of the Binchester Hypocaust'. *Durham Archaeological Journal* 17, 9–12.

Fawcett, W. C. 2004 *A Summary of Excavations at Roman Binchester Pre-1974*. Unpublished manuscript. The Bishop Auckland Archaeological Research Group.

Fawcett, W. C. and Rainbird, J. S. 1973 'The Bath-House, Binchester Fort'. *CBA Group 3 News Bulletin* 4, 5–6.

Ferris, I. M. 1980 'Binchester'. In Coggins, D. and Clews, S. (eds) 1980 'Archaeology in the Bowes Museum'. *Transactions of the Architectural and Archaeological Society of Durham and Northumberland* New Series Vol. 5, 17–18.

Ferris, I. M. 2010 *The Beautiful Rooms Are Empty. Excavations at Binchester Roman Fort, County Durham 1976–1981 and 1986–1991*. Durham County Council Archaeological Monograph.

Ferris, I. M. Forthcoming a. 'A Roman Jet Dog From Binchester Roman Fort, County Durham'. *Transactions of the Architectural and Archaeological Society of Durham and Northumberland*.

Ferris, I. M. Forthcoming b. *A Note on a Seventeenth-Century Copper Alloy Toy Musket from Binchester Roman Fort, County Durham*.

Ferris, I. M. Forthcoming c. *A Note on a Roman Pipeclay Venus Figurine from Binchester Roman Fort, County Durham*.

Ferris, I. M. Forthcoming d. *Excavations by John Rainbird at Binchester Roman Fort, County Durham in 1971*.

Ferris, I. M. And Jones, R. F. J. 1978 'Binchester'. *CBA Group 3 Newsbulletin* 4, 6–7.

Ferris, I. M. And Jones, R. F. J. 1978 *The History of Binchester*. Bowes Museum and Durham County Council.

Ferris, I. M. and R. F. J. Jones 1980 'Excavation at Binchester 1976–1979'. In Hanson, W. S. and Keppie, L. J. F. (eds.) 1980 *Roman Frontier Studies. Proceedings of the XIIth International Limes Congress, Stirling*. BAR International Series 71, 233–254. Oxford.

Ferris, I. M. and R. F. J. Jones 1991 'Binchester - a Northern Fort and Vicus'. In Jones, R. F. J. (ed.) 1991 *Britain in the Roman Period. Recent Trends*. J. R. Collis Publications, Sheffield, 103–109.

Ferris, I. M. and R. F. J. Jones 1996 *Binchester Roman Fort, County Durham, Excavations 1976-1991. Revised Post-Excavation Assessment and Research Design*. Birmingham University Field Archaeology Unit. Unpublished report.

Ferris, I. M. and Jones, R. F. J. 2000 'Transforming an Elite: Reinterpreting Late Roman Binchester'. In Wilmott, T. and Wilson, P. (eds.) 2000, 1–12.

Ferris, I. M. and Jones, R. F. J. 2007 *Binchester Roman Fort. Post-Excavation Completion Project*. University of Bradford Department of Archaeological Sciences. Unpublished report.

Ferris, I. M. and Rátkai, S. Forthcoming *Medieval Activity and Finds at Binchester Roman Fort, County Durham*.

## Bibliography

Fraser, R. 1994 *Binchester Roman Fort. Watching Brief Undertaken for Smiths Gore on Behalf of the Church Commissioners*. Northern Archaeological Associates Client Report.

Geophysical Surveys of Bradford 2007 *Binchester Roman Fort County Durham Geophysical Survey Report 2007/23*. Client Report for Time Team.

Geoquest Associates 2004 *Geophysical Survey of Areas of Land Adjacent to Binchester Roman Fort (Vinovia), Bishop Auckland, Co. Durham*. Client Report.

Hammond, N. n.d. *Binchester Roman Fort in County Durham*. Durham County Council.

Hancox, E. 2001 *Binchester: A Spatial Study of the Jet/Shale and Bone/Horn/Antler Small Finds*. Unpublished M.A. Project, Birmingham University.

Haverfield, F. 1898 'Altar to the Matres Ollototae Discovered at Binchester'. *Archaeologia Aeliana* 15, 225–227.

Herdman, E. F. 1923 *The Wrens of Binchester*. Bishop Auckland.

Hodgson, J. C. 1915 'The Northern Journeys of Bishop Richard Pococke. North Country Diaries Volume ii'. *Surtees Society* Volume 124, 199–253.

Hooppell, R. E. 1879 *Vinovium, the Buried Roman City. A Lecture Delivered in the Town Hall Bishop Auckland*. The Auckland Times and Herald, Bishop Auckland.

Hooppell, R. E. 1880 'On a Votive Tablet with Inscription Recently Found at Binchester'. *Archaeologia Aeliana* 8, 247–255.

Hooppell, R. E. 1887 'Vinovia. Part I.' *Journal of the British Archaeological Association* Vol. 43, 110–123.

Hooppell, R. E. 1887 'Vinovia. Part II.' *Journal of the British Archaeological Association* Vol. 43, 299–306.

Hooppell, R. E. 1891 *Vinovia, a Buried Roman City in the County of Durham*. Whiting and Co., London.

Hooppell, R. E. 1892 'Discovery of a Roman Altar at Binchester'. *Journal of the British Archaeological Association* 47, 268–272.

Horsley, J. 1732 *Britannia Romana*.

Hutchinson, W. 1794 *The History and Antiquities of the County Palatine of Durham*. Newcastle, 346–349.

Jones, R. F. J. 1977 'Binchester'. *Council for British Archaeology Group 3 Newsbulletin* 15, 9.

Jones, R. F. J. 1986 *Excavations at Binchester Roman Fort*. Typescript report in Binchester archive.

Jones, R. F. J. and Clarke, S. 1990 *Binchester Roman Fort: the Furnace Room Excavation 1986-1990*. Typescript report in Binchester archive.

Jones, R. F. J., Gidney, L. and Gillings, M. 1987 *Binchester 1987 Preliminary Report*. Typescript report in Binchester archive.

Leland, J. 1540 *Itinerary* Vol. 1 fol. 74.

Martin, H. 2001 *The Spatial Analysis of Roman Glass from Binchester Roman Fort, County Durham*. Unpublished M.A. Project, Birmingham University.

McIntyre, J. 1932 'Binchester'. *Archaeologia Aeliana* Fourth Series 10, 95–96.

Mowatt, M. R. 1899 'Three Altars Consecrated to the Ollotot Goddesses at Binchester'. *Proceedings of the Society of Antiquaries of Newcastle-upon-Tyne* 5, 127–131.

Noel, M. 1978 *Archaeomagnetic Dating of Samples from Binchester Roman Fort*. Manuscript in the Binchester archive.

Northern Archaeological Associates 1994 *Binchester Roman Fort. Watching Brief Undertaken for Smiths Gore on Behalf of the Church Commissioners*. Client Report.

Northern Archaeological Associates 1995 *Binchester Roman Fort. Watching Brief on the Approach to Binchester Roman Fort*. Client Report.

Northern Archaeological Associates 1997 *Binchester Roman Fort. An Archaeological Evaluation for Durham County Council*. Client Report.

Onodera, M. 2001 *Spatial Analysis of Coins from Excavation at Binchester Roman Fort*. Unpublished M.A. Project, Birmingham University.

Oxberry, J. 1938 'Dr Thomas Sherwood of Snow Hall. A Helper of Surtees'. *Proceedings of the Society of Antiquaries of Newcastle-upon-Tyne* 4.8, 221–231.

Paynter, S. 2006 'Analyses of Colourless Roman Glass from Binchester, County Durham'. *Journal of Archaeological Science* 33[8], 1,037–1,057.

Petch, J. A. 1925 'Binchester'. In 'Roman Durham, 6–9'. *Archaeologia Aeliana* Fourth Series Vol. 1, 1–34.

Pickin, J. 1989 *Binchester Hall Gardens-an Archaeological Examination, March 1989*. Manuscript in Binchester archive.

Pocock, M. and Wheeler, H. 1971 'Excavations at Escomb Church, County Durham'. *Journal of the British Archaeological Association* Third Series XXIV, 11–29.

Proud, J. 1887 'Binchester'. *Journal of the British Archaeological Association* 43, 111–123, 299–306.

Rainbird, J. 1971a *Excavations at Binchester 1971*. Typescript in Binchester archive.

Rainbird, J. 1971b 'Binchester'. *University of Durham Archaeological Newsletter* No. 60.

Rainbird, J. 1972 'Binchester'. In 'Roman Britain in 1971'. *Britannia* 3, 309, 355.

Raine, J. 1852 *A Brief Historical Account of the Episcopal Castle, or Palace, of Auckland*.

Roach Smith, C. 1854 *Collectanea Antiqua* Volume 4, 131–136.

Scarth, H. M. 1880 'On an Inscribed Votive Tablet Found at Binchester (the Ancient Vinovium), County Durham in 1879'. *Archaeological Journal* 37, 129–135.

Skene, P. O. 1822 'An Account of an Inscription Found Near Binchester, County Durham'. *Archaeologia Aeliana* 1, 142.

Steer, K. 1938 *The Archaeology of Roman Durham*. University of Durham Unpublished PhD Thesis.

Still, D. 1997 *Binchester Roman Fort. A Geophysical Investigation of the Fort and Vicus*. Unpublished BSc Dissertation, University of Durham.

Surtees, H. C. 1922 *A History of Byers Green*.

The Archaeological Practice 1990 *Excavation at Binchester 1990*. Manuscript in Binchester archive.

Thompson, J. 1902 *An Account of the Family of Wren of Binchester in the County Palatine of Durham*. The Auckland Times and Herald, Bishop Auckland.

Watkin, W. 1882 'Roman Inscriptions Discovered in Britain in 1881, With Notes on Another Found at Binchester'. *Archaeological Journal* 39, 355–371.

Wessex Archaeology 2008 *Binchester Roman Fort, County Durham. Archaeological Evaluation and Assessment of Results*. Prepared for Videotext Communications Ltd and Time Team. Wessex Archaeology Report 65302.01.

Wittering, C. and Walton, R. 1986 'Binchester'. *CBA Group 3 Newsbulletin* 6, 5–6.

Wright, R. P. 1937A 'Binchester as a Road Centre'. *Transactions of the Architectural and Archaeological Society of Durham and Northumberland* 8, 111–112.

Wright, R. P. 1937B 'The Roman Road from Bowes to Binchester'. *Archaeologia Aeliana* 14, 197–204.

Wright, R. P. 1938 'The Roman Branch Road from Binchester to the North-East'. *Archaeologia Aeliana* 15, 262–268.

# BINCHESTER ON THE WEB

http://binchester.blogspot.com
http://www.channel4.com/history/microsites/T/timeteam/2008/binchester
http://humanitieslab.stanford.edu/Binchester/Home
http://sites.google.com/site/binchesterromanfort
http://vinovium.org

# THE ROMAN NORTH IN GENERAL

Allason-Jones, L. 2001 'The Material Culture of Hadrian's Wall'. In Freeman, P., Bennett, J., Fiemm, Z. T. and Hoffmann, B. (eds.) 2001 *Limes XVIII. Proceedings of the XVIIIth International Limes Congress, Amman, Jordan*. BAR International Series S1084, Oxford, 821–824.

# Bibliography

Bidwell, P. 1996 'Some Aspects of the Development of Later Roman Fort Plans'. *The Arbeia Journal* 5, 1–18.

Bidwell, P. and Hodgson, N. 2009 *The Roman Army in Northern England*. Arbeia Society for XXIst International Limes Congress, Newcastle Upon Tyne.

Birley, A. R. 2001 'The Roman Army in the Vindolanda Tablets'. In Freeman, P., Bennett, J., Fiemm, Z. T. and Hoffmann, B. (eds.) 2001 *Limes XVIII. Proceedings of the XVIIIth International Limes Congress, Amman, Jordan*. BAR International Series S1084, Oxford, 925–930.

Birley, A. R. 2002 *Garrison Life at Vindolanda. A Band of Brothers*. Tempus, Stroud.

Bowman, A. and Thomas, D. 1983 *Vindolanda: the Latin Writing Tablets*. Society for the Promotion of Roman Studies, London.

Breeze, D. J. 1984 'Demand and Supply on the Northern Frontier'. In Miket, R. and Burgess, C. (eds.) 1984 *Between and Beyond the Walls*. Edinburgh, 264–286.

Breeze, D. J. 1993 *The Northern Frontiers of Roman Britain*. Batsford, Lodon.

Breeze, D. J. 2005 'Destruction on Hadrian's Wall'. *The Arbeia Journal* 8, 1–4.

Breeze, D. J. 2006 *J. Collingwood Bruce's Handbook to the Roman Wall*. 14th Edition. Society of Antiquaries of Newcastle-upon-Tyne, Newcastle.

Breeze, D. J. 2007 *Roman Frontiers In Britain*. Bristol Classical Press (Duckworth), London.

Breeze, D. J. 2008 'Civil Government in the North: the Carvetii, Brigantes and Rome'. *Transactions of the Cumberland and Westmorland Antiquarian and Archaeological Society* 3rd Series 8, 63–72.

Breeze, D. J. and Dobson, B. 1985 'Roman Military Deployment in North England'. *Britannia* 16, 1–19.

Breeze, D. J. and Dobson, B. 2000 *Hadrian's Wall*. Fourth Edition. Penguin, London.

Breeze, D. J., Thoms, L. M., and Hall, D. W. (eds) 2009 *First Contact: Rome and Northern Britain*. Tayside and Fife Archaeological Committee Monograph 7.

Brennand, M. and Chitty, G. 2008 *The Archaeology of NW England: an Archaeological Research Framework for NW England*. Liverpool.

Brickstock, R. J. 2000 'Coin Supply in the North in the Late Roman Period'. In Wilmott, T. and Wilson, P. (eds.) 2000, 33–38.

Collins, R. 2004 'Before 'the End': Hadrian's Wall in the Fourth Century and After'. In Collins, R. and Gerrard, J. (eds.) 2004, 123–132.

Collins, R. and Gerrard, J. (eds.) 2004 *Debating Late Antiquity in Britain AD 300-700*. BAR British Series 365, Oxford.

Collins, R. and Allason-Jones, L. (eds.) 2010 *Finds From the Frontier: Material Culture in the 4th-5th Centuries*. CBA Research Report No. 162. Council for British Archaeology, York.

Cool, H. E. M. 2000 'The Parts Left Over: Material Culture Into the Fifth Century'. In Wilmott, T. and Wilson, P. (eds.) 2000, 47–66.

Daniels, C. M. 1978 *Handbook to the Roman Wall with the Cumbrian Coast and Outpost Forts, J. Collingwood Bruce*. Newcastle.

Dark, K. 1992 'A Sub-Roman Re-Defence of Hadrian's Wall?' *Britannia* 23, 111–120.

Dark, K. 2000 'The Late Roman Transition in the North: a Discussion'. In Wilmott, T. and Wilson, P. (eds.) 2000, 81–88.

Dark, K. and Dark, P. 1996 'New Archaeological and Palynological Evidence for a Sub-Roman Reoccupation of Hadrian's Wall'. *Archaeologica Aeliana* 24, 57–72.

Dobson, B. 1970 'Roman Durham'. *Transactions of the Architectural and Archaeological Society of Durham and Northumberland* New Series 2, 31–44.

Dymond, D. P. 1961 'Roman Bridges in County Durham'. *Archaeological Journal* 118, 136–164.

Esmonde Cleary, A. S. 2000 'Summing Up'. In Wilmott, T. and Wilson, P. (eds.) 2000, 89–94.

Evans, J. 1984 'Settlement and Society in North East England in the Fourth Century'. In Wilson, P. R., Jones, R. F. J. and Evans, D. M. (eds.) 1984, 43–48.

Evans, J. 2000 'The End of Roman Pottery in the North'. In Wilmott, T. and Wilson, P. (eds.) 2000, 39–46.

Hanson, W. S. 1987 *Agricola and the Conquest of the North*. Batsford, London.

Hanson, W. S. 2002 'Roman Britain: the Military Dimension'. In Hunter, J. and Ralston, I. (eds) 2002 *The Archaeology of Britain: an Introduction from the Upper Palaeolithic to the Industrial Revolution*. Routledge, London, 135–175.

Hanson, W. S. (ed) 2009 *The Army and Frontiers of Rome. Papers Offered to David J. Breeze On His Sixty-Fifth Birthday and His Retirement from Historic Scotland*. Journal of Roman Archaeology Supplementary Series 74.

Hanson, W. S. and Campbell, D. B. 1986 'The Brigantes: From Clientage to Conquest'. *Britannia* 17, 73–89.

Hartley, B. R. and Fitts, L. 1988 *The Brigantes*. Alan Sutton, Gloucester.

Higham, N. J. 1986 *The Northern Counties to AD 1000*. Longman, London.

Higham, N. J. 1989 'Roman and Native in England North of the Tees: Acculturation and its Limitations'. In Barrett, J. C., Fitzpatrick, A. P. and MacInnes, L. (eds.) 1989 *Barbarians and Romans in North-West Europe: from the Later Republic to Late Antiquity*. BAR International Series 471, Oxford, 153–174.

Higham, N. J. 2004 'From Sub-Roman to Anglo-Saxon England: Debating the Insular Dark Age'. *History Compass* 2 (2004) B1 085, 1–29.

Hodgson, N. 1991 'The *Notitia Dignitatum* and the Later Roman Garrison of Britain'. In Maxfield, V. A. and Dobson, M. J. (eds) 1991 *Roman Frontier Studies 1989 Proceedings of the XVth International Congress of Roman Frontiers*. University of Exeter Press, Exeter, 84–92.

Hodgson, N. 1996 'A Late Roman Courtyard House at South Shields and its Parallels'. In Johnson, P. (ed.) 1996 *Architecture in Roman Britain*. CBA Research Report 94, 135-151. York.

Hodgson, N. 2009 *Hadrian's Wall 1999-2009: a Summary of Excavation and Research Prepared for the Thirteenth Pilgrimage of Hadrian's Wall, 8–14 August 2009*. Kendal.

Johnson, S. 1989 *Hadrian's Wall*. Batsford, London.

Mann, J. C. 1979 'Hadrian's Wall: the Last Phases'. In Casey, P. J. (ed.) 1979 *The End of Roman Britain*. BAR British Series 71, 144–151, Oxford.

McCarthy, M. R. 2005 'Social Dynamics on the Northern Frontier of Roman Britain'. *Oxford Journal of Archaeology* 24/1, 47–71.

Petts, D. and Gerrard, C. 2006 *Shared Visions: the North-East Regional Research Framework for the Historic Environment*. Durham County Council.

Stallibrass, S. 2000a 'How Little We Know, and How Much There Is To Learn: What Can Animal and Human Bones Tell Us About the Late Roman Transition in Northern England?' In Wilmott, T. and Wilson, P. (eds.) 2000, 73–80.

Stallibrass, S. M. 2000b 'Cattle, Culture, Status and Soldiers in Northern England'. In Fincham, G., Harrison, G., Holland, R. R. and Revell, L. (eds.) 2000 *TRAC 99 Proceedings of the Ninth Annual Theoretical Roman Archaeology Conference*. Oxbow, Oxford, 64–73.

Wilmott, T. 1995 'Collapse Theory and the End of Birdoswald'. In Rush, P. (ed.) 1995 *Theoretical Roman Archaeology: Second Conference Proceedings*. Avebury, Aldershot, 59–69.

Wilmott, T. 1997 *Birdoswald. Excavations of a Roman Fort on Hadrian's Wall and Its Successor Settlements: 1987–92*. English Heritage Archaeological Report 14.

Wilmott, T. 2000 'The Late Roman Transition at Birdoswald and on Hadrian's Wall'. In Wilmott, T. and Wilson, P. (eds.) 2000, 13–24.

Wilmott, T. 2001 *Birdoswald Roman Fort: 1,800 Years on Hadrian's Wall*. Tempus, Stroud.

Wilmott, T. and Wilson, P. (eds.) 2000 *The Late Roman Transition in the North. Papers from the Roman Archaeology Conference, Durham 1999*. BAR British Series 299, Archaeopress, Oxford.

Wilson, P. R. 2002 *Cataractonium: Roman Catterick and Its Hinterland: Excavations and Research, 1958–1997*. CBA Research Reports 128 and 129. York.

Wilson, P. R., Jones, R. F. J. and Evans, D. M. (eds.) 1984 *Settlement and Society in the Roman North*. University of Bradford, Bradford.

Wilson, P. R. and Price, J. (eds.) 2003 *Aspects of Industry in Roman Yorkshire and the North*. Oxbow Books, Oxford.

APPENDIX

# Archaeological Excavations, Surveys and Observations at Binchester 1877–2010

It is intended here to provide a summary review of archaeological fieldwork at the site between 1877 and the present day, along with any published references to this work or, in the case of much of the work post-1991, to the 'grey literature' references. All citations here will be found in the Binchester Bibliography on pages 179–84 above.

1877–1889 J. Proud and Revd R. E. Hooppell. Excavation.
The excavations of Proud and Hooppell were extensive and in many ways acted to set the agenda for the interpretation of Binchester for many years to come, almost up to the launching of the major campaign of excavations in 1976. Proud and Hooppell's work included the uncovering of much of the fourth-century commandant's house and bathhouse on which the 1976–1981 and 1986–1991 excavation campaigns were subsequently focused, along with work on the fort's defences and extensive trenching in the vicus (Hooppell 1879, 1880, 1887 and 1891; Proud 1887).

1891 Stray find.
Chance find of an inscribed altar (RIB 1030) by workmen digging pipe trenches just outside the fort to the south-east (Haverfield 1892; Hooppell 1891, 59-62; Hooppell 1892; Watkin 1892).

1911 Stray find.
Chance find of road surface, thought to be Dere Street, by workmen at the sewage works between the fort and the River Wear (County SMR).

1920s (exact date unknown) Stray find.
Chance find, at the time unreported, of inhumation burials by workmen either just inside or just outside the fort to the north by the side of the Bishop Auckland–Newfield road, near Binchester Hall Farm. An oral reporting of this find was made to the author in 1977 by the son of one of the workmen; as the reporter would have been unaware of what now is known to be an extensive Anglo-Saxon cemetery at Binchester, the report has the ring of authenticity about it. The find was not reported at the time because the workmen were apparently afraid of losing their jobs if they held up the work.

1929 J. McIntyre. Observation and collection.
Collection of Roman finds from a number of pits outside the fort to the south of Hooppell's vicus structures (Steer 1938, 134–154). The pits themselves were not recorded. One of the more unusual finds was reported as being 'a coin mould of Caracalla' (McIntyre 1932). Part of a pipeclay Venus figurine was also recovered.

1934 Stray find.
Chance find of an inscribed building stone (RIB 1040).

1937 K. A. Steer. Excavation.
A series of eight trenches was excavated across the line of the fort wall and in places the fort ditch was recorded. Note was made of walls of buildings extending over the line of the backfilled ditch (Steer 1938 and Steer 2010 in Ferris 2010, 540–541).

1955 B. Dobson and M. Jarrett. Excavation.
Excavation was centred on a small rectangular structure on the inner face of the south-east wall of the fort that showed up on an aerial photograph of the site and which was initially interpreted as an interval tower. The structure was finally interpreted as being a ballista-platform (Dobson and Jarrett 1957).

1964–1969 W. C. Fawcett. Excavation.
The Bishop Auckland Archaeological Research Group was periodically involved in the clearance work necessary for the construction of a shed over the partially cleared fourth-century bathhouse on the site (Fawcett 1971, 2001, 2003 and 2004; Fawcett and Rainbird 1973).

1971 John Rainbird. Excavation.
Excavation connected to the extension of the Binchester Hall Hotel. The full sequence of deposits down to natural was sampled. The most significant horizons dated to the second century and included features associated with metalworking on a large scale. Skeletons excavated in the upper horizons were at first thought to be sixteenth-century in date, but are now known to date to the Anglo-Saxon period (Rainbird 1971a, 1971b, and 1972; Ferris 2010, 542-543; and Ferris Forthcoming d).

1972 W. C. Fawcett and J. Rainbird. Excavation.
The 1972 excavations were limited to inside the covered part of the fourth-century commandant's bathhouse, and more specifically to uncovering half of the third room of the bathhouse and the plunge bath at the north-east end of that room (Fawcett and Rainbird 1973).

1976–1981 I. Ferris and R. F. J. Jones. Excavation.
Excavation in, around and beneath the fourth-century commandant's house (Ferris 2010).

1977 I. Ferris. Watching brief.
Pipeline watching brief inside the fort and in the vicus (Ferris 2010, 107–110).

1978 I. Ferris. Excavation.
Excavation of the so-called Squash Court Trench in the former garden of Binchester Hall Hotel. The Roman sequence was sampled down to natural. The most significant horizon was represented by a number of Anglo-Saxon inhumation burials (Ferris 2010, 105–106).

1979 S. Dockrill. Geophysical survey.
Geophysical survey inside the fort, principally around the fourth-century commandant's house outside the area of excavation (Dockrill 1980 in Ferris and Jones 1980, 249–253).

1978/1979 I. Ferris. Fieldwalking.
Fieldwalking to the east of the fort (Ferris 2010, 109–111).

1983/1984 RCHME. Survey.
Measured survey as part of the Durham Magnesian Limestone Survey. Survey unpublished.

1986–1991 S. Clarke and R. F. J. Jones. Excavation.
Excavation in the northern praefurnium of the bathhouse of the fourth-century commandant's house (Ferris 2010).

1987/1988 University of Bradford. Geophysical survey.
Further geophysical survey, principally inside the fort, in its south-east corner (Ferris and Jones 1991, 104 Figure 14.1).

1988 Observation.
Observation by Bowes Museum staff of unauthorised groundworks in the north-western part of the retentura recorded the presence of walling and metalling. In the former Binchester Hall Hotel gardens a stone pila, tufa and opus signinum floor fragments were recovered (Britannia 1989, 277).

1989 J. Pickin. Observation.
A visit was made by John Pickin to view and record an area against the south wall of Binchester Hall Hotel gardens where levelling was taking place for the laying of a lawn, which had led to the disturbance of human remains here. Following the collection of stray human bones, the cleaning of the area revealed three or possibly four inhumation burials in situ, aligned east–west but badly disturbed (Pickin 1989).

1989 S. Clarke. Observation.
Observation by Simon Clarke of unauthorised excavation near the Binchester Hall Hotel recorded the probable destruction during these works of a significant stretch of two stone walls and a mortar floor of a Roman building in one area (Clarke 1989). Deeper excavation still in a second area allowed the deposits here to be examined in section. Overlying the Roman horizons was a black garden soil containing disarticulated human bones, itself overlain by modern building rubble.

1990 The Archaeological Practice. Excavation.
Excavation near the Binchester Hall Hotel revealed four main phases of activity (The Archaeological Practice 1990): in Phase a, defined by the excavators as the earliest phase and dating to the second century, the area was levelled by a number of episodes of spoil dumping, the dumping being interrupted by the use of temporary timber structures, before the upper surface of the dump was roughly surfaced; in Phase b a ditch was cut into the upper dump surface and demolition deposits were dumped here; in Phase c a number of graves was dug here, with six graves being wholly or partially excavated; in Phase d a garden soil was laid over the area.

1991 RCHME. Survey.
Measured survey/resurvey as part of the Durham SAMs Project. Survey unpublished.

1994 R. Fraser, Northern Archaeological Associates. Watching brief.
A watching brief during tree clearance and replanting to the south of the fort on the upper slopes of Binchester Plantation recovered occasional scatters of Romano-British pottery. No archaeological features were recorded (Fraser 1994).

1995 P. Abramson, Northern Archaeological Associates. Evaluation.
Evaluation consisted of the excavation of two trial trenches in the former Binchester Hall Hotel garden. In both trenches Roman stone walls were encountered; in the smaller, more northerly trench, the walls were associated with a cobbled yard surface and formed a small stone structure with internal rammed gravel floor and in the larger, southern trench a wall was associated with a demolition deposit on its south side. A single inhumation burial, presumably part of the Anglo-Saxon cemetery here, was found in the larger trench (Abramson 1997).

1996 G. Speed, Northern Archaeological Associates. Watching brief.
A watching brief on the removal of topsoil in an area for new car parking led to the recovery of some Romano-British pottery and stray human bones, but no archaeological features or deposits were encountered (Durham County HER).

1996 Northern Archaeological Associates. Watching brief.
A watching brief on the approach to Binchester was largely negative (Durham County HER).

1996 K. Buxton, Central Archaeological Services, English Heritage. Excavation.
Excavation at Binchester Hall Farm, for a new sheep dip, was directed by Kath Buxton (Buxton 2008). Deposits of the Flavian to Hadrianic periods were recorded, along with a possible Antonine abandonment horizon. A Roman stone building of third- to fourth-century date was recorded fronting onto Dere Street and part of its interior was excavated, including a hearth. Part of a post-medieval building, 'possibly a dovecot or horse-engine house', was also recorded on the site.

1996/1997 D. Still. Geophysical survey.
Geophysical survey of both the fort and vicus (Still 1997).

2004 M. Noel, Geoquest Associates. Geophysical survey.
Extensive geophysical survey around the fort and vicus by Geoquest Associates (Geoquest Associates 2004).

2005 D. Graham, Archaeological Services Durham University. Evaluation.
An archaeological evaluation was carried out in the area around the former Binchester Hall Hotel (Archaeological Services University of Durham 2005). Four trenches were excavated and Roman deposits and features were encountered in all four trenches. In a trench north of the hall a metalled surface and a possible road base were found. West of the hall two trenches were excavated, locating part of a Roman barrack building that had been damaged during illegal excavations in 1989 and a number of east–west-aligned inhumation burials. In the fourth trench, to the south-east of the hall, two later gullies were found cutting mixed Roman deposits, again with disturbed human remains being recorded.

2007 *Time Team*. Excavation and geophysical survey.
The *Time Team* campaign involved extensive geophysical survey around the fort and vicus by Geophysical Surveys of Bradford (Geophysical Surveys of Bradford 2007), significantly enhancing the Geoquest Associates survey of 2004.
    A number of trenches were excavated. One trench in the vicus was opened to examine part of one of the stone buildings first uncovered by Proud and Hooppell in the late nineteenth century, but excavation here was limited and it was concluded that the structure had been robbed of stone subsequent to Hooppell's work here. A second trench was dug across the line of the double ditch defences of the already-known earlier fort here, defences which show up on aerial photographs. A possible oven was encountered, along with a possible road surface and traces of timber buildings inside the fort. Two further trenches in the vicus most significantly located a row of three stone-built mausolea. The most elaborate mausoleum contained an inhumation burial in poor condition and two pottery vessels deposited as grave goods, provisionally dated to the second century (Wessex Archaeology 2008).

2007 Archaeological Services, Durham University. Watching brief.
Watching brief at Binchester Hall Farm (Archaeological Services University of Durham 2007). A few sherds of Roman pottery were recovered during observation of the demolition of a barn; a cobbled surface exposed might possibly have been the line of Dere Street through the fort.

2009–2013 Durham University, Stanford University, Durham County Council International Research Project. Excavation, geophysical survey, field survey.
Excavation of a barrack building and later overlying structures commenced in 2009 and continued in 2010. Also in 2010 an area was opened up in the vicus to examine parts of a number of stone buildings here. Work in both areas is still ongoing. The geophysical survey area has now been extended beyond the areas surveyed in 2004 and 2007. It is also intended to conduct wider field survey in the next few years to help set the site in its broader landscape context (Archaeological Services, University of Durham 2010).

# Index

Image references are in **bold** at the end of the relevant entry.

Abramson, P. 187
Acanthus decoration on copper alloy handle 148
Aerial photographs of site 18, 58
Aesculapius 33, 35, 148, 151, 152, 153, **14**
Agricola, Gnaius Julius 40–1, 158, 161
Agricola, Sextus Calpurnius 57
Ala Vettonum 15, 25, 35, 108, 152, 161, 162, **14, 62, 94**
Altars 24, 108, 146, 148, 162, **15, 62, 86, 94**
Amphorae 65, 138, 143–4
Ancaster 152
Anglo-Saxon amber beads 125, **72–3**
Anglo-Saxon antler objects 128, **72–3**
Anglo-Saxon burials/cemetery 19, 76, 124–31, 156, 158, 165, 169, **71–4, 95**
Anglo-Saxon church at Escomb 130, 131, 161, **75**
Anglo-Saxon copper alloy brooches 124, 125, 165, **71–3, 95**
Anglo-Saxon glass beads 125, **72, 95**
Anglo-Saxon iron Francisca axe 124
Anglo-Saxon objects 124, 125–8, **71–3, 95**
Anglo-Saxon pottery 125, 128, **72–3, 95**
Animal bones 43, 52, 54–5, 84, 117–21, 123, 136, 142–3, 164, **23, 66–7**
Animal carving 86, 109, **42**
Anthropomorphic carving 85, 109, **90**
Antiquarian interest in site 23–38, **6–15, 93, 96, 97**
Antler/bone working 49, 121, 122, 141, **68**
Antonine abandonment 65, 71, 161
Antonine Itinerary 17
Antonine Wall 57
Apicius 144
Archaeological Services Durham University 188
Argonne roller-stamped ware 113–14, 123
Armea tiles 146, **85**
Athlete, possible, painted on wall plaster 99, **53**
Atys 153
Auckland Castle 24
Augustina, Aelia 148

Bacchus/Bacchic cult 26, 147, 148, 149
Badger 123
Ballista platform 58
Barracks 59, **92**
Bath 165
Bathhouse, of mid-fourth century 27, 28, 29, 32, 84–100, 102–5, 106–8, 109–14, 165–7, 169–71, **6, 8–9, 41–53, 55, 97**

Beads 54, 125
Bell Burn 25, 156
Benwell 130
Bernicia 130
Binchester Crags 50, 105, 141, 142
Binchester Flatts Farm 27
Binchester Hall 24, 26–7, 134, 135
Binchester Hall Hotel 42, 55, 59, 128, 135, 150
Binchester Hall Nursing Home 135
Binchester pennies 24
Binchester place name 17–18
Binchester Plantation Woods 33, 128, 135
Bird bones 52, 55, 84, 123, 143, 155–6, **70**
Birdoswald 124, 139, 158, 164, 165, 167, 168, 169, 171
Bishop Aldhun 131
Bishop Auckland 15, 24, 131, 169
Bishop Auckland Archaeological Research Group 186
Bishop van Mildert 134
Bishop's Park, Bishop Auckland 24, 156
Black burnished ware 53, 65, 70, 75, 78, 83, 99, 102, 137, 138, **37**
Bone dice 54, 70, 99, 102, 113, **83**
Bone objects 54, 70, 99, 141, **81, 83–4**
Bone pins 146, **84**
Bone weaving combs 54, 141, **81**
Bone/antler working 49, 121, 122, 141, **68**
Bowes 153, 162
Brigantes/Brigantia 39, 40–1, 168
Britannia capta coins 41
Brithdir 142
Brooches 54, 124, 125, 165, **71–3, 95**
Bruce, J. Collingwood 25
Buck, Nathaniel 24
Butchery practices 143
Buxton, Kath 188
Byers Green 29

Cade, John 26, 148
Caerhun 56
Caerleon 124
Caerwent 124
Caldarium 32, 92–3, 107, **48**
Camden, William 24, 25
Camulodunum 40
Cannel coal object 128, **72–3**
Canterbury 124
Caratacus 40
Carbon 14 dating 76, 108, 114, 123, 128, 164, 165, 167, 169

Caricature, graffito on tile 139, 163
Carlisle 142, 143
Carrawburgh 56
Cartimandua 40
Carved and sculptured stones 85, 86, 109, 42, 90
Carvoran 130
Cats 84, 123, 143
Catterick 70, 138, 139, 142, 143, 167, 169
Ceramic tile and brick 54, 65, 70-71, 99, 102, 123, 136, 139, 79, 85
Cerialis, Quintus Petillius 40, 41, 161
Cess 43, 119
Charcoal stores 83, 101, 54
Chester-le-Street 95, 111, 164
Chesters 130
Children in forts 145
Christian church 33
Christianity 148
Church Commissioners 135
Circular bath house 32, 10, 96
Cirencester 124, 152
Cistern 58
Clarke, Simon 186, 187
Claudius 40
Closing deposits 155
Coarse pottery 41, 43, 49, 53, 65, 70, 76, 83, 98-9, 112, 113-4, 121, 136, 137-8, 164, 165, 37, 89
Cockerels 148, 149
Cockerel hairpin 148
Coins 24, 41, 64-5, 71, 76, 78, 87, 97, 105, 109, 111-2, 113, 119, 121, 136, 165
Coin supply to site, end of 76, 165
Concangium 95
Constans 77
Constantius Chlorus 57
Convivium culture 143-5
Copper alloy Anglo-Saxon brooches 124, 125, 165, 71-3, 95
Copper alloy eagles 148-9
Copper alloy patera 54
Copper alloy seal box 48, 49, 54, 153, 155, 163
Copper alloy strigil 33
Copper alloy toilet implement 54
Coprolites 119
Corbridge 15
Corner tower 18
Crambeck wares/pottery industry 83, 99, 102, 121, 138
Cremation urns 24, 156
Crucibles 50
Cultural vandalism 26-9
Culvert 30, 58, 7, 93
Cuneus Frisiorum 15, 25, 161

Danubian rider gods 153
Defences 18, 19, 29-30, 41-2, 58, 74, 4, 7, 93
Deira 130
Dere Street 15, 33, 41, 74
Derwent, River 41
Diana 152, 153
Dice 54, 70, 99, 102, 113, 83
Diet, in fourth-century praetorium 143-5
Diocletianic army reforms 169
Ditch 58
Dobson, Brian 19, 186
Dockrill, Steve 186
Doctor, with Ala Vettonum 35, 152, 162, 14
Dog coprolites 119
Dogs 43, 55, 84, 119, 123, 143, 148, 150-3, 87

Dumped deposits 50-5, 119-24
Durham, County 71, 169
Durham County Council 15, 19, 20, 188
Durham University 19, 20, 188

Eagle on altar design on intaglio 149-50, 86
Eagles, copper alloy 148-9
Earl Northman 131
East coast trade 138
East Yorkshire calcite gritted ware 121
Ebchester 15, 161
Enchainment 129-30
English Heritage Central Archaeological Services 188
Equites catafractariorum 161
Escomb 131, 169
Escomb Church 130, 131, 161

Facepots/headpots 33, 153, 88
Fair, Peter 25
Fawcett, W. C. 186
Fendoch 48
Fieldwalking 186
Finewares 41, 43, 49, 53, 65, 70, 83, 99, 112
Finger ring with intaglio 149-50, 86
First fort 39-56, 16-23
Fish bones 55
Flints 39
Flora, statue of 36, 105
Fort size 42, 66, 161
Fortuna 26
Fox 123
Francisca throwing axe 124
Fraser, R. 187
Fulvianus, Marcus Valerius 26
Furnaces 115-17, 65

Gallic auxiliary unit 161
Gaming counters 54, 70, 99, 102, 113, 122, 83
Garrisons 15-7, 161
Gates 58
Gaunless, River 15, 24
Gemellus 25
Geology 142
Geophysical survey 18, 19, 71-4, 76, 32-3
Geophysical Surveys of Bradford (GSB) 188, 33
Geoquest Associates 188, 32
Glass vessel with Greek inscription 43, 140
Glass vessels 43, 49, 54, 65, 83, 99, 112-13, 122, 136, 139-40, 164
Glass working waste 140
Graffiti 83, 123, 139, 146, 155, 162, 37, 79, 85, 89
Graffiti caricature on tile 139, 163
Graham, D. 188
Gravegoods 75, 125-8, 35, 71-3
Great barbarian conspiracy 77
Greta Bridge 164
Grimm, Samuel Hieronymous 25

Hadham ware 99, 121, 138
Hadrian 41
Hadrian's Wall 41, 56, 57, 71, 160, 164-8
Hairpins 145-6, 148, 84
Half-timbered building 61-6
Hammerscale 142
Hare 123
Harrold southern shell tempered ware 99
Hearths 50-6
Headquarters building 59

# Index

Heatlie, W. 30, 11-13, 93, 96-7
Heronbridge 148
Holt 142
Honorius, Emperor 77
Hooppell, Revd Robert Eli 6, 18, 19, 27, 29-38, 58, 62, 71, 74, 76, 81, 84, 87, 88, 90, 95, 105, 128, 131, 138, 146, 153, 157, 185, 7-15, 93, 96, 97
Horsley, John 24, 25
Housesteads 56, 130, 139, 168
Human bones 75, 119, 124-30, 136, 156, 157, 71-2, 74
Huntcliff 99
Hunting 152-3
Hutchinson, William 24, 135
Hypocausts 32, 61-3, 66, 70, 81-3, 84-95, 107, 6, 8-10, 25-6, 39, 43-50, 96-7

Inchtuthil 48
Industrial activity 50-6, 115-7, 132-3, 21-2
Intaglios 149-50, 86
Iron shield boss 70
Iron window grille 54

Janus face 149
Jarrett, Michael 19, 186
Jet and shale in late Roman assemblages 122
Jet and shale objects 83, 122, 145-6, 148, 150-3, 87
Jet and shale working 49, 54, 65, 70, 83, 99, 122, 141
Jet dog knife handle 148, 150-153, 87
Jock's Bridge 15
Jones, Rick 186
Jupiter 37, 147, 148, 149, 15, 62, 94

Kiln, misidentification of 30
Kitchens 64, 101, 27, 54
Knife handle in form of jet dog 148, 150-3, 87

Laconicum 32, 90-2, 46
Lakenheath 125
Lamp chimney 48, 49, 153
Lanchester 15, 161
Late Roman army 164, 167, 168
Late Roman houses 75, 109-14, 168-71
Late Roman transition in the north 164-71
Latrine pit 43, 48
Lead seal, inscribed PBR 163
Leaf shaped flint arrowhead 39
Leg VI 15, 123, 131, 139, 161, 80
Leg IX Hispana 17, 162
Leland, John 18, 23, 134
Limitanei 168
List inscribed on ceramic tile 139, 162, 79
Lydney Park 151, 152
Lyon, Charles 27
Lyon, Mary 26
Lyon, Thomas 25, 26
Lyon family 25, 26, 27, 134
Lysons, Samuel 25

Magnesium Limestone 142
Mancetter 65, 70, 138
Manchester 56, 130
Matres Ollototae – see Mother Goddesses
Mausolea in vicus 74-5, 157, 34-5, 91
McIntyre, J. 39, 148, 185
Medical instrument 153
Medieval activity 61, 70, 132-4, 158, 76-7
Medieval brooch 134
Medieval pottery 132, 134, 136

Mercury 65, 147, 148
Mercury flask 65, 148
Mesolithic flint 39
Metalworking 50-6, 115-17, 132-33, 142, 21-2, 65
Military equipment 20, 99, 163
Mithras 30, 152, 153
Morbio/Morbium 161
Mortaria 65, 70, 138, 155
Mother Goddesses/Matres Ollototae 25-6, 35-6, 37, 148, 151, 152, 153, 15

NCON tile stamps 82, 84, 95, 139, 80
Nemonius Montanus, tombstone of 26, 156
Nemonius Sanctus 26, 157
Nene Valley pottery 65, 70, 99, 121, 138
Neolithic flint 39
Newcastle 56
Newstead 56, 142, 164
Newton Cap Flatts pit 27-9
Niccolo intaglio 149-50, 86
Ninth Legion 17, 162
Nodens 152
Noel, Mark 188
Northern Archaeological Associates 187, 188
Notitia Dignitatum 161
Numerus Concangiensium 15, 82, 84, 95, 112, 139, 161, 80

Ollototae, Matres 25-6, 35-6, 37, 148, 151, 152, 153, 15
Orpheus 152, 153
Otter 123
Oxfordshire pottery 70, 99, 138

Pagans Hill 150, 151
Painted wall plaster 43, 49, 65, 70, 84, 99, 102, 136, 53
Pallet of animal bones 52, 23
Pan 149
Panther copper alloy key handle 148
Patera, copper alloy 54
PBR inscribed lead seal 163
Piercebridge 41, 56, 111, 130, 143, 161, 164, 167, 169
Pickin, John 187
Picts 77
Pipeline watching brief 58, 71, 186
Pits 42-3, 48
Placename, meaning and significance of 17-18, 26
Pomponius Donatus 37, 15
Praefurnia/furnace rooms 91, 97-8, 106-7, 109, 111, 47, 49-52, 61, 69
Praetorium/commandant's house, of timber 43-50, 16-20
Praetorium/commandant's house, first stone 61-6, 24-7
Praetorium/commandant's house, second stone 66-71, 28-30
Praetorium/commandant's house, third stone mid-fourth century 76-114, 165-171, 38-63
Praetorium foodways 143-5
Pre-Columbian syphilis 129-30, 74
Prehistoric flints 39
Priapus 24
Principium 59
Proud, John 18, 19, 29-38, 58, 62, 71, 74, 77, 84, 146, 153, 185, 7-14, 93, 96, 97
Provinciae Britanniae Inferioris lead seal 163
Ptolemy 17, 39, 168

Quintianus, Tiberius Claudius 25

Rainbird, John, 1971 excavations of 19, 55-6, 128, 142, 150, 186, 87
Raine, Canon James 27

Ramparts 18, 29-30, 58, 4, 7, 93
Ravenna Cosmography 17
Ravens, bones of 123, 155-6
RCHME surveys 186, 187
Red deer 43, 55, 123, 143
Religious belief 136, 147-57, 34-5, 87-8, 91
Research aims and objectives 20-1
Rhenish ware 65, 138
Rhineland 151
Ribchester 55-6, 130, 142
Ritual deposits 48, 49, 54, 63, 65, 78, 136, 153-6, 37, 89
Ritual knife 150-3, 87
River Derwent 41
River Gaunless 15, 24
River Tees 41, 164
River Tyne 41
River Wear 41, 138, 148
Roach Smith, Charles 27, 28, 29, 32, 6
Road 29, 52, 58, 66, 83
Rocester 43
Roe deer 55, 123, 143
Rolfe, H. W. 28-9, 6
Roman army 20, 42, 66, 99, 137-43, 159-63, 164, 167, 168
Rooftiles, ceramic 54, 65, 70-1
Rooftiles, stone 50, 54, 65, 70, 105

Saint Cuthbert 130-1
Salus 35, 148, 152, 14
Samian pottery 41, 49, 53, 54, 63, 65, 70, 137, 138, 153, 155, 78
Saxons 77
Scargill Moor 153
Scotland 40-1, 57
Scots 77
Sculpture 36, 85, 86, 105, 109, 14, 42, 90
Seal boxes 48, 49, 54, 153-5, 163
Secundus, Julius 148
Septimius Severus 57
Serpent/snake 35, 149, 14, 86
Sewingshields 56
Sexing small finds 145
Shells 55, 65-6, 136, 143
Sherwood, Thomas 26
Shield boss 70
Silenus 149
Silver spoon 144, 82
Sixth Legion 15, 123, 131, 139, 161, 80
Slags 50-6, 122, 134, 136
Slaughterhouse 117-21, 66-7
Sleaford 125
Southern shell tempered ware 121, 138
South Shields 56, 111, 139, 143, 150, 156, 158, 164, 167, 168
Spacer bobbins 32, 138
Speed, G. 187
Spennymoor 29
Spong Hill 129
Stanegate 41
Stanford University 20, 188
Stanwix 56
Statue bases 63
Statue of Flora 36, 105
Steer, Kenneth 19, 58, 71, 186
Stilicho 77
Still, D. 188
Stone fort 57-114
Stone praetoria/commandants' houses: first 61-6, 24-7; second 66-71, 28-30; third 76-114, 165-71, 38-63

Stone robbing 26, 61, 70, 134
Stone roof tiles 50, 54, 65, 70, 105, 123, 136
Stone roof tiles with graffiti 123
Stone stopper/lid 78, 37
Strigil 33
Styli 163
Surtees, Robert 26
Syphilis, congenital 129-30, 74

Tacitus 40, 41
Taranis 149
Taylor, J. W. 30, 32, 7-10
Tees, River 41
Temples 147
Tepidarium 32, 86-8, 43, 45
Terra sigillata – see samian pottery
Textile production/repair 54, 141, 81
The Archaeological Practice 187
Theodosius, Count 77
Tile stamps 82, 84, 95, 123, 80
Tiles with graffiti 139, 146, 162, 79, 85
Timber fort/buildings 41-50, 16-20
Timber praetorium/commandant's house 43-50, 16-20
Time Team 20, 41, 42, 74-5, 157, 188, 33-5
Tombstones 25, 36, 156-7
Townley Greyhounds 150
Tuberculosis 129
Tufa 95, 99, 105, 121, 123, 142
Tyne, River 41

Valkenburg 48
Vellocautus 40
Venus 147, 148
Venus figurines 148
Venutius 40
Verulamium 165
Via principalis of fort 58, 66, 83
Vicus 17, 18-19, 24, 29, 32, 33, 71-5, 3, 10-13, 31-5, 91, 96
Vindolanda/Chesterholm 17, 56, 130, 144
Vindolanda praetorium diet 144-5
Vinotonus 153
Vinovia/Vinovium 15, 17, 18, 26, 168
Virius Lupus 162
Votive deposits 48, 49, 54, 63, 65, 78, 136, 153-6

Wales 55
Wall plaster, painted 43, 49, 65, 70, 84, 99, 102, 136, 53
Watling Street 33
Wear, River 15, 18, 19, 24, 41, 138, 148
Wear Valley 39, 169, 1
Weaving combs 54, 141, 81
Well, in Binchester Plantation Woods 33, 13
West Auckland 131, 169
Whitby 150
White tailed eagles, bones of 123, 156, 175, 70
Window glass 43, 140
Wint Hill 152
Women in forts 113, 145-7, 84-5
Wren/Wrenne family 26-7, 134
Wren, Sir Christopher 134
Wren, Farrer 26
Wrenne, William 134
Wroxeter 165, 169, 171

Year zero event 164
York 15, 43, 53, 57, 124, 137, 143, 150, 160